'After years of surveillance and wiretaps, federal authorities felt ready to begin a broad assault on the Philadelphia Family. By the time the indictments were actually executed in early 1982, half of those named were dead.

Nothing like it had ever been seen in Philadelphia before. Indeed, not since Chicago during Prohibition had so many mobsters been murdered so quickly. The prosecutors could not update the indictments fast enough to keep up with the killings. Yet they could not know that the "hard work" of Nicky Scarfo's clan of Calabrese was just beginning.'

'As a US Senator, I have heard testimony of hardened criminals, terrorists and mobsters, but none more chilling than of the cold-blooded havoc wreaked by the Atlantic City mob.'

Senator William V. Roth, Jnr

'Joe's testimony was the most crippling thing that ever happened to the Family.'

Philip Leonetti,
former underboss of the Philadelphia Mafia

THE
PLUMBER

The True Story of
How One Good Man Helped Destroy
the Entire Philadelphia Mafia

JOSEPH SALERNO and
STEPHEN J. RIVELE

CORGI BOOKS

THE PLUMBER
A CORGI BOOK 0 552 13847 9

First publication in Great Britain

PRINTING HISTORY
Corgi edition published 1992

Copyright © Joe Salerno & Stephen J. Rivele 1990

The rights of Joe Salerno & Stephen J. Rivele to be identified as authors of this work have been asserted in accordance with sections 77 and 78 of the Copyright Designs and Patents Act 1988.

This book is set in 10/12pt Plantin by
Kestrel Data, Exeter

Corgi Books are published by Transworld Publishers Ltd., 61–63 Uxbridge Road, Ealing, London W5 5SA, in Australia by Transworld Publishers (Australia) Pty. Ltd., 15–23 Helles Avenue, Moorebank, NSW 2170, and in New Zealand by Transworld Publishers (N.Z.) Ltd., 3 William Pickering Drive, Albany, Auckland.

Printed and bound in Great Britain by
Cox & Wyman Ltd., Reading, Berks.

To the memory of
Monsignor Edward J. McLaughlin
—J.S.

Contents

Acknowledgments

There are many people I would like to thank for their help and support during these past ten years. The debt I owe to some of them will be clear from the text. Others, however, I cannot name because to do so might place their lives in danger. I hope they will understand, and accept my thanks anonymously, just as I must give it anonymously.

My gratitude and respect go to the many law enforcement agencies and officers who helped me. Among them I would like to single out the Philadelphia office of the FBI, especially agents Klaus Roher, Jim Maher, Gary Langan, Gary Scalf, Charlie Kluge, and agents Richard Ross, Jim Darcy, and Larry Schneider of the Linwood, New Jersey office.

I am also grateful to the Philadelphia office of the Department of Justice's Organized Crime Strike Force, and in particular to Special US Attorneys Joel Friedman, Arnold Gordon, Louis Pichini, Joseph Peters, and Al Wicks.

The officers of the Atlantic County Prosecutor's Office were with me from the first. I especially wish to thank County Prosecutor Jeffrey Blitz and Lieutenant Joseph Khoury for their confidence in me, and for their courage and integrity. My gratitude and friendship are also due to Captains Edward Hepburn and Andrew Allegretto, Investigator Dennis McGuigan, and Chief Bernard McBride.

My family and I want to thank the Wildwood Crest

Police Department for their protection, and in particular Detectives Donald Sheehan and Tom Stocker. We also thank the Philadelphia Police Department, with special thanks to Detectives Michael Chitwood and John Main.

The New Jersey and Pennsylvania State Police provided protection for me and my family. I am especially grateful to New Jersey State Troopers Manny Ridegway and Joe Regerri, and to Trooper George Taylor for his encouragement and support while I testified.

I want also to acknowledge my gratitude to Ron Chance of the US Department of Labor, and Stephen Cass Weiland of the US Senate Permanent Subcommittee on Investigations.

The Salerno family stood by me throughout this ordeal, and I want to thank them all. I also want respectfully to honor the memory of my grandmothers, Amelia Salerno and Carmella Adelizzia, who died while I was in the Witness Protection Program. I am grateful, too, for the support of the Adelizzi, De Meo, Spay, Ippolito, Hall, and Thomas families.

My publishers and I would like to thank the Pennsylvania Crime Commission and the *Atlantic City Press* for the use of their photo records, and Arthur Soll for his help with photo researching.

Finally, my special thanks to to Joel Gotler, Ruth Cohen, and the staff of Knightsbridge Publishing for making this book possible.

JOE SALERNO

Preface

I do not know who or where Joe Salerno now is. To do the interviews for this book, we met for a week at a motel in a neutral city, to which we both traveled. When we were finished, he returned to the life he now leads, and I left to research and write his book. I never asked him, nor did he tell me, his new name.

Joe Salerno is a hero: the kind of hero who is indispensable to our society's survival. He does not wear medals, nor parade himself before the media. Indeed, the very nature of his heroism obliges him to remain anonymous. Instead, he is an ordinary citizen who came forward in the face of a great evil in an effort to help government put an end to that evil. That the effort was successful is a tribute to his courage and to his faith, for Joe Salerno never stopped believing in the system, regardless of how badly it abused him.

His victory was a victory for all of us who value our laws and the protection from crime they afford. Ironically, however, for Joe Salerno that victory was only partial. He can never recover his true identity, nor will his old way of life be restored to him. He has paid a price for his heroism, and continues to pay it, living as he does in a peculiar exile: among us, but a stranger both to us and to himself.

Joe Salerno's accomplishment cannot be minimized. He helped put an end to a seventy-seven-year-long criminal conspiracy which, in its final phase, had grown to a level of power and violence such as had never been seen before. While there were others who also contributed to ending that reign of terror by coming forward and testifying, Joe Salerno was the first. His unprecedented action proved that it was possible to speak out against the evil and survive. And, unlike the witnesses who came after him, Joe was always a law-abiding citizen; never a criminal.

Joe's story has been authenticated by every government and law-enforcement official to whom I have spoken. Because he is still in some danger, however, I have made certain alterations to the narrative. The name of every place in which Joe lived or had meetings after he entered the Witness Protection Program has been changed. The names of a number of people with whom he dealt have likewise been changed.

I feel privileged to have had the opportunity to tell Joe's story. I hope that other Americans will come to understand the service he has rendered us and will realize the debt we owe him. And I hope that they will wish him well, as I do.

S. J. Rivele
February, 1990

This book is an opportunity for me to explain to my family and friends what I have experienced during the past ten years. The change in my identity and the circumstances in which I lived kept me isolated, even from those who cared about me. Not even my sons really understood what happened, to them and me. Nothing in our previous lives could have prepared us for this experience; sometimes it was hard to tell the difference between nightmare and reality.

I also want the public to know that what happened to us can happen to anyone. The kind of people I testified against don't make distinctions between innocent and guilty; their evil will destroy anyone. And if it isn't stopped, that evil will spread until no-one is safe — not families, not parents, not even children.

I am sure that even among those who have been convicted and will spend the rest of their lives in jail, there are some who now understand how destructive such evil can be. Their lives are finished. And for myself, I know that my life will never be the same.

I saw what such people are capable of. I watched them commit a murder in cold blood, and I knew then that I had to make a choice: to join them, to run, to remain silent, or to cooperate with the law. I thank God I had the strength to make the right decision and to see it through to the end. It is my hope that through this book, others may be spared from having to make that kind of decision.

I want to thank those in the Witness Protection Program who helped to protect me. But I think it is important to understand that this program has serious problems, and that it often doesn't distinguish between cooperating citizens and criminals. This has caused a lot of unnecessary anguish to people trying to assist the government. That is a shame, since the only way to stop this evil is to stand up and speak out against it.

Without witnesses, there can be no prosecutions and convictions. And without protection, there will be no witnesses. But unless that protection is complete, caring, and compassionate, witnesses may be discouraged from coming forward. I believe that basic changes are long overdue in the way in which the program is run and witnesses are treated.

It hasn't been easy, but my experience has taught me that while our system of laws is imperfect, it does work. Though it may take a long time, it does bring justice, even to the most powerful and the most evil. I have seen it with my own eyes, and so have they.

Now that it is over and the guilty have been punished, it is important to me that the truth about what happened come out, especially for the sake of the innocent ones who suffered.

Joe Salerno
February, 1990

Prologue

South Philadelphia, where Joe Salerno grew up, is a self-contained culture. Italian-American, Catholic, intensely proud of its heritage, it is as homogeneous a neighborhood as any in the United States. It is supported by an infrastructure of merchants, craftsmen, and professionals, who share Old World ties and New World ambitions. Cementing them all is the church, toward which the Italian-Americans of South Philadelphia have the same complex emotions as did their ancestors in Italy.

Ringed by neighborhoods of Irish and blacks, Italian South Philadelphia is a world which turns upon itself. It is insular, sometimes suspicious, often intolerant of outsiders. Indeed, Joe Salerno's recollections of his boyhood include an ongoing defense of his homeland.

We were always havin fights with Irish kids that came into the neighborhood. Nothin really serious, not like gangs today; we never had any weapons. It's just that we were taught to stick with our own kind, the Italians, and to keep the others out. So there'd be fights, but if anybody's lip got cut, if there was any blood, we'd stop and say, 'Here, let me help you.'

Loyalty to neighborhood and defense of one's own kind were the outward face of South Philadelphia. Inwardly, its families prized traditional values and consciously kept them alive. Education was one and success through hard, honest work. Family was central, with all the

17

protectiveness and devotion which that implies. Family also meant generosity and celebration, with food playing an indispensable role.

Another value was respect for authority, in all of its forms: parents, elders, teachers, clergy, and the law. The Salernos were proud of their reputation as honest business people and law-abiding citizens. Law and order were valued in their home as much as in any other household in South Philly.

The other great value was religion, which embraced every aspect of life and death, from pre-birth to eternity – whether the living resented the fact or not.

For the culture to be retained, as Joe Salerno early learned, it had to be defended. While South Philadelphia's youths often did this with their fists, some of their elders had more sophisticated and sinister methods.

Organized crime had always been part of the landscape. Inherited and imported from Italy, the *Cosa Nostra* (literally, 'our thing') had evolved in the old country in part as a form of communal self-defense against outside oppressors. It was a way or surviving by any means, so long as those means served the needs of the group – the 'Family.'

In the New World, cultural and economic oppression compelled the retention of the institution. But after Italians had been assimilated into American culture, the institution changed. Survival was transformed into self-aggrandizement, and defensiveness became antisocial activity. A cultural defense mechanism had mutated into a criminal conspiracy.

South Philadelphia was a natural locus for the *Cosa Nostra*, but Philadelphia itself was never a leading center of organized crime. In the South Philly in which Joe Salerno grew up, there were rackets, numbers, some gambling and prostitution, the occasional shooting. But it never reached the levels seen in New York or Chicago. The mob was present, but not predominant. Its activities were expressed in anecdotes, never anarchy.

Soon, however, events and personalities would transform the Philadelphia Family's low-level and languid operations into a vicious criminal conspiracy such as the city, and the nation, had never seen. And neither the neighborhood, nor Joe Salerno, would ever be the same again.

PART ONE

BOY FROM THE NEIGHBORHOOD, 1963–1979

I

Crossing the Walt Whitman

Joe Salerno was born into a thoroughly Italian family. Both of his grandfathers had been immigrants – from Naples on his mother's side, Calabria on his father's. His maternal grandfather had fought with the Italian Army in Ethiopia in the 1920s. His father's father had joined the American Expeditionary Force in Europe during the First World War.

In 1918 the elder Salerno returned with the army to America, where he married an Italian girl and settled in South Philadelphia. Illiterate and non-English speaking, he worked as a laborer, but he saw to it that his nine children had an education. The eldest of these, Joe's father, became a plumber. By the time Joe was born, in 1944, Joseph, Sr, was building a successful plumbing and heating business in South Philly.

Like most Italian boys from the neighborhood, Joe was enrolled in Catholic schools. The discipline of the grade-school nuns was harsh; that of the high-school priests, brutal. Joe was an average student who liked math and history. But he was also a tough, self-reliant kid, with a limit even to the respect for authority that had been drilled into him at home.

Tardiness was not tolerated at Joe's high school, Bishop Neuman. For every minute a student was late, he was slapped in the face once, in front of his classmates. There were beatings for other infractions: talking in class, disrespect, sloppy work. Joe took his share of punishment for two years, and then came a turning point.

A priest caught me and another guy smokin in the bathroom. He made me throw the cigarette into the toilet, then he said he was gonna put my head in after it. I told him, 'No way.' He asked if I wanted to get tough with him, and he hit me. I couldn't take that, so I swung at him, ran out, and left school.

Knowing that the incident meant expulsion, Joe hid all day in a bowling alley to avoid facing his parents. When at last he called, his father told him that it was all right, that he should come home. As it usually does in South Philly, family had prevailed over every other tie, and the ability to 'come home' in the face of adversity remained sacred.

Joe transferred to South Philadelphia High School, where for the first time he came into contact with young people from outside the closed Catholic environment. He had never before socialized with Protestants and Jews. Doing so gave him a perspective, however limited, on life beyond the neighborhood.

After graduating, Joe went to work for his father's plumbing and heating company. He resisted his parents' efforts to have him attend a local college; he wanted to work, earn money, and establish his independence. He began plumbing school at night and worked full-time during the day. He found that he enjoyed the classes and had a natural ability for the work.

By now, Joe, Sr, was an important plumbing contractor with a busy, varied work schedule. Apprenticing with his father and uncles, Joe was exposed to every aspect of big-city plumbing. The work was arduous, and sometimes dangerous.

We used to tap into mains thirty, forty feet under the street. I'd climb down inside a thirty-inch-wide sleeve, and they'd lower the tools on a rope. First you'd cut through the top of the main with a jackhammer. The mains were cast iron, but in the old sections, they'd be oak. Then you'd straddle the hole. The water would be rushing past under your feet like a tidal wave, and the noise would almost deafen you.

Then a crane would lower the new line so you'd be squeezed back against the sleeve. There was hardly room to move, and the hole was full of sewer gas. You'd take oakum in your hands and make a gasket between the line and the main, and then you'd pour hot metal over that and seal it. By the time you climbed out you were dirty and sweaty, and grateful to be back in the air.

Even routine repair jobs had their challenges. In the historic sections, where Joe did much of his apprenticeship, he had to work with fixtures that were more than 100 years old. These brittle antiques had to be handled with soft gloves and with tools sheathed in canvas. Joe learned techniques known to the profession for centuries – for example, the art of rolling hot lead in the hands to form ferrule joints.

It was tough, demanding physical and mental labor, but Joe was good at it. He enjoyed the challenges and the variety, and the sense of accomplishment that his skills gave him. And he enjoyed having money of his own to spend.

Though he still lived at home with his parents, brother, and sister, Joe bought a car and began to strike out on his own. The great symbol of his emancipation was the

Walt Whitman Bridge, the handsome suspension span that connects South Philadelphia and southern New Jersey. In the early years following his high school graduation, Joe crossed the bridge often in search of a world other than his own.

It was a big thing for me, crossin the Walt Whitman. It meant gettin away, gettin out, and meetin different kinds of people. Sometimes I'd go with my friends, sometimes just by myself, to meet new people. Even though it was only a few miles, for me it was like goin to another country.

It was on one of these trips, to Cherry Hill, the shopping-mall suburb of Camden, that Joe met a blonde girl in a new 1963 red Cadillac convertible, Barbara Hall.

He had never met a girl like her. Her parents were the affluent owners of a fuel-oil company, and her background was totally different from his: upper class, non-Italian, New Jersey suburbia. He was nineteen, she was eighteen, and he was overcome. He decided after their first date that he would marry her.

Joe and Barbara saw each other every day for months, despite their families' objections. His parents wanted Joe to marry someone from the neighborhood, a good Italian girl. Hers objected to the apprentice plumber from South Philly. It was Barbara's parents who finally acted. At Christmas they sent her to stay for a while with relatives in Montana.

Although there was little contact between the two while Barbara was away, Joe was waiting at the train station when she returned in February. Four months later they were married.

The marriage represented Joe's first real break with South Philadelphia. The couple moved to the New Jersey suburb where Barbara's parents lived. Now a registered plumber, Joe put a sign on the front lawn and went into business for himself.

For seven years Joe built his plumbing business, and during that time the couple had two sons, Johnny and Michael. But there were also problems bred by the differences in Joe's and Barbara's backgrounds. The distance between South Philly and South Jersey, the short span of the Walt Whitman, intruded into their relationship.

In 1971, Barbara's parents sold their business and moved to the Jersey shore. Joe and Barbara followed, settling on the little, undeveloped island of Brigantine, north of Atlantic City.

They did not know it, but they had arrived at a critical time. A new tide was sweeping toward the coastal communities surrounding the aging matriarch of the shore, Atlantic City. A movement was under way to legalize gambling in New Jersey. In 1974, an initial effort at statewide legalization was defeated. Intensive behind-the-scenes maneuvering produced a second referendum, which passed in 1976. Casinos, regulated by the state but operated by private concerns, were to be permitted in Atlantic City.

The vote was hailed as a new lease on life for the decaying resort. It would bring new tax money, new investment, new construction, and new jobs. Atlantic City would become the Las Vegas of the East, a mecca for gold and glamor. Gambling was greeted as the salvation of the city; nothing short of a miracle.

But warnings were also being sounded. Organized crime in Philadelphia and New Jersey, long low-level and nearly dormant, was awakening to the promise of unprecedented wealth. Already, plans were being laid in cramped offices and back rooms by men accustomed to dealing with petty extortionists, loan sharks, and pimps.

Now they were eyeing the greatest prize of all, dropped into their laps by the voters of New Jersey.

Among these men were some who understood instinctively that whoever was most cunning and most ruthless would rise to the crest of the tide. And so they prepared to meet that tide with a viciousness calculated to overcome any opposition.

In the midst of all this was Joe Salerno, an honest plumber who had come to the coast in search of opportunities for his business and a better environment for his family.

The tide would soon overtake him as well.

2

From Boo Boo to the Docile Don

In 1911, a young Sicilian named Salvatore Sabella arrived in Philadelphia. Like thousands of other immigrants, he was looking for a new life. Unlike them, he was fleeing not only from poverty and oppression but from a murder conviction as well.

Settling in South Philadelphia, Sabella gathered a group of young toughs around him, Sicilians and Calabrese, and formed the city's first Mafia Family. They called themselves the Black Hand, and by the 1920s they had organized the petty rackets and gambling in Philadelphia's Italian neighborhoods.

Sabella established structural and ethnic rules for his organization that would forever determine the shape of the Philadelphia Family. The Family was to be headed by a boss who, like Sabella, was to be a Sicilian. He, in turn, would appoint an underboss, also Sicilian. But there was to be a third figure of authority, that of the *consigliere*, or counselor. This was largely an honorary position, though an important one, and it was to be filled by a Calabrian.

This structure enabled the dominant Sicilian faction to maintain control while acknowledging and appeasing the smaller Calabrian group. It was a delicate balance, intended to promote stability and harmony within the Family.

Below these men were the *capos*, each of whom controlled a group of soldiers. Here, too, the mix of Sicilians and Calabrians was to be maintained. All members were to be 'made men,' which meant that they had to be formally inducted through a ritual of oaths and bloodletting.

A limited number of soldiers would be recruited from time to time from among mob associates, but the Family would remain small and close-knit. In order for an associate to become a made man, he would have to perform 'hard work' – that is, commit or participate in a murder.

Sabella's Black Hand activities were carefully proscribed, both in nature and in geography, for at that time Philadelphia's underworld belonged to the Jewish mob. This mob was split between two factions, which vied for control of gambling and Prohibition-era bootlegging. Max 'Boo Boo' Hoff led one group, while the other was headed by the Haim brothers. In 1926, war broke out between the factions. After two years and many murders, Harry Stromberg and Irving Wexler, known as 'Waxie Gordon,' emerged as the leading figures in the Jewish organization. With the backing of national syndicate boss Meyer Lansky, Stromberg eliminated Gordon and became Philadelphia's unchallenged leader.

Sabella, meanwhile, hoped to exploit the Jewish mob war to strengthen the Mafia's position. But his involvement in the Jewish struggle caused dissension among the Italians, and soon Sabella was faced with a power struggle of his own. In the course of it, he was indicted for two murders. It was the beginning of the end for the Family's founder.

In 1929, Al Capone and Lucky Luciano called a summit meeting in Atlantic City to determine the future course of organized crime in America. Sabella had hoped that the conference would bring formal recognition of his Black Hand as Philadelphia's leading crime group. Instead, Sabella was not invited, and the city was represented by Harry Stromberg. As far as the rest of the country was concerned, Philadelphia was still controlled by the Jewish mob.

This rebuff of Sabella, along with his imprisonment, forced a change in the organization's leadership. One of Sabella's lieutenants, John Avena, took control of the Family, inheriting the dissension that had been created during Sabella's involvement in the Jewish war.

But by now the Family was hopelessly split. In 1936, Avena was murdered by the Lanzetti faction, whose members had worked as gunmen for the Jewish mobsters during the 1920s war. They were prolific and ruthless killers, and their murder of Avena left the Family in chaos.

While the end of Prohibition had weakened the Jewish mob, creating an opening for the Mafia, its internal fighting was preventing it from exploiting the situation. If it were to overtake the Jews, the Family would first have to resolve its disputes and unite. It seemed that only an outside force could effect such a union, and this force would have to come from New York.

New York had long been the capital of the criminal underworld. Along with the Chicago mob, New York's five Families controlled the national crime commission, which dictated policy and resolved disputes across the country. The Philadelphia Family had grown up deep in New York's dense shadow, and it seemed only logical that New York should step in.

Following Avena's murder, the New York Commission appointed Joseph Bruno as boss of Philadelphia. The move set a precedent by which New York reserved the right to anoint the head of the Philadelphia Family.

Joe Bruno ran Philadelphia from his headquarters in New Jersey. He carefully respected New York's dominance of North Jersey, turning his attention instead to the largely neglected southern part of the state. Taking over the scattered rackets there, he placed South Jersey, including the resort town of Atlantic City, under Philadelphia's control.

New York did not object. As far as crime was concerned, South Jersey was a wasteland, and Atlantic City, its heyday over, was no more than an elegant anachronism declining into slum.

Joe Bruno managed the Philadelphia Family until his death, from natural causes, in 1946, when, with New York's approval, Joe Ida took over. By now the Jewish mob was in decline, and the Italians enjoyed increasing control of the Philadelphia-South Jersey operations. These included such traditional criminal activities as loan sharking, extortion, bookmaking, and gambling. There was also some drug trafficking, but this had always been frowned upon by the Family, and it remained confined to splinter groups on the periphery.

Ida was an absentee boss who preferred to allow his subordinates to run things. His underboss, Marco Reginelli, took advantage of this, controlling the Family's operations through a group of young, aggressive *capos*, or chiefs. Among these was the leader of the Family's gambling operations, Angelo Bruno.

Reginelli died in 1956, and Ida retired to Italy the following year. It was a period of flux within the Family, with the potential for the kind of bloody power struggle that New York wished to avoid.

The acting underboss, Antonio Pollina, assumed control and immediately began plotting to eliminate his rivals. His first target was the man he feared most, Angelo Bruno. Bruno went to New York and presented the

Commission with proof of Pollina's plot to kill him. He applied for permission to take control of the Philadelphia Family himself. The Commission agreed, giving Bruno authority to kill Pollina. Instead, in a gesture typical of his methods, Bruno confronted Pollina with the authorization and warned him to flee. Pollina did so, and Bruno became boss.

Bruno had migrated to Philadelphia from Sicily as a child in 1911, the same year in which Salvatore Sabella had arrived. He had grown up during the formative years of the Black Hand and had lived through the war of the 1920s. Bruno understood the history of the Family, and he grasped its unique position in the orbit of New York. As a young man, he had been arrested for minor crimes and had had a taste of prison.

All of these factors combined to make Angelo Bruno a cautious and conservative leader. He knew that violence could lead to chaos, and that excess only drew unwanted attention. These, he felt, the Family could not afford. What the Philadelphia Family needed, Bruno believed, was stability, controlled growth, and good relations with New York. Its leadership had to reflect the realities of its position: Philadelphia would never be New York or Chicago, but for a small, well-run Family it could be enormously profitable. And for that, what was needed was not flamboyance or risk-taking, but competence and compromise.

Through the late fifties and into the sixties, Bruno molded the Philadelphia mob into a model of an efficient criminal enterprise. Its main money-maker was gambling, especially numbers and crap games, run by capo Frank Narducci. Bruno had always enjoyed good relations with the city's Jewish gangs, and as their power waned he gradually absorbed their gambling interests into his own.

The profits from gambling were channeled into an extensive loan-sharking operation, under capo Frank Sindone. As income from this area grew, Bruno diverted the Family's money into established, low-risk ventures such as Caribbean casinos, as well as into such legitimate investments as real estate, vending machines, trucking, and liquor distribution.

Bruno kept the Family small and unobtrusive. At the time of his accession to the leadership, there were roughly seventy members. He maintained this number, 'making' new members only as older ones died or became inactive. The scale of the Family's business was tailored to keep the membership prosperous.

The boss set the tone for his Family's behavior himself. He continued to live in the same modest South Philadelphia row house in which he had been raised. He dressed simply and eschewed display, and he insisted that his subordinates do likewise. Once, when one of his capos bought a new Lincoln Continental, Bruno ordered him to return it and buy a less ostentatious car.

New York was satisfied with Bruno's leadership. The Commission gave him a free hand, and it even accorded him special marks of respect. For example, when the Kennedy administration was waging war on organized crime during the early sixties, the Commission was forced to declare a moratorium on membership in order to prevent infiltration. To compensate Bruno, who needed to make new members just to maintain the status quo, the Commission ceded several lucrative gambling territories in North Jersey to the Philadelphia Family. Ironically, this gesture planted the seeds for dissension that would eventually prove disastrous for the boss.

Later, after years of proven stability and competence, Bruno was given the highest honor of all: he was made a member of the New York Commission itself and accorded the honorary title of Don.

Bruno professed little tolerance for two things: drugs and violence. Though he managed to keep narcotics trafficking out of the mainstream of Family business, it was far too lucrative an operation to be suppressed altogether. A few family members dealt in methamphetamines, or speed, which had an important market in Philadelphia. The leader of this group was a contemporary of Bruno's, Pete Casella. In 1959, Casella was convicted of narcotics trafficking. He spent fifteen years in prison, a fact which seemed to vindicate the boss's ban on drugs.

Bruno's prohibition on violence earned him the nickname 'The Docile Don.' He became famous for settling disputes through compromise, both inside and outside the Family. His twenty-two years as boss were remarkable for their lack of violence; during his reign, murder virtually disappeared as a problem-solving tactic.

With such tight control of the Family, membership became a valuable commodity. To be inducted, it was almost always necessary to have relatives who were already in the group. Another requirement was long service on the streets. In the late 1950s, an opening occurred, and one of Bruno's capos, Nick Piccolo, nominated his nephew, Nicodemo Scarfo, to become a made man.

Scarfo seemed to have all the qualifications. His Uncle Nick's three brothers, Dominic, Joe, and Mike, were also members, and Scarfo's father, Phil, had been a member of the Genovese Family of New York. Scarfo himself had been working for several years in the Family's numbers operation and had proved energetic and capable. What was more, he was Calabrian, and his membership would

35

help maintain the balance between Calabrese and Sicilians in the Family.

The troublesome point was Scarfo's capacity for violence. He was known to have a vicious, moody temper and to harbor grudges. In 1948, at the age of nineteen, he had knifed a man during a quarrel.

Nonetheless, with the backing of his uncles, Nicky Scarfo performed the ancient induction ritual and became a soldier in Angelo Bruno's Philadelphia Family.

For the next few years, Scarfo continued to work in Frank Narducci's numbers operation. Then, in 1963, he got into an argument in a South Philadelphia diner with an Irish longshoreman. The two men wanted to sit at the same table. It was a confrontation flared by hubris and culture. Scarfo pulled a knife and stabbed the Irishman to death.

This was the kind of excess that Bruno could not tolerate. Scarfo was sentenced to two years for involuntary manslaughter, but he served only three months. After his release, he was summoned to a meeting with the boss. Bruno informed him that he was exiled from Philadelphia forever. He was to leave at once, for Atlantic City.

When Scarfo arrived there in 1963, Atlantic City was well into its decline. The once-great hotels were now decaying hulks marooned amid slums and ghettos. Middle-class tourists avoided the city, moving southward to Wildwood and Cape May. There was little left to attract summer visitors but the threadbare quaintness of the boardwalk. There was even less for new year-round residents like Nicky Scarfo.

Nonetheless, Scarfo accepted the boss's decision in silence: like Bruno himself, Nicky respected the value of Family discipline. Where he differed from the boss, however, was in his understanding of the nature of the Family's business. To Scarfo, Bruno was a racketeer, primarily a business operator. Nicky, in contrast, saw himself as a gangster. In his mind, the distinction was crucial.

For Scarfo, being a gangster was the aim of Family membership. Racketeers were managers; gangsters were men of action. Gangsters stood above racketeers and that despised criminal class, drug dealers, in that they wrote and carried out the rules of the underworld. Their characteristic attitude was one of ambition and uncompromising action, and their principal weapon was violence.

Scarfo identified with the classic gangsters of the thirties. He idolized Al Capone and educated himself about Capone's career. He saw himself as the last of that breed, the repository of the Old World values. To be reduced to operating in the seaside shambles of Atlantic City must have been a blow to his pride. Still, Nicky set about taking over the place. If it was a shambles, at least it would be *his* shambles.

He began by muscling into partnerships in bars. Atlantic City was a convenient meeting place for mobsters from North and South Jersey, Philadelphia, and New York, and Scarfo made his bars available to them.

He also began to organize his own gang. Nicky was close to his young nephew, Philip Leonetti, and was grooming him for membership in the Family. Philip would be his right-hand man in Atlantic City, the one person he could trust and count on. Nicky and Philip were joined by two commuters from Philadelphia, the Merlino brothers, Lawrence and Salvatore (known as Chuckie). Together, the four men formed the nucleus of the new organization-in-exile.

Nicky bought an aging apartment house at 26 North Georgia Avenue, in the center of town, as well as the

37

storefront office next door, at number 28. He and his associates moved into the apartment building and set up a cement contracting business, Scarf, Inc., in the office. These, and the bars, became their base of operations. Scarf, Inc. would serve both as a front for the group's illegal activities and as a means for penetrating the construction industry and its associated labor unions.

Within a few years, Scarfo had established a traditional underworld operation in Atlantic City that involved extortion, loan sharking, gambling, and some narcotics. He kept a low profile while building his business, avoiding contact with the law. But by 1971, the law could no longer ignore him, and Scarfo was called to testify before a New Jersey State Commission of Investigation looking into organized crime. When he refused to testify, he was ordered jailed for contempt of court.

Ironically, the two-year term he served in New Jersey's Yardville Prison boosted Scarfo's career, for he found himself in the company of several major mobsters, including Jerry Catena, underboss of New York's Genovese clan.

Nicky had always enjoyed good relations with the Genovese Family. They were Calabrians, as he was, and his father had been a member. Catena, for his part, was impressed with the tough little soldier from Atlantic City. It was an important connection, one that Scarfo would later use to his advantage.

Nicky was released during the first furor over legalized gambling in New Jersey. Gambling, he knew, would radically alter his situation within the mob, and he spent the two years between the defeat of the 1974 effort and the 1976 casino referendum gearing up his operations to greet its almost certain passage.

His penetration of the construction industry and of Local 54, the union of restaurant workers, bartenders, and hotel workers, now placed him in a potentially potent position. Construction would skyrocket when gambling passed, and the local would be at the very center of casino operations.

Nicky moved quickly to expand the membership of his gang, recruiting young, tough Italians, especially Calabrians. He tightened his grip on the construction trades, too, reaching out from Scarf, Inc. into electricity, carpentry, and plumbing, thus positioning himself to reap the power and money which the start-up phase of gambling would bring.

When the Atlantic City casino ordinance passed in 1976, the wheel came full circle for Nicky Scarfo. The exile that Bruno had imposed on him proved suddenly to have been the greatest boon possible to his career. Far from being removed from the center of things in Philadelphia, he was now at one end of a national axis of activity, anchored in Las Vegas.

Thirteen years earlier, Nicky had been banished to a backwater. Now, overnight, the whole country would be coming to him.

By late 1977, casino construction was under way in earnest, and Nicky was in the thick of it. Scarf, Inc. had contracts on five of the first nine casinos, and it funneled work to dozens of subcontractors. In return for padded payrolls, protection, and other rake-offs, Scarfo guaranteed an absence of labor and delivery problems. It was a small price to pay to keep gambling on schedule.

Meanwhile, Nicky's colleagues were taking note of his growing power. Mobsters from all over the East Coast now acknowledged him and treated him with respect. As the boss of the Vegas of the East, Scarfo became one of the most sought-after mobsters in the country. And he had his supporters in Philadelphia as well.

When Angelo Bruno's longtime underboss, Ignazio Danaro, died, Bruno appointed Phil Testa to replace him. Testa, a Calabrian, had worked with Scarfo in Bruno's gambling operations, and the two had become friends. Then, in 1977, Bruno's consigliere, Joe Rugnetta, died, and Testa nominated Scarfo to replace him.

The gesture was a mark not only of the friendship between the two, but also of Testa's vision. Testa was looking beyond the Bruno era to the future of the Family. He saw its traditional sources of income drying up, with drugs and casino operations replacing them.

Testa felt that bringing Scarfo back into the fold, in a position of importance, would be a step toward Philadelphia's control of both drugs and casino gambling. Also, if Scarfo were consigliere, two of the top three leadership positions would be held by Calabrians.

Bruno refused. Scarfo was too young and hotheaded to be consigliere. Besides, Bruno wanted the Family out of the casinos and drugs. It was the second time Nicky had been rebuffed by the boss. He was disappointed and angry, but he appreciated Phil Testa's patronage.

Despite his resentment over Bruno's rejection, Scarfo offered no overt protest. He knew that Philadelphia, like Atlantic City, was changing. Bruno was old, and his leadership was obsolete. His lieutenants were becoming impatient with the restraints he placed on their ability to branch out and benefit from the narcotics and gambling booms.

Even the Docile Don could not rein these men in forever. Something was bound to change, and when it did, Nicky wanted to be sure he was in the right position. He began to draw closer to the Calabrese faction of the Family, led by Testa. When the transition came, it would probably not be docile. And if blood was to be spilled, Nicky wanted to be on the side of his own blood.

3

'Crime Don't Pay'

Joe Salerno was doing well in Brigantine. He had bought
a house on the bay and obtained a contractor's license.
With a reputation for honesty and quality work, he had
gradually taken on most of the plumbing jobs on the
island; his truck, with 'Salerno Plumbing and Heating'
stenciled on the door, was a familiar sight. The name
stood out, for there were few Italians in the traditionally
Anglo-Irish community.

Joe stood out, too. His thick black hair, trim black
moustache, and dark eyes advertised his Italian ancestry.
And his strong South Philly accent was unmistakable.
Nonetheless, Joe was determined to become assimilated
into the community. He joined the Elks, the Lions, the
Chamber of Commerce, and, of course, the Knights of
Columbus.

He usually worked in tandem with other contractors,
especially in the cement business. While the concrete
footings and foundations of a structure were being laid,
Joe would rough out the plumbing system, then come
back later and finish the work. It was natural, then, for
Joe and the cement contractors to find each other work
and to socialize.

What was more, several of the area cement contractors
were Italian-Americans. And despite his determination
to leave behind his South Philly origins and become

integrated into the community, Joe still enjoyed the company of his own kind.

On a fall day in 1972, Joe was driving to a job in his plumbing truck when a man hailed him from the sidewalk.

'I seen your truck around town,' the man said. 'You're Italian, huh?' He introduced himself as Eddie Cipresso, from South Philadelphia. He owned a seventy-five-unit motel in Brigantine, and he offered Joe his plumbing business, saying he would rather work with his own kind than with the Irishman he normally used.

Joe had heard of Eddie Cipresso. He was supposed to have been involved in the numbers rackets in South Philadelphia in the old days and to have served a prison term for it. But that had been a long time ago, and Cipresso had since gone straight, retiring to Brigantine.

Joe gladly accepted Cipresso's offer, and he soon started work at the motel. A cement contractor was already on the job when Joe arrived. His name was Alfredo Ferraro, and he spoke broken English with an unusual accent. He explained that he was an Italian, but that his family had lived in Argentina. He had another Italian friend from Argentina, he told Joe, named Vincent Falcone. A few days later, he introduced Joe to Falcone.

Vincent Falcone was in his thirties, a tall, well-built man with thick sideburns and a bushy moustache. He was married and had a child. Like Alfredo, he spoke with a heavy accent.

Joe liked Vincent, and he offered to help him find jobs. Gambling was almost certain to pass at the next election, and there would be plenty of work for everyone.

'I don't want any big jobs,' Vincent told him. 'It's better if you stay small, work private, and get your money from the customer. Me, I like to do the work myself.'

This struck Joe as a modest, honest attitude, and he was soon referring people to Vincent for driveway and paving jobs and for room-addition foundation work.

Joe, Alfredo, and Vincent began socializing together, meeting for cheese steaks at lunchtime or having dinner after work in Atlantic City. They were sometimes joined by another young Italian-American who worked for Alfredo. His name was Philip Leonetti.

When I first met Philip, he looked like he was fifteen. He had those kind of looks, a baby face. But one thing I noticed about him, he never smiled at anything. And when he laughed, he had to force himself. He had a way of starin, just starin at you and not sayin anything, like he was tryin to decide whether to trust you. And his eyes sometimes would get a look in them that was just cold-blooded; it could freeze your blood, that look. The more I got to know Philip, the more I thought, this is a guy who's never loved anybody in his life.

When the gambling referendum passed in 1976, there was a construction boom such as South Jersey had never seen. Marshes that had once been home only to green-head flies and mosquitoes were being filled for housing tracts; hotels were sprouting up out of the sand; and acres of reeds were transforming into condominiums.

There was more work than Joe Salerno and his contractor friends could handle, not only in Brigantine, but in Atlantic City as well.

In 1977, Joe was working a job in Brigantine when Alfredo Ferraro walked over to him.

'C'mere, Joe, there's somebody I want you to meet.'

Joe asked who it was.

'Philip's uncle,' Alfredo replied.

Joe followed him across the job site to where a small

43

man in his forties was squatting next to a concrete wall. He was wearing a trench coat and a suit and tie, and his thick hair was brushed back from his forehead. He was clearly wealthy, and the other men at the site seemed to treat him with respect.

'Nicky,' Alfredo greeted him, 'this is Joe Salerno.'

The man did not stand, and Joe had to stoop to shake his hand. Nonetheless, he could see that Nicky was diminutive, scarcely more than five-and-a-half feet tall.

'What do you do, Salerno?' he asked Joe.

Joe said that he was a plumber.

'Good,' Nicky replied. 'That's good. I hear you're a pretty nice guy. I'll do what I can for ya.'

Joe thanked him and said that if he had any work, he could direct it to Alfredo.

'That's nice,' Nicky nodded approvingly. 'I like that.' Then he added confidingly, 'You know, it's all damn Irish down here, but you're my own kind. Anything I get, I'll throw it your way.'

They shook hands again, and Nicky left. Joe watched him drive off in a new black Cadillac sedan.

'He's a good man,' Alfredo remarked.

Joe knew that Philip's Uncle Nicky was Nicodemo Scarfo, who controlled a cement contracting business in Atlantic City called Scarf, Inc. He had never worked with the company, and apart from those few facts he knew nothing about Nicky Scarfo or his business.

Gambling brought changes not only to the shoreline but to Joe Salerno's home as well. After the referendum passed, Joe's wife, Barbara, announced that she wanted to go to work as a dealer in the casinos. Joe did not like the idea, but he agreed to her going to school to learn the trade.

Barbara attended school several nights a week, leaving Joe to fix dinner and tend to the children after work. There were three boys now – Johnny, 11, Michael, 10, and a baby, Tony. It was not long before the new schedule irritated Joe, and arguments began.

In Joe's view, it was traditional for the wife to stay home and raise the kids, and besides, there was no need for Barbara to work. Joe was doing well, and there was enough money. What was more, he did not want her working in the casino atmosphere. Already, it was changing her: she was losing weight, and she was dressing and grooming differently. Joe saw Barbara as being seduced away from home by the glitter of gambling.

Barbara's new plans became the focus of all the tension in the marriage. The arguments grew into fights, and the fights became intolerable. Finally, Joe threatened to move out. Barbara called his bluff.

'Go ahead,' she told him. 'Leave.'

Joe felt that he could not back down, yet he had no place to go, and there were his sons. He did not want to be separated from them. Still, the situation at home had become impossible.

That was when Philip Leonetti called.

'My Uncle Nicky has a job for you,' he said. 'He's got a problem at his place on Georgia Avenue.'

Joe drove over to Nicky Scarfo's brick apartment house at 26 North Georgia Avenue in Atlantic City. The plumbing was as ancient as the building, and the boiler had cracked. It was the winter of 1978, and Scarfo, his relatives, and his tenants were freezing.

'You're supposed to be a good plumber,' Scarfo grumbled at Joe in the storefront office of Scarf, Inc. 'Get the goddamn heat on.'

It was an enormous job. The boiler was a million BTUs and heavy as a battleship. Joe special-ordered a new unit, and then hired two men to help him disconnect the old one and haul it out. The job took five days of heavy, dangerous, dirty work, punctuated by Scarfo shouting down the vents, 'When are we gonna get that goddamn heat?!'

Joe estimated the cost at $25,000 for equipment and labor. Scarfo paid Joe's discounted price for the boiler, but he offered nothing for the labor. Joe paid the men from his own pocket, and billed Nicky for their salaries. He left the bill at the Scarf, Inc. office with Nicky's son, Chris, a stocky seventeen-year-old with slicked-back hair. The next day, Chris Scarfo came to the job site where Joe was working and handed him back the bill.

Across it were scrawled the words 'Crime don't pay.'

Joe was bewildered. At first he thought it meant that Scarfo was accusing him of cheating, but he knew that was not so. He asked Chris to explain.

'You better ask my cousin Philip,' the boy said, and walked away.

Later, Joe showed the bill to his contractor friends and asked them what he should do about it. Alfredo Ferraro shook his head. 'Just don't do anything to upset the Little Guy,' he told Joe. Vincent Falcone seemed to agree.

Joe wanted to know what they were talking about. 'Look,' Eddie Cipresso said, 'these guys are no good. You don't wanna get too involved with them.'

When Joe asked if he was supposed to eat the money for the labor, they told him yes.

The next time he saw Philip Leonetti, Joe mentioned the bill. 'We'll make it up to you some other way,' Leonetti told him.

Joe knew that Scarfo owned apartments in Atlantic

City. He told Philip that it might be necessary for him to move out of his house, and he asked if Philip could help him find a place.

'I got an idea,' Philip replied slowly. 'A friend of my uncle's got a house in Margate. Needs some plumbing work. You can stay there while you do the work.'

The friend was Salvatore 'Chuckie' Merlino. Although the house in the beach community of Margate, south of Atlantic City, had no heat or water, it was a godsend for Joe, given the pressures at home.

He moved into Chuckie Merlino's house in September. The separation from his wife and sons was painful, and he was in a continual state of depression. Though he called his sons and stopped at his home to see them, his wife remained adamant. She was determined to pursue her career, and if that meant separation, so be it.

In his isolation, Joe spent more time with his contractor friends, including the group at Scarf, Inc. When the work on the Margate house was done and Chuckie was ready to return, Joe again had to find a place to live. This time, Nicky himself suggested a solution.

'Listen, Joe,' he said one day at the Scarf, Inc. office, 'you don't need Brigantine. This is where it is now. Forget about your wife, and don't worry about your kids. They'll be all right. You come and stay here. We'll take care of you.'

He offered to rent Joe an apartment at 26 North Georgia Avenue for $200 a month. In his distraught state of mind, Joe accepted both the apartment and the implied offer of a closer relationship with Scarfo and his associates. If he could not have the companionship of his wife and family, Joe could at least count on these Italians, who understood and sympathized with him. He also enjoyed the respect they commanded everywhere, the free meals in restaurants, the best seats at shows, the deference in the new casinos. It was a consolation to his wounded self-respect. But it was also the beginning of a manipulation that was to grow more complex and pointed as the months went on.

4

'Did You Ever Wanna Be a Gangster?'

At the time he met Joe Salerno, Nicky Scarfo was building an army to use in his conquest of Atlantic City. He was surrounding himself with young, tough South Philadelphia Italians, securing their loyalty through favors, debts, and sometimes fear.

Still smarting from the disgrace of his exile to the coast, Scarfo was working to create a counterweight in Atlantic City to Angelo Bruno's fading authority in Philadelphia. The weight had to be tipped so far in his favor that no-one who replaced Bruno in the succession that was sure to come would be able to challenge Scarfo. To do this, Scarfo had to recruit as many soldiers as he could, as quickly as possible.

This recruiting campaign was not accidental or haphazard, as Joe Salerno would eventually realize. It was a carefully plotted and ruthlessly executed scheme to wed troops to Scarfo in such a way that divorce was impossible.

Joe was already at loose ends because of his marital problems. Besides the apartment at 26 North Georgia Avenue, Joe began using the office at Scarf, Inc. as a business contact point. Nicky was finding him plumbing jobs in the frantic casino-construction boom, and Joe was also being integrated into Scarfo's circle. He was even invited to the regular Sunday dinners at Scarfo's apartment.

The next step in Scarfo's seduction of Joe Salerno came when a contractor defaulted on Joe.

In the midst of a major plumbing job Joe was doing in the affluent coast town of Longport, the general contractor suddenly went bankrupt. Joe was left with $45,000 in obligations for materials and labor, which he paid off. Other bills were piling up, and the mortgage payments on his house in Brigantine were falling behind. By Christmas of 1978 Joe needed cash badly.

Joe knew by now that Philip Leonetti had friends who loaned money at steep interest. He went to Philip and explained his problem.

'How much do you need?' Philip asked.

Joe told him he could get by with $10,000.

Philip thought it over a moment, the empty stare, which Joe had often noticed before, in his eyes.

'I'll see what I can do,' Philip said at last, 'but I gotta go to Cherry Hill.'

The drive to Cherry Hill and back normally took a good two hours. Leonetti returned in twenty minutes.

Philip drew an envelope from the front of his trousers and handed it to Joe. In the envelope were a hundred $100 bills.

'Interest on this is usually 500 a week,' Philip said, 'but since you're a friend I got it for 250. It's the best I could do.'

Even this rate meant that the debt would double in ten months, but Joe had some big jobs coming up, and he expected to be able to pay Philip back quickly. He did not ask, nor did Leonetti volunteer, where the money had come from.

1979 brought a new way of life for Joe. During the day he worked out of Scarf, Inc., trying to pay his debts and keep his business afloat. The evenings he spent with

Scarfo, Philip, and Chuckie and Lawrence Merlino. They were usually joined by Alfredo Ferraro and Vincent Falcone.

Later in the evening, after the group had broken up, Joe would go to his house in Brigantine to visit with his wife and sons. His encounters with Barbara were not happy ones, and Joe was now virtually a stranger in his own home.

As the months went on, the Scarfo circle drew tighter. The men would have dinner together, or they would go to the local bars for drinks. Nicky was always at the center, holding court, and barmen and waiters treated him with the appropriate deference. There was a specific reason for this, as Joe learned suddenly one night.

The barman at the My Way, the group's usual rendezvous, dropped a newspaper in front of Nicky and pointed out an article that detailed Scarfo's ties to Local 54, the union of restaurant workers, hotel workers, and bartenders. The barman, who was himself the secretary of the local, made a joke about the article.

Scarfo flew into a rage.

'I put you where you are!' he shouted at the barman, his voice rising to a thin screech. 'And I put that fat bastard downstairs where he is, and don't either of you ever forget it!'

The 'fat bastard,' Joe knew, was Frank Gerace, president of the local and one of Scarfo's associates. Control of the union, which was at the very heart of the casino service industry, would give Scarfo a stranglehold on the city, and for him it was no joking matter.

Joe had other occasions to witness Scarfo's unpredictable, violent temper.

If we were in a restaurant and the service didn't please him, he'd turn the table over. One time he took a sledgehammer to a bar that was bein built in his house because it was takin too long. He was always wantin to show he was boss, even to his wife. At one of the Sunday night dinners, she put the pasta on the table. Nicky tasted it, told us it was overcooked, and threw the plate against the wall.

Philip Leonetti, Joe learned, was cast in the same mold as his uncle.

One time I went over to Phil's apartment and he had his girlfriend there. She was a waitress at the Brajole Café. While we were talkin, Philip took a bread knife from the kitchen, grabbed her around the head, and put the knife to her throat. He nicked her so that he drew blood. When he saw the way I looked, he said to me, 'Don't worry, she don't mind. It doesn't hurt, and besides, it shows her who's boss.'

Scarfo demanded respect, and even emulation. When he ordered a drink, he expected everyone in his party to order the same. He dictated to his companions how to dress and what jewelry to wear. He prohibited the use of cologne by men in his presence, on the grounds that it was effeminate. And he criticized continually even the most inoffensive behavior of everyone who worked for him.

He used to carry mint candies in his Cadillac, and if there weren't any, he'd complain. 'You guys, I can't trust you for anything,' he'd say, and he'd make Philip stop at the first candy store and run in and buy some. And he was always complaining about the way people drove. 'Easy on them brakes,' he'd say. 'When are you guys gonna learn to drive?' If you let the gas get below a half he'd chew

*you out: 'Suppose I had a meetin in Philly,' he'd say.
'You'd have to stop for fuckin gas!'*

*Sometimes we'd pass a restaurant or a bar and he'd
tell me, 'I oughta get a piece of that place, Joe; find out
who owns it, and I'll go and lean on him.' Once I went
with him to a jewelry store to pick up a watch. When the
jeweler went in the back, Nicky said to me, 'See that guy?
He showed me disrespect. I should kill him, but hell, you
can't kill everybody.'*

On the subject of his height, Scarfo was particularly
sensitive. No reference to it was ever allowed, and though
among themselves his associates referred to him as 'Little
Nicky' or 'The Little Guy,' no-one dared to use these
terms within his hearing.

More sinister was his anger at those he took to be his
enemies. He liked to talk about the murder of the
longshoreman he had committed years earlier. On several
occasions he described to Joe with relish how he had
'stuck a knife into the Irish motherfucker and twisted it
into his guts.'

Still, even within his own circle Scarfo was carefully
close-mouthed, and he demanded the same of those
around him. He often said to Joe, 'If I tell you something,
remember, you're like this . . .' and he pressed his stubby
index finger to his lips. 'Otherwise,' he would add, 'you
get this,' and he would make a shooting gesture toward
his head and chest.

Conversations in the office or in Nicky's apartment
were schizophrenic: general discussions of politics, personalities, or gambling were punctuated by Scarfo's brief
asides to individuals. In these, he would take Philip, Joe,
or one of the others into a corner, speak briefly, and
demand silence.

The Little Guy talked in circles. He never looked you in the eye, and he never discussed criminal matters straight out. Instead, he'd say things like: 'Gambling's comin, Joe. Everything's gonna be all right. We been here a long time . . . we're the main ones now. Don't worry, you're gonna be OK . . .'

He had a statue in his apartment of a Mexican bandit, with bandoliers filled with bullets, and he'd point at that and say, 'We gotta be like him, Joe, we gotta take care of things.' Then he'd look at me and tell me never to repeat to Philip or the others what he had said.

Occasionally, after one of the Sunday dinners at 26 North Georgia Avenue, Nicky would take Joe to the window, which overlooked the casino skyline.

'You see this, Joe?' he would say, gesturing toward the city. 'One day I'm gonna own this place.'

These suggestive, vaguely sinister asides seemed calculated to confer a measure of confidentiality. Without revealing anything specific, they implied a trust between the Little Guy and his interlocutor and, as Joe was to learn, served as a signal that something specific was being planned.

The first real indication that something *was* planned was the disappearance of Alfredo Ferraro. In late summer of 1979, Ferraro dropped out of sight, with no explanation and no word to Joe. Then Vincent Falcone stopped visiting the Scarf, Inc. office and attending the Sunday dinners at 26 North Georgia Avenue.

Nothing was said openly about the absences, but one Sunday when Alfredo's name came up, Nick grumbled, 'That no-good Alfredo, I'd like to cut his guts out and fry em in a pan.'

On Vincent Falcone there was silence.

It was around this time that Philip approached Joe to tell him that his grandmother, who also lived at 26 North Georgia Avenue, needed new kitchen cabinets. Joe replied that he had a friend in South Philadelphia who made them, so he and Philip drove to Philadelphia in a Scarf, Inc. truck.

As they were crossing the Walt Whitman Bridge, Joe half-jokingly asked Philip exactly what business he and his Uncle Nicky were in.

Philip regarded him stone-faced for a moment, and then he reached under the seat and took out a copy of *Philadelphia* magazine. He pointed to an article entitled 'The Boardwalk Mob.' 'This is who we are,' he told Joe. 'This is what we can get away with.'

The article identified Scarfo as a member of the Philadelphia-South Jersey *Cosa Nostra*, and it named Philip as a suspect in the unsolved murders of a former municipal court judge and an Atlantic City gambler.

Philip's sudden frankness confirmed Joe's suspicions and explained the early warnings given him by Ferraro, Falcone, and Eddie Cipresso. It also explained the 'Crime don't pay' message Scarfo had sent him. Yet up to this point Scarfo and his group had not asked Joe to do anything illegal, nor had he been party to any of their operations.

On the other hand, he was still living in Nicky's building and was getting jobs from him, and he still owed Philip $11,000 in principal and interest on the loan – the payments for which were falling behind.

He asked Philip where the loan money had come from.

'Where do you think it came from?' Philip replied. 'It was my uncle.'

That summer, Nicky Scarfo and Chuckie Merlino made a brief trip to Italy. Then, half a dozen times following their return, Nicky would make a peculiar excursion. 'C'mon, Salerno,' he would say when Joe stopped at the Scarf, Inc. office. 'Let's take a little ride down there.'

'Down there' was Margate, and an apartment building that Joe did not recognize. While Nicky peered through the tinted windows of the Cadillac, Philip would cruise around the building several times. Then Nicky would order him to drive back to Atlantic City.

The trips were never explained to Joe. What he did not know was that his friend Vincent Falcone kept an apartment in that building, which he used on occasion. Joe also did not know something much more significant.

Just before leaving on the trip to Italy, Chuckie Merlino had spent an evening drinking with Vincent. During their conversation, Vincent had remarked that he thought Philip Leonetti and his uncle were both crazy and should be banned from the contracting business. Chuckie related this conversation to Nicky Scarfo in Italy. Scarfo then swore that when he returned to Atlantic City, he would murder Vincent Falcone.

It is likely that Scarfo summoned Alfredo Ferraro and ordered him to set Vincent up to be killed. It is customary in such matters to use someone close to the victim, since the trust between the two makes access easier. Instead, Ferraro left town, but not before warning his friend that Nicky intended to kill him.

Vincent now carefully avoided Nicky and began taking steps to protect himself. On his side, Scarfo became convinced that Falcone was plotting to kill *him*. It was his paranoid obsession with Vincent that triggered the trips to the building in Margate. Nicky's problem was how to get to Falcone.

The obvious answer was Joe Salerno.

Vincent had been one of the first friends Joe had made on the Jersey shore, and though Vincent knew that Joe was involved with Scarfo's group, the two still met occasionally for drinks. In their conversations, Vincent said nothing to Joe about the warning he had received, but Joe could see that his friend appeared uneasy.

By now, Joe was determined to get out of his financial obligation to Scarfo. His plumbing business was being bankrupted by his debts, but he needed cash to repay Philip. Then he contracted hepatitis on a job and was laid up for a month. His payments fell behind, and Philip began to threaten him. In desperation, Joe turned to his family.

Joe's parents owned a motel in the beach town of Wildwood Crest, and Joe drove down there to see his father. He gave him few details of his dealings in Atlantic City, saying only that he had borrowed loan-shark money and needed to repay it at once. His father took out a bank loan for $10,000 and gave the money to Joe, asking no more questions. Joe repaid Philip all but a thousand dollars of the interest, which Philip told him to forget.

A few nights later, Joe accompanied Nicky, Philip, and the Merlino brothers to the opening of an Italian restaurant in Philadelphia. The guest of honor was Angelo Bruno's underboss, Phil Testa. During the dinner Nicky took Joe aside.

'Hey, Joe,' he began, glancing to right and left to avoid his eyes, 'you got any guns?'

Joe replied that he had, at his father's house.

Nicky nodded. 'I want you to bring em around sometime so I can look at em.'

Joe had been trying to limit his contacts with Scarfo, and the request immediately put him on his guard. He managed to make excuses for not producing the guns for a few weeks, but at last, in October, Nicky pinned him down. It was time for Joe to drive to South Philadelphia to pick up the kitchen cabinets he had ordered made for Philip's grandmother.

'Now would be a good time to bring back those "chandeliers," ' Nicky remarked.

There was no way Joe could get out of it. After picking up the cabinets, he stopped at his parents' house and told his father that he wanted his guns because he planned to go hunting. His father handed them over – a 30.06 hunting rifle with scope, and a .32-caliber Colt revolver.

Joe delivered the guns to Nicky at the Scarf, Inc. office. Nicky looked them over approvingly and told Philip to put them in the trunk of the Cadillac. Nothing more was said about the matter.

The following Saturday afternoon, Nicky and Joe were alone at Scarf, Inc. Nicky asked Joe where his people came from. Joe answered that his father's family was from Calabria.

'Ah, you're like me, Calabrese,' Nicky replied. 'We're good people. Anybody in your family in the law?' Joe told him no.

'C'mon,' Nicky said, 'we'll get some lunch.' He took Joe to the Brajole, a nearby Italian café, which was deserted. After they had ordered, Nicky leaned across the table. 'You ever wanna be a gangster, Joe?' he asked in an undertone.

Joe asked him what he meant.

'Well, you see, there's three kinds of criminals,' Nicky explained. 'There's drug dealers, there's racketeers, and there's gangsters. We're the ones – we're the gangsters. We don't hire nobody. The others, if they want somethin done, they come to us. Now you and me, we're Calabrese. We're where it came from. Not the Sicilians, us. You understand?'

Joe answered that he did.

'Good,' Nicky replied. 'We'll talk about this again.'

It was now all very real to Joe – in fact, too real. He knew now what he was dealing with, and he was scared, for he saw himself being drawn in deeper and deeper. He had been trying to pull away from Scarfo and his people, but it seemed that every move he made to free himself only served to tie him tighter. They had him, and they had his guns. What would happen next he did not know, but he knew that he feared it.

5

'You're One of Us Now'

Joe ordered bicycles for his sons for Christmas, and in December he began work on a plumbing job at one of the new casinos in Atlantic City. He was worried all the time now, convinced that Scarfo was planning to murder someone, using his guns.

He remained in contact with his wife and saw his sons as often as he could. He began to long for their former days together in Brigantine, when work was going well and he had had no cares except the usual domestic challenges of running a household. He hoped that Christmas might bring relief, from both his marital difficulties and his involvement at Scarf, Inc.

One afternoon in early December, Philip Leonetti and Lawrence Merlino appeared at the Scarf, Inc. office together. They chatted with Joe for a few minutes, and then Philip said to Lawrence, 'How bout we take that ride now?' As the three men walked out to Lawrence's black Thunderbird, Joe noticed that Merlino was carrying a small brown paper bag. Joe asked if his gun was in the bag.

Philip turned on him. 'I told you not to mention them guns no more,' he said.

Joe was now sure that the bag contained his revolver, and he became frightened of what might happen. Merlino slipped the bag under the driver's seat, and he and

Philip climbed into the front. Joe got in the back. They set off in the direction of the Atlantic City Expressway.

The longer they drove, the more apprehensive Joe became. He knew too much about their operations, he told himself, and so they had decided to kill him. Or they were planning to kill someone else but had to get rid of Joe first. They would murder him in the car and dispose of his body somewhere in the woods.

Lawrence and Phil drove on in silence. Finally, Joe pulled himself up between the front seats, resting an elbow on each, so that he could watch their hands.

'What are ya sittin up for?' Philip asked him. 'Sit back, relax.'

Joe told them he was hungry and that they should stop for something to eat. He repeated this several times until Merlino finally pulled in at a restaurant. After the meal, the three drove back to Scarf, Inc.

That evening, Joe and Lawrence went to a nightclub together.

Lawrence was drinkin so I started to pump him. I said, 'Y'know, this afternoon, the way you guys were actin, I thought you were gonna do somethin to me.' And Lawrence says, 'No way. Don't ever say nothin like that.' So I was trying to get him drunk, and I said, 'But really, if you did do somethin in a car, how would you get rid of it – the body, and stuff?' Lawrence shrugs, and he says, 'Oh, we can always get rid of a car or a body. But let's not talk about it; we ain't gonna do nothin.'

Joe's apprehensiveness evidently triggered a response on Scarfo's part. Shortly after the incident, Nicky took him aside and confided that he was going to kill a Philadelphia mobster named Tony De Pasquale. 'He

61

showed me disrespect,' Scarfo told Joe. 'He spit in my face.'

Then, with a rare direct look, Scarfo fixed Joe's eyes. 'If somethin happened in front of you,' he asked, 'would you be all right?' Joe knew he could not show fear, so he replied that he would.

'That's good,' Nicky nodded. 'Now, what I want you to do, I want you to stick close to Philip. I want you to hang around with him at the office every afternoon between four and six. Understand?'

Joe answered that he did.

'Good,' Nicky said. 'And remember, you don't repeat a word of this to anybody. Not Philip, not Lawrence, not Vincent Falcone.'

Joe knew he was trapped. Scarfo *was* planning a murder, and Joe was sure his gun would be used. He could not go to the police, since the others could name him as an accessory. And he had a wife and children who would be in danger if he made any move to prevent the murder. He had no choice but to play along with Scarfo, hoping for some opening through which to escape.

As Nicky had instructed, Joe was at the Scarf, Inc. office every afternoon. The curtains at the front were thrown wide open, and Joe was seated at a desk in the window. What the purpose of this display was, he did not know.

There was, at least, one good piece of news: the rift between Nicky and Vincent Falcone seemed to have closed. Joe did not know what had caused Vincent's absence, but Nicky assured Joe that he had put word out on the street that their difficulties were resolved. Nicky even told Joe that he intended to make Vincent the business agent for the local cement workers' union. It was an important job, paying $75,000 a year, with the use of a new car. Joe was not surprised, therefore, when

Vincent stopped in at the office one afternoon in mid-December.

Joe greeted him, and then Philip shook his hand.

'Let me get my uncle,' Phil told him, and he went upstairs for Nicky.

Scarfo came down, smiling, and took Vincent's hand.

'How ya doin, Vince, how ya been?' he beamed. 'We ain't seen ya in a while. You should come around more often.'

The rest of that week Vincent stopped in to pay his respects to Nicky, as he used to do, each afternoon between four and six.

On Sunday morning, 16 December, Nicky stopped Joe as he passed the Scarf, Inc. office on his way upstairs to his apartment. 'Joe,' Nicky greeted him, as always shaking his hand, 'today we're gonna have a party, and I want you to be there.'

Joe tried to demur, saying he was going to see his sons. Nicky cut him off. 'Philip and Vincent are gonna be there, and Chuckie and Lawrence are comin down from Philly. It's a Christmas party, Joe . . . you'll come.'

Upstairs, Joe phoned his wife. He told her he was on his way over. 'I'm just about to leave with the kids,' she answered. She said they were going to collect firewood.

'I gotta talk to you,' Joe said. 'I'll go with you. Wait until I get there.'

When he arrived at the house in Brigantine, Barbara, his sons, and several neighbor children were dressed and waiting at the car. They all climbed in together and drove to the frozen forest around the town of Absecon.

While the children played and shouted and gathered wood, Joe told Barbara what had been preoccupying him for the past weeks.

'I don't know what to do,' he began. 'I think somethin's gonna happen today.'

Barbara asked impatiently what he was talking about.

'I don't know,' Joe replied. 'They might do somethin to somebody . . .'

'Well, *what*?' she demanded.

'Maybe hurt somebody, I don't know. But I'm scared.'

Barbara began to berate him, telling him that if anything did happen it was his own fault for associating with that kind of people.

'Look,' he cut her off, 'I just wanted to tell you, if anything happens to me, you know who I'm with.'

She responded with silence.

When the children had finished, they all drove back to Brigantine. On the way, Joe picked up a Christmas tree.

They spent the rest of the morning setting up the tree and decorating it. The familiar, festive gestures were welcome to Joe, whose mind had been in a turmoil for so long.

Then the phone rang.

'He wants you over here,' Lawrence Merlino told Joe.

Joe answered that he did not feel like partying, and that he and his family were trimming the tree.

'You can do it later,' Merlino said. 'He wants you now. We're gonna go out. It's a party. You gotta get over here.'

I couldn't get out of it. I got in the car. It only took five minutes to drive over to Georgia Avenue. I went into the office. Philip was there, Lawrence was there, and Vincent. Vincent shook my hand. He said they'd told him I was coming. Then Philip went out to the back and I went after him. 'Look, Philip,' I told him, 'I don't feel like goin to a party today.' He says, 'C'mon, man, Chuckie's comin down, he wants to see you.' Then, for a split second, he gave me that look, and he says, 'C'mon, you'll have a good time.'

That brief, lethal glance made it clear to Joe that he had no choice.

As the men talked and got ready to go, Joe tried to convince himself that he was letting his imagination run away with him. Philip and Lawrence seemed perfectly at ease, as did Vincent Falcone. Joe knew that Nicky had promised Vincent the job with the cement workers' union, and he also felt that he and Vincent were secure in each other's presence.

They climbed into Lawrence's Thunderbird – Merlino and Leonetti in front, Joe and Vincent in the back. As they drove, Philip and Vincent talked casually about evenings they had spent together and women they had known. Joe began to let himself believe that his fears had been exaggerated.

Merlino drove through the city, and Joe was surprised when he suddenly turned south. 'We gotta make a stop,' Philip said. 'We're gonna pick up my uncle in Margate, at Phil Disney's.'

Joe knew that Phil Disney was a business acquaintance of Scarfo's who enjoyed cultivating the society of gangsters. They pulled up at a two-story apartment building on the beach and climbed the stairs to the upper floor. The door to Disney's apartment was open.

The apartment was a small L-shaped room, the broad leg of which was the living room, while the narrow end was a combination dining area and kitchen. These two were bordered by a low counter, which served as a bar.

Nicky Scarfo was seated on the sofa watching a football game, half-glasses perched on his nose, his legs propped on a coffee table. He greeted them and said that Phil Disney had gone out for a few minutes. 'Let's wait for him,' Nicky offered. 'Vincent, go and make some drinks. There's plenty of booze in the kitchen.'

Vincent walked around the dining-room table to the bar. He reached for the Scotch, knowing that Nicky insisted that everyone drink Scotch and water. He poured two drinks and placed them on the table, near where Phil and Joe were standing. Lawrence had moved to the far side of the table, and Nicky still sat watching the game.

Vincent returned to the counter for more glasses, again turning his back toward the others.

Philip is standin right next to me. I pick up my drink, and I'm about to take a sip when out of the corner of my eye I see Philip make a move. He takes a step in front of me and leans over toward Vincent. He's got a gun in his hand – my gun – and he puts it to the back of Vincent's head and . . . BOOM!

The bullet blasted into Falcone's skull, destroying his brain instantly. His body was seized in a convulsive spasm, and for a moment he stiffened and shuddered violently. Then he relaxed, half-turned, his hands limp across his stomach, his legs crossed, and slid to the floor. He sat there motionless, leaning against the corner cabinets, his eyes open and staring.

It happened so fast, I've still got the drink to my lips. Philip's got the gun down by his waist, and he turns toward me and puts his face up close to mine. His eyes are full of that look of his, and he says to me, 'Joe, he was a no-good motherfucker.'

Nicky comes up to me on the other side and says, 'You OK?' I can't show them how scared I am, so I say, 'Yeah, I'm fine.' 'Good,' Nicky says. 'You're one of us now.'

Nicky goes over to where Vincent is sittin. He pulls

open Vincent's jacket, crouches down, and listens to his heart. 'I think we should give him another one,' he says. 'Give me the gun.'

'No,' Philip says, 'I'll do it.' Philip steps over to Vincent, puts the gun to his chest, and BOOM!

Nicky then began giving instructions. He told Philip to wipe the gun, wrap it, and dispose of it. Lawrence and Joe were ordered to move the dining-room table into the living room. Then they laid the body out on the floor.

Nicky reaches into Vincent's pocket, takes out his keys, and gives them to Lawrence. 'You know what to do with these,' he says. Then Lawrence and Philip leave.

Now I'm alone with Scarfo and Vincent. There's a cardboard box by the sofa with a blanket and twine in it. Nicky gets it and says to me, 'Joe, I need your strength. You know how they used to tie people up in the cowboy days? I want you to do that.'

Joe knelt down and rolled Vincent over on to his chest. Blood was gathering on Vincent's shirt front. His face was distorted by the shock, and his forehead was buckled out where the bullet had struck it from behind. In the hair beside his right ear was a bullet hole, from which blood was trickling out on to his collar.

Joe put Vincent's hands behind his back and tied his wrists together. Then, following Nicky's instructions, he bent Vincent's legs up, bound his ankles together, and tied them to his wrists.

Then Nicky tells me, 'Wrap him in the blanket, but leave the face exposed.' I tie the blanket around the body, and Nicky says, 'I love this . . . I love it. The big shot is dead.' Then he bends down to the body and closes the eyes. He takes the end of the blanket and throws it over Vincent's face, and he tells me, 'Now tie that part up, too.'

Joe took a piece of the twine and secured the blanket around Vincent's neck. There had been surprisingly little blood, some stains on the cabinets and a few smears on the floor.

By now it was dusk, and a chill silence had settled. Lawrence, who had been dispatched to get Vincent's car, had been gone a long time. In the apartment were Nicky, Joe, and the blanketed body.

Then, outside the window, Joe saw a police car roll to a stop. Nicky's Cadillac was parked a few yards away from it at the curb. While Joe and Nicky watched, the policeman took out a thermos and poured a cup of coffee.

'We should warn Lawrence not to come back right now,' Nicky said. He told Joe to call him at the Scarf, Inc. office.

Joe reached for the phone, but Nicky stopped him

'No, don't call from this phone. There's a phone booth at the corner.'

Joe made his way to the phone booth, staying out of sight of the policeman. He had a powerful urge to run, to get as far away as possible. But there were his wife and children to think of, and, too, they had used his gun.

Instead of calling Scarf, Inc. Joe called Barbara. She was not home. His son Michael answered the phone.

'When you see Mommy, tell her that I'm OK,' he said.

Then he called Lawrence Merlino, who was still at the office.

'OK, I won't come,' Lawrence said, 'but give me a call back.'

When Joe returned to the apartment, the police car was gone. He went back to the phone booth and told Lawrence it was safe to come.

As he walked again to the apartment, his mind was fighting the shock he felt. Vincent was dead, lying on the floor of Phil Disney's dining room, and though he had had no part in it, Joe knew he was involved.

Philip, he now understood, was mad – a homicidal lunatic. And Nicky had schemed out the whole business, from insisting on seeing Joe's guns to putting him on display in the Scarf, Inc. window as a signal to Vincent that he would be safe there.

It all came clear now to Joe. Nicky had lied about wanting to kill Tony De Pasquale to divert Joe's attention from Vincent. And he had lied to him about offering Vincent the union job in order to allay his suspicions. They had used him to lure Vincent to his death, exploiting Vincent's trust in him. And they had used his gun.

He realized that, for the moment at least, he had no choice: he must play along with them. For his own safety and that of his family, he must seem to be, as Nicky had said, one of them. But beyond that everything was dim and confused, and his mind was in too much tumult to imagine a way out.

When Joe got back to the apartment, Nicky was drinking. Joe explained what had happened and said that Lawrence was on his way.

'Good,' Nicky grunted, downing another Scotch. He was becoming drunk. 'What the hell's takin him so long?'

It was dark by the time Lawrence pulled up to the foot of the stairs. He had changed his clothes and was wearing gloves. Nicky also put on soft driving gloves, and gave a pair to Joe.

He ordered Joe and Lawrence to carry the body down and put it in the trunk. Joe took the legs and Lawrence the torso, and they started down while Nicky watched.

It was a heavy and awkward burden, and they

struggled with it until, near the bottom of the stairs, Lawrence dropped his end. Joe strained to keep the body from tumbling while Lawrence regained his grip. Finally, they reached the car.

As they were about to heft the body into the trunk, Nicky called to them.

'Wait, I want somethin outa that car.'

He was drunk now, and he had to hold the railing as he hurried down the stairs.

'There's somethin in here I always wanted,' he muttered. Joe saw him reach into the spare-tire compartment and take out a gun. It was wrapped in a jogging suit, which Nicky also took.

When they had locked the body in the trunk, Nicky went back upstairs and closed the apartment door.

'I'm gonna drive this car,' he told them, taking Vincent's keys from Lawrence. 'You two follow me in my car, but not close. After I get out I'll walk for a while, then you pick me up. But stay back.'

Joe got into the front seat of Nicky's black Cadillac, and Lawrence drove. Nicky led them, weaving, through the deserted Margate streets to the home of a contractor with whom Joe had worked. Across the street, new homes were under construction. Nicky parked Vincent's car in front of the unlit, bare-ribbed structures.

Scarfo got out and walked for a few blocks while Lawrence followed at a distance. At last Scarfo stopped, and Lawrence pulled over. Nicky came to the driver's-side door, so Lawrence slid over and Joe got into the backseat.

Nicky began driving toward Georgia Avenue, but suddenly he stopped and made a U-turn.

'We forgot somethin,' he said.

In a few minutes they were back at Phil Disney's apartment. Nicky opened the door with his key.

'Salerno,' he said, 'get a washcloth or somethin from the bathroom and wipe everything down. And use cold water – don't use any hot water.'

Joe did as Nicky instructed, sponging up the blood on the countertop and floor. He started to move the table back into the dining room.

Nicky stopped him. 'No – leave it there.'

Again they climbed into the Cadillac and started off for Georgia Avenue. At the office of Scarf, Inc., Nicky gave more instructions.

'Take off everything you've got on – shirts, shoes, underwear, everything – and put it in a bag. Take a shower and get changed, and bring the clothes back here.'

Joe made his way up to the apartment and did as he had been told. His gestures were strangely mechanical, numb, detached.

I wasn't really thinkin, because I was in a state of shock. I just felt I was in so much trouble now that I'd never get away from these people, that I'd have to be with them forever. Then, in the next minute, I'd tell myself, no, no way could I ever be one of them. I'd seen what they'd done, and I knew what they were doin to me. But I couldn't collect my mind enough to reason out what I should do.

When Joe went back to the office, Philip Leonetti and Lawrence Merlino were waiting. They had been joined by Lawrence's brother, Chuckie.

Joe put the plastic bag containing his clothes into a larger one, which already held those of Nicky and Lawrence.

'So,' Chuckie said to Joe, 'lights out, huh?'

Joe nodded.

'You did a good job,' Chuckie told him, and turned to Nicky. 'I told you he'd do a good job.'

'I didn't know it was gonna be him,' Joe said.

Chuckie then told Joe the story about Vincent's remark, and the trip to Italy. 'So we decided the guy's no good,' he concluded, 'and we killed him. Forget it.'

Nicky was putting on his trench coat to leave. 'It's over with,' he grumbled. 'Next we're gonna get that other guy, that Alfredo. And Tony De Pasquale. He don't know you, Joe – you could walk up to him in a bar and shoot him right in the face.'

His expression brightened suddenly. 'But tomorrow what we're gonna do, we're goin over to Philly, to the Camac baths, and get some steam. I want all you guys there. Then we'll go out, we'll eat, we'll drink; we're gonna relax. Tomorrow,' he declared, 'is a holiday for us.'

6

'We Have an Informant Who Says You're Next'

That night, Joe accompanied Philip and the Merlino brothers to dinner at one of the casinos. They picked up some women and went to a bar for drinks. Nicky had clearly been in earnest when he said they were going to celebrate.

Anxious as he was to get away from them, Joe knew he dare not show any discomfort. However, when he was alone for a moment with Philip, he could not help but repeat his surprise that the target had been Vincent.

'Let me tell ya somethin,' Philip said. 'If I could bring that bastard back to life, I'd kill him again. But don't worry,' he added, 'it's over with now. Everything's gonna be all right.' And he shook Joe's hand.

The group broke up after midnight. 'C'mon,' Philip said to Joe, 'let's take a ride.'

Philip drove to a dumpster near the Brajole Café, where they often went for drinks, and he and Joe disposed of the bag containing their clothes.

Philip then headed for the boardwalk at Mississippi Avenue. He pulled over at an open sewer drain, handed Joe a small green cardboard box, and told him to drop it into the drain.

Joe opened the car door and tossed the box out. It missed the drain and fell open in the street. Philip cursed and told him to get it. When the car's dome light shone on the box, Joe saw that it contained .32-caliber cartridges. He gathered them up and threw them into the sewer.

Before Philip left him, he told Joe that he and Nicky had some business the next morning in Philadelphia and would be leaving early. Joe was to go to his parents' home in South Philly and wait for a call telling him where to meet them.

Joe drove immediately to his house in Brigantine and woke Barbara. 'You can't believe what they did,' he told her. 'They killed Vincent.'

Barbara turned on him furiously. 'You *knew* they would!' she said. Joe insisted that he had not known, but Barbara refused to believe him. They argued for an hour, until Joe finally convinced her that he had not been involved.

'Well,' she concluded, 'you'd better get out of this house.'

It was now nearly three in the morning. The others had said they were leaving early: if they did not find Joe at his apartment at 26 North Georgia Avenue, they would become suspicious. Joe drove to the apartment, where he lay awake for the rest of the night. Around seven, he heard Philip and Nicky leave. A few hours later, he drove to South Philadelphia.

In the kitchen of his parents' home, Joe told his mother that he thought he might have to move away. He was tired of Jersey, he said, and he had had an offer from a friend to join him in the plumbing business in Florida.

His mother tried to dissuade him. It was because of his business and marital problems that he felt that way, she said. Things would get better; he didn't have to move.

All morning Joe waited at the house for the phone call

74

from Nicky, dreading it. Hours went by and it did not come. By afternoon he had decided that he would not go to the Camac baths. He was sure that it was a setup, and that they intended to kill him.

At last the phone rang. It was Philip.

'My uncle's not feelin too good,' he told Joe, 'so we're cancelin this afternoon. Go back to Georgia Avenue and meet us there.'

Once again, Joe had no choice. He made the long drive back to Atlantic City and pulled up at the Scarf, Inc. office. In the office were Nicky, Philip, Lawrence Merlino, and two other men. Joe recognized one of them as Salvatore Testa, Phil Testa's son. The other he knew from his old neighborhood. He was Frank Narducci, Jr, whose family lived behind Joe's parents. Joe had known Frank and his brother, Phil, since boyhood. He had heard that they were connected with Testa's gang.

Joe was looking for some excuse to leave. Several times he had caught Nicky staring at him, and it unnerved him. At last he said to Nicky that he wanted to spend the week before Christmas with his family. 'Good,' Nicky replied. 'That's a good idea. You get away for a while, cause there's gonna be a lot of heat on once they find our friend.'

From Scarf, Inc., Joe drove back to Brigantine.

Barbara was displeased to see him, but Joe insisted that he could not go back to Georgia Avenue. He needed some time away from them to think. Reluctantly, she agreed to let him stay and sleep on the sofa.

The rest of Monday and all day Tuesday Joe stayed in the house, trying to decide what he should, or could, do. He felt keenly that his entire family was in danger now, but he feared that he was too deeply involved to do anything to save them. By Wednesday he was hopelessly confused and growing desperate.

Joe had had no word from Nicky since leaving the office three days earlier. Nicky's silence was almost as sinister as his presence. Joe felt that he had to find out what Nicky and Philip were up to, and so that afternoon he called Georgia Avenue.

Philip's mother answered the phone. She told Joe that Nicky and Philip were at Scannicchio's Restaurant, not far from the office. Joe knew the place well. It was popular and busy. He felt that nothing could happen to him there, so he drove over in the hopes of getting some idea of what Nicky and Philip were planning.

He found them seated at a back table. He joined them, and Nicky ordered him a drink. Both Nicky and Philip seemed to be in a good mood, and they made small talk for a while. Then Joe brought up the subject of the gun.

'When they find this guy,' I said, 'it'll make the front page of all the papers. They'll see that he was shot with a .32.' I reminded them that I had just picked up the gun at my dad's a couple of weeks before, and I said he might get suspicious. 'Don't worry about that,' Nicky says. 'There's plenty of .32s in the world.' But I could see what I'd said bothered him a lot.

After a few minutes Nicky said he had to go, and he left. Philip asked me for a ride home, but when we got outside he turned to me. 'You never shoulda said that to my uncle about the gun,' he said. 'You got him worried.'

And I said to myself, now I know what's goin on. They used me to get to this guy, they killed him with my gun, they've still got the gun, and now they're not talkin to me. They've got me, they've got the kids, they've got all of us under their thumb. And now they're afraid I'm gonna talk.

Joe returned to the house in Brigantine, and to another

sleepless night. The next day – Thursday, 20 December – the police found Vincent Falcone's body.

To the Atlantic County prosecutors, it was unmistakably a gangland killing. The bullets in the head and chest, the trussing, the trunk of the car: they had seen it several times in the past few years. The investigators immediately contacted their informants in the mob, trying to anticipate who might be next. To their susprise, a name they did not recognize rose to the top of the hit list.

When the news of Falcone's murder appeared that evening on television, Barbara Salerno seemed to grasp the full reality for the first time.

'You're sick,' she said to Joe. 'I told you something like this would happen if you hung around with those people. Now what are we going to do?'

Joe shook his head. He had been torturing himself with that question for days, and he had to admit that he still had no answer.

'I gotta do something,' Joe said. 'I gotta take off – I gotta run.'

'What about the kids?' Barbara demanded.

'I know, I know,' Joe replied. 'You're right . . . I can't run. I don't know what to do.'

All day Friday Joe stayed in the house, afraid to go out. He had not slept in days, so he began to drink until he passed out. By Saturday, a week after Falcone's murder, he was a shambles.

Saturday morning I was in the livin room, and I saw three men get out of a car out front. They came up the steps, and I knew they were cops. I didn't know until that moment what I was gonna do, but when I saw them I decided.

The men introduced themselves as detectives from the Atlantic County Prosecutor's Office. They told Joe they wanted to talk to him.

I asked what they wanted to talk about. They said, 'We've got an informant who says you're next.' In my own mind I knew that these people were gonna kill me, but when I heard it from someone else, I knew it wasn't just me, just paranoia – it became real. I said to them: 'What do you mean, "next"? For what?' They asked me, 'Do you know Vincent Falcone?' I said I did. They said, 'Do you know that he was murdered?' I told them, 'Look, I know everything you want to know, but I'm not gonna talk here in my house, in front of my family.' They asked if I was willin to go with them to the prosecutor's office. I said yes.

Joe followed the detectives in his own car across the Brigantine Bridge to the prosecutor's office in Atlantic City. By now his anxiety was at fever pitch. The detectives led him into an enormous, open room filled with desks and chattering typewriters. After his days of seclusion, Joe felt unnerved by all the activity, and he asked to be taken into a smaller room.

Once there, the detectives crowded around Joe, who sat hunched at a little table. One of them opened a folder and dropped half a dozen photographs in front of him. They were photos of Vincent Falcone's body, including an enlarged close-up of his face.

'Do you know what happened?' they asked.

Confronting Vincent again – wrapped in the blanket in which he had tied him, his face smeared with blood, his eyes closed and swollen, his skin blue – pushed Joe over the edge. Yet his reaction was not one of hysteria but of fierce determination.

'I'm not gonna say anything to you,' I said. 'I don't care if you put me in jail; I'm not sayin one word unless you get my wife and kids out of that house and get them protected. Then I'll tell you what went on.' They said to me, 'Don't worry, we'll take care of it.' I said, 'No, I want it done now. My car's parked right outside; these people will know I'm here, and I'm scared they'll do somethin to my family. Lock me up if you want, but I want it done right now.'

The detectives arranged to have Barbara and the boys moved to a neighbor's house, where they were put under police guard. Only after Joe had called the neighbor and verified that they were safe did he agree to make a statement.

For the next twelve hours, Joe went over his relations with Scarfo and the murder of Falcone again and again. The detectives badgered and challenged him, trying to break down his story.

As the hours wore on and the detectives became convinced that Joe was telling the truth, the prosecutors were called out of their homes and their beds to join the interrogation. By midnight, the office was brilliant with light and filled with people. The excitement was scarcely suppressed: at last they had a witness willing to testify against the Scarfo organization.

At one point, in the middle of the night, Joe was bustled into an unmarked car with five detectives and driven to Phil Disney's apartment, where he pointed out the crime scene. On the way back, the detectives received a radio message that the prosecutor was on his way to a judge's home to apply for arrest warrants.

They swung the car around and headed for the judge's house. While Joe lay on the floor of the backseat, the detectives and the prosecutor hurried into the house. In the living room, the judge, in pajamas and robe, signed warrants for the arrest of Nicodemo Scarfo, Philip Leonetti, and Lawrence Merlino. The charge was murder in the first degree.

On Sunday morning, Leonetti and Merlino were arrested at 26 North Georgia Avenue. Scarfo was picked up later at his mistress's apartment. When the detectives told him that he was charged with the murder of Vincent Falcone, he grumbled: 'How in hell did you put that together?'

It was only later, when all three were assembled at the county prison, that they realized it had been Joe Salerno who had talked.

PART TWO

A MARKED MAN,
1980–1982

7

'Have You Ever Heard of the Witness Protection Program?'

It was early Sunday morning, 23 December, before Joe got back to Brigantine. The detectives drove him to the neighbor's house where his wife and children were under police protection, and together the family moved back into their own home.

The atmosphere by now was bizarre. The house was decorated for Christmas; colored lights sparkled on the eaves and sashes, and the tree glistened at the front window. But the place was ringed with unmarked police cars in which detectives watched with machine guns.

There were police inside as well, armed with shotguns, while in the house, the mantle was decorated with holly, and there were a few presents already under the tree. The three boys were almost as excited by the nearness of Christmas as they were by the armed strangers. Barbara, however, maintained a stony silence, scarcely speaking to Joe. For Joe, there was only fear, uncertainty, confusion, and more fear.

In the midst of everything, relatives began arriving. Joe's father and mother had heard about the murder and Scarfo's arrest and had hurried to the house. Joe's sister, Lisa, and brother, Thomas, also came, as did an aunt and uncle. Barbara's family, too, began to arrive. By

Christmas Eve, the house was overflowing with family and police.

Joe tried as best he could to explain what had happened. Reactions ranged from crying and hand-wringing on the part of his family to rueful reserve from his in-laws. The question in everyone's mind, however, was the same: What would happen next?

It was then that the first phone call came. The police had bugged Joe's phone, hoping to intercept some talk of the murder. It was Philip Leonetti's voice on the line, asking Joe to come down to the county jail to see him.

'I can't,' Joe replied. 'I've got 9,000 cops here.'

Philip hung up.

The detectives supposed that Scarfo wanted to see Joe to threaten or bribe him into silence. It was a tactic he was believed to have used in an earlier murder case. In that case, a truck driver, the only witness to the killing of a gangster rival of Scarfo's, had initially agreed to testify against him. After meeting with one of Scarfo's lawyers, however, the man claimed that he could not remember anything. The charges were dropped.

The call from Philip put everyone on edge. When Joe's in-laws offered to have Christmas dinner at their house on the other side of Brigantine, Joe accepted, and the police agreed to escort the family there.

It was there that the second call occurred. When Joe's father-in-law answered the phone, an anonymous voice warned him that they would all pay for what Joe was doing.

Whatever pretense of a normal Christmas the family had managed up till now was destroyed. After the exchange of gifts, the detectives took Joe and his family back to their house.

The third call came the next morning. By now, everyone tensed when the phone rang. While the detectives looked on, Joe reluctantly picked up the receiver.

'Hello . . .'

'Your family's gonna be dead,' the caller told him, and hung up.

The Salerno family was now under twenty-four-hour police protection in their home, but the situation was becoming untenable. Joe was thoroughly paranoid, and Barbara was continually upset. The three boys were not allowed out, and they were growing more restless every day. And with the telephone threats, everyone – including the police – was in a constant state of anxiety.

The Atlantic County Prosecutor's Office decided to apply on Joe's behalf for the family's admission into the federal Witness Protection Program. The program had grown out of efforts by Attorney General Robert Kennedy to fight organized crime during the early sixties. The first breakthrough was the defection of mafioso Joe Valachi. His violation of *omertà*, the ironclad code of silence, encouraged other mobsters to come forward, and the Justice Department realized that there had to be some way of ensuring the safety of these witnesses.

With no specific guidelines to follow, a protection program had been organized piecemeal. At first, it merely provided witnesses with safe houses, but gradually the program took on the responsibility of relocating them and changing their identities. The program's authority and details were never formally debated by Congress, and it lacked even a fixed title. It was variously referred to as the Witness Security Programme, the Witness Relocation Program, and the Witness Protection Program.

Equally haphazardly, the programme was entrusted to the US Marshal's Service. The Marshal's Service had previously been responsible for process serving and for guarding prisoners. Though it was now also to be entrusted with hiding witnesses and creating new identities for them, the service was perhaps the only law-enforcement agency that had no undercover or intelligence experience. It was also one of the few agencies that had no vested interest in witnesses' safety.

Nonetheless, within a few years the Witness Protection Program had a budget of $11 million and a staff of more than 200, and it was creating new lives for some 500 witnesses each year. Almost all of these people were criminals, a fact that permanently colored the program administrators' perceptions of them.

This was a feature of the Witness Program of which Joe Salerno would become painfully aware. For the moment, however, he accepted without protest the Atlantic County prosecutors' offer of protection.

In my state of mind, I couldn't think things out, so I just followed along with what the prosecutors said. I didn't know anything about the Witness Program; I'd never even heard of it. What I didn't realize was that the prosecutors didn't know anything about the program, either. They said they'd take care of all our bills and we'd have no financial worries, that it would be like a new start.

I didn't really believe they could keep us safe, but I felt it was the only thing I could do.

It would be several days before the Marshal's Service could process the family's application; in the meantime, the Salernos could not stay where they were. On the morning of 27 December, two unmarked police cars pulled up to the house.

*There were four detectives, and this sergeant, Joe Khoury,
was in charge. He was a big guy, very official, did
everything by the book. He told me they were goin to
relocate us for a while and that we should pack enough
clothes for about a week. I told my family we were leavin,
and Barbara started cryin, and everybody was throwin
stuff into suitcases. When we were ready, I asked where
we were goin. The detectives said they couldn't tell us,
and Barbara started cryin again.*

Sergeant Khoury had not told Joe where they were
going because he did not know himself. One thing he had
decided, however: since it was midwinter, the mob would
likely assume that the group would be traveling south.
Instead, they would go north.

In two cars, they drove first to upstate New York and
stopped for the night in a small town. Khoury had been
given several hundred dollars in cash to cover their
expenses. They were to stay at motels, use false names,
and leave no records of their passage. Not even the
prosecutor's office was to know where they were, though
Khoury was to call in every evening.

Over dinner that first night, Khoury told the Salernos
the names they would be using on the trip. They also
had to learn the cover story that had been prepared for
them.

For the three boys it was a grand adventure: traveling
to strange places, using new names and a made-up story
about their past. They competed with one another to
share rooms with the policemen, on whom they played
ceaseless practical jokes, tying their shoelaces together or
hiding their toothbrushes.

For Joe and Barbara, it was a death blow to their
already damaged relations. They drove in different cars
and slept in separate rooms, taking turns sharing beds

with the boys. They rarely spoke to each other, and when they did it was usually to argue. When the arguments grew too heated, the detectives would mediate, telling them that the situation was only temporary, that the government would relocate them soon and they would have a normal life again.

The little convoy logged hundreds of miles during the first week. They drove through New England, never staying more than one night at any motel. Every time a stranger approached or someone in a restaurant stared at them, Joe would panic and insist on moving on.

At the end of the first week they headed west, toward Ohio. The family had now been in a dozen different towns in half a dozen states. Packing, loading the cars, and leaving had become a science: all nine of them could be ready to move on fifteen minutes' notice.

Each evening Joe Khoury phoned in to the prosecutor's office, speaking with his superiors in a pre-arranged code. And each evening he was told it would be a few more days until the Marshals were ready to interview the family.

By now the detectives had run out of money, and the Salernos had none. They could not use credit cards, nor could they draw on their own bank accounts, so a detective was dispatched from New Jersey. He drove all night through a snowstorm, and at an anonymous roadside rendezvous he handed Khoury an envelope stuffed with cash.

On New Year's Eve they were in Buffalo, trying to enjoy a dinner out to celebrate the holiday. When Sergeant Khoury phoned in, he was told to report to the US Marshal's Service in New York City at nine the following morning.

The group returned to the motel to pack and get a few hours' sleep and then left for New York. They drove all night, traveling 400 miles over unlit, icy roads. At nine o'clock the next morning they pulled up in front of the federal building in Manhattan. It was New Year's Day, 1980, and the streets were deserted. Two armed marshals met them at the curb and escorted them into the empty building.

In a large office, a marshal inspector was waiting with an Atlantic County prosecutor. Joe, Barbara, the boys, and the four detectives went in.

The marshal inspector was impatient and abrupt. 'Have your lives been threatened?' he asked as soon as they had sat down. Joe replied that they had.

Then he asked: 'Have you ever heard of the federal Witness Protection Program?' I said we hadn't. 'Here's exactly the way it is,' he said. 'You'll never see your family or friends ever again. There will be no phone conversations with your family. We're going to take you to a place in the United States – we haven't decided where yet – and we'll change your names and social security numbers.' All this he said very coldly. He didn't ask anything about us or our situation.

Barbara started cryin hysterically. Then my oldest, Johnny, started cryin, since he understood what was happenin. Then Michael began cryin too, and when the little one, Tony, saw them, he started. So everybody's sittin there cryin, and the marshal tells us the meeting's over. It all hadn't taken twenty minutes.

The family and the detectives bundled back into their cars and set off again. This time, Joe Khoury told them, they were going to Detroit. The US Marshal's Office there would handle their relocation.

The brusque interview in New York had unsettled them all, family and detectives alike. In the hectic days of travel, they had become a close-knit little group. Joe had grown friendly with Sergeant Khoury and had come to depend on him; the whole family, especially the boys, had become attached to their protectors.

Amid all the confusion and anxiety they had shared, the one hope they all held was that the government would understand their situation and give them a new start in circumstances that would be familiar to them. Their first contact, however, had been far from reassuring.

Indeed, for Joe it had been a disaster. He blamed himself for having gotten his family into this situation, and the marshal inspector's attitude only made him feel more guilty. He had no idea what the Marshals knew about him and his reasons for entering the program, and the inspector had not seemed to care.

In a gloomy state of mind, they began the long drive to Detroit and a new life, the nature of which none of them – not even the detectives – could imagine.

8

'Just Another Case'

Nicky Scarfo, Philip Leonetti, and Lawrence Merlino were held in the Atlantic County jail over the Christmas holidays in lieu of $150,000 bail each. By New Year's they had produced the bail, in cash and property, and they were set free, pending trial.

The Atlantic County prosecutors, meanwhile, labored at building their case against the three. It was not an easy task. Investigators were sent to dig through a toxic-waste dump in search of the bag containing the suspects' clothes. After days of filthy, exhausting work, they found nothing. The bullets, however, were recovered from the sewer where Joe had thrown them. Joe's gun, the murder weapon, was never found.

Microscopic tests at Phil Disney's apartment provided scant proof that the murder had even occurred there. There were some traces of blood in the kitchen and on the banister, but it could not be typed. The Margate police were able to substantiate Joe's story of a patrol car pulling up to the house at the time of the murder, but the officer could not remember seeing Scarfo's car. And, predictably, the defense began assembling a parade of witnesses who claimed that the defendants could not have been at the scene at the time of the murder.

As they prepared for trial, the prosecutors realized that their case rested almost entirely on Joe Salerno's testimony and the willingness of the jury to believe him beyond a reasonable doubt.

Back at 26 North Georgia Avenue, Scarfo and the others seemed far from troubled. They went about their business as usual, displaying unconcern, even disdain, for the indictment. Indeed, on their visits to the casinos they wore T-shirts printed with bold letters declaring JUST ANOTHER CASE.

The Salerno family and the detectives arrived at the federal building in Detroit late on a Friday afternoon. The family was escorted to the office of a marshal inspector, but the detectives were not allowed to accompany them; the Salernos were now formally out of Atlantic County's jurisdiction.

The parting in the corridor surprised them all by its emotion. Barbara and the children cried, and the detectives, too, seemed near tears. Barbara kissed them, and they hugged each of the children. Joe shook hands with all four detectives. Sergeant Khoury gave Joe some cash, and then, spontaneously, the two hugged each other. The bond that had developed between the family and the detectives was now to be broken with a strange finality: from that moment on, the Salernos were to become different people, whom no-one from the past was to know.

The detectives left, and Joe, Barbara, and the children entered the office.

The marshal inspector, a middle-aged black man, was a war veteran, and his office was decorated with patriotic memorabilia, military medals, and a large American flag. Joe found this fact encouraging. The marshal greeted them cordially, but he was evidently in a hurry to go home.

'It's late in the day,' he said to us, 'so I really don't have too much time.' He handed me a telephone book and told us to pick out a name. 'I can give you about ten minutes,' he said. Barbara was cryin. This was goin to be our name for the rest of our lives. I flipped through the book and chose a name at random.

Then the marshal took our fingerprints and said he had some documents for us to sign. There was a stack of papers about a half-inch thick, but there was no time to read them, so we just signed. I never did know what they said. The marshal then told us to surrender any identification we had – driver's licenses, credit cards, anything with our name on it. When we did, he put it all in a big walk-in safe marked 'Classified Information.' This safe must have held the identities of hundreds of people, and now ours was in there, too – our whole past, locked up forever.

While the boys played near the safe, the marshal hurriedly informed Joe and Barbara that they must never return to the Philadelphia–South Jersey area, which he referred to as 'the danger zone.' Any property they still possessed there that had any traceable identification, such as serial numbers, would be forfeited. He promised that they would shortly be issued new social security numbers, along with new birth certificates for the children.

They were to be relocated the next day. A home would be found for them, and a subsistence payment of $1200 a month provided until they were self-supporting. Their clothes and furniture would be forwarded to the new house.

The marshal stressed that there must be no direct communication with their families or friends. Messages must be sent through the Marshal's Service, which alone was to know their whereabouts. There were to be no phone calls. No-one – not even the Atlantic County prosecutors or the FBI – was to know who or where they were. Any violation of the regulations, he concluded, could result in denial of subsistence or dismissal from the program – or worse.

'We've never lost a witness who followed our instructions,' he told them as he gathered up his things to leave, 'so if you do that, everything will be fine. However,' he continued, 'one or two of our witnesses have been killed, but they broke the rules.'

The inspector accompanied them downstairs, where armed marshals had a car waiting. Joe asked where they were to be sent. The inspector replied that he did not know; this decision was to be made by others the following day.

The Salernos were driven to a motel in Detroit and left alone. It was the first time since the detectives had come to the house to interview Joe that the family had not been surrounded by police. The sudden isolation had a powerful effect on them. Weeks of anxiety and anger spilled out.

Barbara assailed Joe for subjecting them to this madness – new identities, a new home, and they did not even know where they were going.

The boys alternated between crying over their lost home and relatives and expressing curiosity about their new life. Would there be kids where they were going? Would they go to school? Would they have to take a boat to get there?

Joe tried to put the best face on things, saying that where they were going might not be so bad. He had done nothing wrong; on the contrary, he was helping the government, so they were bound to be treated well. Besides, the trial would start soon. Once Scarfo and the others were convicted, they might be able to go home.

Again, Barbara refused to talk to Joe. In the long

silences, he tried hopelessly to tell himself that this could not be true, that it would not last long, that something was bound to happen to get them out of it.

The next morning was brittly clear and sunny. The marshal inspector they had seen the day before came to the motel and informed Joe and Barbara that their location had been chosen. They were to fly to Topeka, Kansas, where a house would be found for them.

On the flight, Barbara tried to make casual conversation, expressing interest in their new home for the first time. Joe took this as a good sign and allowed himself to relax a little. The marshal who met them in Kansas had little information to offer, however. He took them to a hotel in the city and told Joe that they were looking for a house for them to rent and a school for the boys to attend. He gave them their first month's subsistence, $1200 in cash, and then left, assuring them that he would be back in a day or two to take them to their new home.

In fact, the Salernos remained at the hotel for more than a week, during which time the initial excitement about their relocation dissolved. They had brought only enough clothes for the first few days of travel, but they had now lived in them for nearly a month. They were afraid to leave their room; they knew no-one, nor could they make any phone calls. The tentative truce between Joe and Barbara broke down, and the arguments started again.

At last the marshal returned and informed them that he had found them a house on the outskirts of Topeka. Without telling them where it was, he piled the family into his car and set off.

The drive to the house was the Salernos' first view of the area in which they would live, and it could not have been more alien to them. It was January, and the rolling

Kansas landscape was frozen and bare. As the icy road wound outward from the city, there was nothing to see for miles, except hedgerows among the snowy, stripped cornfields. The family felt as far from Philadelphia and the Jersey shore as it was possible to be.

The marshal pulled up at a small, neat single home in a new development in the suburb of Jasper. The sight of the house, at least, was reassuring. The marshal had a key and let them into the house, which was empty.

While the boys explored, the marshal explained to Joe and Barbara that the rent was $500 a month. This would be their home indefinitely; they were given no choice. Furniture would be rented for them until their own arrived by truck from Brigantine. To avoid its being traced, their furniture would be brought via a circuitous route and transferred from one truck to another several times. Their clothes would be sent the same way. There was no telling when they could expect them. Until the rented furniture came, they would stay at the hotel.

Joe took the marshal aside.

I tried to explain to him the kind of life we'd been used to in Brigantine. I told him that the $1200 wouldn't do it, with $500 a month in rent and three kids. I said I had to get to work as fast as I could and I needed some kind of transportation. He said they'd arrange all that. They'd find me a job, and they'd give me money to buy a car – $300. I asked what kind of car I could get for $300 and no credit. He just said that that was the allowance.

Barbara and the boys moved into the house after three more days at the hotel. On the morning they were to move, Joe was driven directly from the hotel to his new job. On the way, the marshal, one whom Joe had not seen before, explained that they had placed him with a plumbing company in the village of Silcott, some forty miles out in the countryside. The owner had agreed to let Joe drive to and from work in one of the company trucks until he found his own transportation.

Joe asked how much his new boss had been told about his situation. The marshal waved him off, telling him not to worry. 'Just do your job,' he said, 'and everything will be all right.'

Joe then raised the vital question of his plumbing license: with his new name and new social security number, how could he become certified? Again the marshal responded by telling him not to worry.

But Joe *was* worried. So far, he had dealt with four different marshals in four different towns. It was not like the Atlantic County Prosecutor's Office, where he had come to know and trust Sergeant Khoury. The lack of rapport bothered him.

For the first time, Joe began to feel the confines of the Witness Program. The Marshal's Service was his only link to both his past and his future. For the time being he was totally dependent upon the Marshals not only for protection and subsistence, but also for things as fundamental as his very identity and others' perception of him. To feel comfortable with this he needed continuity and information, and so far, at least, these had not been forthcoming.

And there was the question of work. Joe was thirty-four years old, and had been a plumber for fifteen years. He was a skilled craftsman and was used to earning good money. If his seniority were now stripped away from him, would he have to start all over? And how much *did* his employer know about him? Did he assume that Joe was a criminal?

When they arrived in Silcott, the marshal introduced Joe to his new boss, a genial, elderly man who was recovering from heart surgery and was glad of the help. After the marshal left, the owner quizzed Joe to assure himself he knew the profession.

He told Joe that he could start him at seven dollars an hour. For a man who had been earning forty dollars an hour and had owned his own business, this was not easy to accept. But Joe thanked him, and the owner gave him a truck and a handful of routine repair jobs.

Although Joe spent most of that day lost among the featureless farms in a truck that had no heat, he was grateful to be working again. The people he met were strange to him – farmers with accents so strong he had trouble understanding their speech – but the work was familiar and welcome.

With each job that day, Joe grew more relaxed. He determined that he would do well and make up to his family for all that had happened. Perhaps the situation could still be saved; perhaps through hard work and patience they could have something like a normal life again.

It was late by the time he finished his last job and made his way back to Silcott among the unlit country lanes. The office was closed, so Joe started back to the house in Jasper.

That was when he realized he had no idea how to get home.

The marshal had not given him his new address, and Joe had not even made a note of the street. He had only seen the house once, and he was not sure that he could recognize it. The phone was not yet connected, and when he stopped to call the Marshal's Office, there was no answer.

Joe drove around Topeka for hours, searching for some landmark he remembered. It was now nearly midnight, and the temperature was below zero. Street after unfamiliar street went by. There was not a soul out, but in any case, he could not even ask directions.

All his anger and self-accusation oozed out in the freezing truck. What had he done? He began to shout at himself, beating on the steering wheel. He had seen a man murdered before his eyes, and he had now uprooted his family and lost his home, his relatives, and his business – perhaps forever. *What in God's name had he done?*

I knew then that this whole Witness Program thing was a big mistake, that it wouldn't work for me. I couldn't sleep, I was afraid all the time. Worst of all, I couldn't talk about it to anyone, I couldn't even risk makin friends. I had nothin to look forward to but my next breath. I told myself I should have stayed in Philadelphia and had it out with these people, and if they killed me, so be it.

Barbara was right: it was all his fault. They were fighting constantly, and the boys were complaining that they would never see their friends again. The little one, Tony, had just learned how to spell his name, and now Joe had had to teach him a new one. And here he was, a grown man with a family, and he could not even find his way home.

He started to cry. How could he have gotten into this situation? And how would they ever get out? Then he became aware of the pain in his feet.

He was shivering uncontrollably, and his feet were freezing. He became frightened that he would get frostbite, so he stopped the truck, took off his boots, and began massaging his feet. The pain was intense, and as he continued searching for the house, he sat on first one and then the other foot to keep them warm.

At last, after hours of driving, he spotted a supermarket

that he thought he remembered. In a few minutes he was in the development in Jasper, scrutinizing every house in the lights of the truck. It was after midnight when he finally found the house.

He had no key, so Barbara let him in. The boys were long asleep in anticipation of their first day at the new school. The rented furniture, which had arrived that morning, was all strange to Joe, and the house seemed unwelcoming.

He told Barbara that he had gotten lost on his way back, but he said nothing about the ordeal. There was no point in upsetting her any further. What they needed to do now was to make a home of this place. Perhaps, despite everything that had happened, that could still be done. Joe hoped it was not too late. Or maybe it was: Barbara had made up his bed on the new rented sofa.

9

Death of the Docile Don

At about the same time that Joe Salerno was being relocated to Kansas, Angelo Bruno was returning to Philadelphia from a trip to Sicily. The aging boss was in poor health, and he was facing a federal indictment for racketeering. It was the beginning of a wide-ranging assault on the Philadelphia-South Jersey Family, which Bruno had ruled with relative stability for twenty-two years. Now it was becoming apparent to others, if not to Bruno, that his rule had outlived its usefulness.

But pressure from law enforcement was not the only, nor the most important, challenge to the Docile Don. If the Philadelphia Family was stable, it was also growing older and more stagnant. A younger generation, eager to assert itself, was chafing under Bruno's old-fashioned strictures.

There were fortunes to be made through narcotics, which Bruno abhorred, and through Atlantic City gambling, which he seemed to ignore. Among the leaders of the dissident faction was Bruno's own consigliere, the Calabrese Antonio Caponegro.

Caponegro, known as 'Tony Bananas,' saw the end of the Bruno era approaching and was determined to hasten it. Indictments were pending, and there was no leadership in either the methamphetamine industry or casino gambling. Caponegro knew that he could count on the support of several key members of Bruno's organization after the old man died, but that might be years away. The time to act was now.

Accordingly, Caponegro traveled to New York City to consult a member of the Genovese Family whom he had known for years, Frank Tieri. The circumstances under which they had met had not been propitious.

Caponegro controlled a lucrative numbers operation in the Newark area, a holdover from the 1960s when New York had ceded parts of North Jersey to the Philadelphia Family. Tieri was also active in the area, and he challenged Caponegro's incursion. Caponegro appealed the dispute to the New York Commission, which, acting on Angelo Bruno's recommendation, ruled in favor of Caponegro. Caponegro supposed that the matter had ended there, but Tieri was not a man to forget or forgive.

When Caponegro approached him with a plan to murder Bruno and take over the Philadelphia Family, Tieri assured Caponegro that he would support him before the Commission. Caponegro returned to Philadelphia believing that his coup was now officially sanctioned. He recruited the support of his brother-in-law Alfred Salerno, a Bruno soldier, and of capos John Simone and Frank Sindone, and ordered the assassination.

On the evening of 21 March, 1980, Bruno was returning home after dining at a South Philadelphia restaurant. He stopped briefly to buy a newspaper, then had his driver pull up in front of his narrow row house on Snyder Street. Before he could get out of the car, a man walked up to the open window, shoved a shotgun against his ear, and fired.

When the New York Commission learned of Bruno's murder, Caponegro was summoned at once. His puzzlement turned to shock when he was told that the hit had not been authorized by the Commission, nor even considered by them.

Caponegro turned helplessly to Frank Tieri, who sat coolly watching the proceedings. When he identified Tieri as the man who had authorized the hit, Tieri categorically denied it. The commissioners ruled that Caponegro had murdered a Commission member without authorization, and they sentenced him to death.

Caponegro and Alfred Salerno were taken to an isolated house in the mountains of upstate New York, tortured for days, and killed. Their bodies were later found in garbage bags in the South Bronx, naked and mutilated, with twenty-dollar bills stuffed into their rectums as a sign that they had become too greedy.

Within a few months, John Simone's body was found in the woods of Staten Island. He had been shot three times in the back of the head. Then Frank Sindone's body was discovered in a dumpster in South Philadelphia. His hands were tied behind his back, and the marks on his knees indicated that he had been kneeling when three bullets were pumped into his ear.

Frank Tieri, meanwhile, was given Caponegro's numbers operations in Newark.

The deaths of Bruno, his consigliere, and two capos threw the Philadelphia Family wide open. With New York's blessing, Bruno's underboss, Phil Testa, became the new boss. In a clean break with Bruno's tradition, Testa appointed narcotics trafficker Pete Casella as his underboss. For consigliere, he chose Nicky Scarfo.

For Scarfo, the murder of Bruno was a watershed. He could at last return from his exile in Atlantic City to Philadelphia, and to a position of power and security. What was more, for the first time in its history the Family was controlled by Calabrians.

Scarfo took the lead in expanding the Family's

membership, and dozens of new members were made within a few months. Most of these were drawn from Scarfo's own circle; among them were the Merlino brothers and many of the young toughs Scarfo had recruited from his headquarters on Georgia Avenue. By the end of 1980, Scarfo's faction dominated the Family. The years of patient building were paying off.

The problem now was the Falcone case. The trial had been set for that summer, and the fact was interfering with Nicky's efforts to consolidate his new position in Philadelphia and run Atlantic City. His lawyers assured him that the state had virtually no case, but Nicky knew better.

There was the unresolved matter of Joe Salerno, the plumber who was going to testify against him. After decades of labor, Nicky was near the top of the Philadelphia Family, and the possibilities for increasing his power were virtually limitless. Only the plumber threatened him now, but the plumber could not be found. Unless that could be done, Scarfo knew, the Falcone case would go to trial.

Meanwhile, he could now look out from Georgia Avenue at the casino skyline, as he had done with the plumber, and say that he really did own the place. And he could look to Philadelphia as well.

10

'If I Were You, I Wouldn't Testify'

At the Salerno home, things were going from bad to worse. Barbara found the adjustment to life in Kansas difficult, and with every frustration and every setback, another argument started.

The arguments took on an unvarying theme: it was Joe who had put them in this awful position by associating with 'those people.' She had warned him, she had said no good would come of it, and now look at what had happened.

Joe had no response. What she said was true, but the continual reminders did nothing to help. He did his best to placate her, even ignoring the fact that she was calling her parents on the phone, a violation of the Witness Program rules.

There was now no contact between Joe and Barbara except arguments and the most mundane exchanges. Their marriage had virtually ceased to exist. Joe appealed to the marshals for some kind of help, but they had nothing to offer.

His own frustration sometimes broke out in anger, and the fights with Barbara became more heated. At the height of some of them she would tell him to leave.

Then one night I called her bluff. 'You want me to leave?'
I said. 'OK. I don't know anybody, I got no place to go,

*but I'll leave.' But there was no bluff. She said, 'Good,
it's better than fighting all the time.' I couldn't back down,
and I couldn't go on like this, so the next day I left.*

*I got an efficiency near where I was workin. It was
twenty-five dollars a week, all I could afford, and what
a place. It was so tiny you had to climb over the bed to
get to the bathroom. The sink stuck out over the toilet, so
you had to put your legs under it to sit down. And right
over your head was a hot-water heater on a shelf that
sloped down, so that I thought, any minute this thing's
gonna fall and kill me, right here on the toilet.*

It was about this time that Sergeant Khoury contacted
Joe through the Marshals to tell him that the Falcone
murder trial had been scheduled for June. He and the
prosecutors would arrange to meet with Joe at neutral
locations to begin preparing him for his testimony.

For Joe, this was a period of severe depression and
anxiety. He was cut off from his family, and he felt
particularly the absence of his sons. He had few friends,
for he was far too anxious about his safety to trust anyone.
He was almost totally isolated.

His work, and the pride he took in it, helped. Nonetheless, adjusting to life and work in the Midwest was
difficult, at times even perilous.

*One morning they sent me out on a job at a farm way out
in the country. My boss says, 'Take this road to the first
viaduct, then turn right to the second viaduct . . .' I'd
never heard the word viaduct before, but I didn't want
to admit I didn't know what it was. I was drivin down a
back road, and it started rainin. I was headin for a bridge,
but the road was slick, and the truck was slidin to the
right. I hit a post on the end of the bridge and flipped
over into the stream.*

My truck was fillin up with water, so I kicked out the windshield and crawled out. I climbed up the embankment, and there at the top was this giant dog. I've always been afraid of dogs, so I ran back down and jumped into the stream. The dog followed me down, and while I was trying to get under water, he started lickin my face. I figured maybe the dog's OK, so I climbed back up and started walkin to a farmhouse nearby, with the dog following me.

On the fence there was this big sign, BEWARE OF THE DOG, and I was hopin that maybe this was the dog they meant. I went up to the house and knocked. A farmer came to the door. He was wearin overalls, and his cheeks were full of tobacco. I asked if I could use his phone to call my boss. 'I had an accident with my truck,' I said.

He chewed up a big wad of tobacco and spit it out.

'Now don't tell me you ran off that viaduct *back there,' he said.*

So now I know what the hell a viaduct is.

In Kansas, Joe had to learn a new kind of plumbing: wells and irrigation work. It was something for which his city skills scarcely prepared him. Almost all of his work was on farms, where there were no sewers or mains. The water table was high – often just six or eight feet below the surface – so the water for farmhouses and animals was drawn from wells.

Driving wells was heavy, monotonous work. Joe would attach a conical stainless-steel head containing filters to a five-foot length of pipe. To the top of this he would fix a driving tool, a big, double-handled sleeve that sat over the pipe. Then, with sheer muscle power, he would pound the drive into the half-frozen earth and twist it down, adding another five-foot length as the pipe disappeared. When it had gone about ten feet, he would remove the driving tool and replace it with an old-fashioned pitcher pump.

When the pump was primed, the water could be drawn up. At first the water would flow brown and muddy, and Joe would have to pump out twenty gallons by hand before clear water appeared. Then he replaced the pitcher pump with an electric one, hooked it to the line running to the house, and turned it on. The job often took a whole day's backbreaking labor.

Irrigating cattle was more onerous. The huge herds consumed thousands of gallons of water, forcing the search for new sources deeper and deeper. Often, the big casement wells had to be sunk one or two hundred feet deep.

When the jet pump at the bottom of one of these wells failed, it was necessary to replace it, together with the pipe to which it was attached. To do this, Joe would have to winch the pipe and pump out by hand, several hundred pounds of mud-soaked metal. He would muscle up each six-foot section on a block and tackle, drill it through with a pin to hold it, torch it off, and winch again. It took a whole day just to remove the old pump.

The next day, Joe would rig a new pump to a twenty-foot length of pipe and lower it into the casing. Then he sectioned together a new line, one length at a time, and eased it down into the well. It was dirty, demanding work. If the pump was lost, either during removal or replacement, the well might have to be abandoned, and a new one drilled.

Once the new pump's in place and the whole line's secure, you connect the pump wire to the electricity, and you hook the pipe up to the hose that serves the trough. Now the whole time you're doin this, the cattle are standin around watchin you, cause they haven't had a drink in two days and they're just waitin for that water. So before you turn on the pump, you make sure that all your tools are over the fence. Then you throw the switch, and you hear the pump kick in, and you can smell the water comin up. And you get yourself over that fence as fast as you can, cause those cattle will trample you to death.

Joe usually worked alone. This suited him, since he preferred to avoid conversation with strangers. But occasionally one of the farmers would chat with him while he worked. Invariably he would be asked about his accent, and he would then produce a cover story about being from New York or Boston, and having relatives in Kansas who had talked him into moving out that way. Sometimes a local would comment on his name, remarking that it did not sound Italian, although he clearly was.

When the combination of his being Italian and coming from back East arose, Joe would often be asked if he knew anything about the Mafia. Though he learned to deal with such incidents, they added to his anxiety. Others were more frightening.

One time I was drivin a well on this farm way out in the middle of nowhere. There was nobody around for miles, and nothin but a dirt road leadin out to where I was. I was just hookin up the pump to the pipe when I saw a car comin up the road. I couldn't imagine why anybody else would be out there.

The car pulled up and three men got out, wearin business suits. They were between me and my truck, so I couldn't get away. I was just kneelin there, watchin them come toward me. One of the three guys walked over to me, carryin a briefcase. The other two were kinda hangin back by the car, and I was thinkin, this is it – they found me.

The guy with the briefcase said hello. I said hello. Then he said, 'Do you go to church?,' and before I could figure out what to say, he opened up the briefcase and handed me a pamphlet. They were Jehovah's Witnesses.

In May, Joe received a call at work from the Marshal's Service, informing him that he would be flying to Oklahoma City to meet with the Atlantic County prosecutor. Joe asked what arrangements would be made about his job. He was told that he would leave from work on Friday evening, and that the meetings would be on Saturday and Sunday.

The marshal who drove Joe to the airport in Topeka told him that every time he traveled in connection with his testimony, he would use a different name. When he arrived at any destination, he was always to be the last person off the plane. A marshal would be waiting for him at the airport, would identify himself, and would take him to the meeting.

Joe was looking forward to this. He considered the prosecutors and detectives to be friends, and he had not spoken to a friend in months. And he was relieved that the work of testifying was actually under way. He still held the hope that Scarfo's conviction might make it possible for him and his family to return home. Then, perhaps, all their problems could be solved.

The Atlantic County officials were waiting for Joe at a motel in Oklahoma City. Joe Khoury and the detectives from the family's first travels were there, along with the prosecutor. Joe greeted them warmly. Over the next two days, they took him through his relations with Nicky Scarfo and the others, and once again he told the story of Vincent Falcone's murder. Though he had told the story dozens of times, it still shook him to relive the event.

The prosecutor explained to Joe the structure of the trial and the four phases of his testimony. He would first be examined by the prosecution and would give his direct testimony. Next, the defense attorneys would cross-examine him, trying to break down his story. There would be three of them, one for each defendant.

Following this, the prosecutor would examine again, in redirect, endeavoring to clarify points which had been challenged by the defense. The defense would then question him a final time.

The prosecutor then took Joe through his direct examination, as he would do on the stand. He assured Joe that all that was required of him was to tell the truth, clearly and in detail. Then he gave him a taste of cross-examination, challenging parts of his story and suggesting that he had made the whole thing up.

Joe did well, and he began to feel optimistic about the trial. The prosecutor was more reserved, telling him that while they felt they had a good chance of winning, the lack of hard, physical evidence was a problem.

They arranged to meet again for further preparation in about a month. Joe was reluctant to see them go: they were a link with his old life, and, perhaps more important, they were people who understood his situation and with whom he could talk freely.

Joe was in the habit of driving from Silcott to Jasper every few days after work to visit with his sons. He would call before he came and offer to cook Italian dinners for the family, but Barbara usually refused. And so he would spend a few hours at the house, playing with Tony and helping Michael and Johnny with their homework. Then he would make the forty-mile drive back to his room.

About two weeks after his meeting with the prosecutors, Joe stopped in unexpectedly at the house. He parked in the driveway as usual and went in through the kitchen. At the kitchen table sat Barbara, with her mother and father.

> *I was at a loss for words. I couldn't believe it. Then my father-in-law said to me, 'Joe, let me buy you a drink.' I said, 'I don't want a drink.' Until that moment I had never had bad words with my in-laws, ever. I said, 'Do you know I could get killed because you're here?' My father-in-law says, 'Don't worry about that — nobody followed us.' I said, 'How did you pay for the trip? Did you use a credit card?'*
>
> *It was the first time I'd ever seen him on the defensive. He tried to come back at me, and I went into a rage. I told him exactly what I thought about him and what he'd done. Years' worth of stuff came out.*
>
> *'Old as you are,' I said, 'I oughta kick your ass.' It got so bad that Barbara and her mother had to leave the house. 'Big man,' I told him, 'millionaire — look at you! Now I know what you are. Your precious daughter — why the hell don't you leave her alone? You're gonna get us all killed!' I didn't let him get a word in. Finally, I said to him, 'If anything happens to the kids, it's on your conscience, not mine.' And I got in the truck and I left.*

Joe was frantic about his in-laws' visit. His only thought was to call the Marshals and ask for their advice. When he did so, the Marshals refused to believe him. He told them that his in-laws were leaving Topeka the next day. The Marshals demanded that he point them out at the airport when they left.

The following afternoon, a marshal picked Joe up and drove him to the airport, where he identified his in-laws as they were boarding the plane.

'You know what this means?' the marshal told Joe as they drove away from the airport.

'What?' Joe asked.

'You've violated the rules of the program. We're going to have to cut off your subsistence.'

Joe protested that he had known nothing about it, and he pointed out that it was he who had called the affair to their attention. 'I'm not a criminal,' he said. 'I've never done anything in my life.'

'That's not the point,' the marshal cut him off. Then he added, 'You know, if I were you, I wouldn't testify.'

Joe was stunned. He asked what the marshal meant.

'You're in the program,' the marshal said. 'They can't find you. If you were smart, you'd stay here, because once you testify, they'll use you for the rest of your life.'

When I heard that, I thought, where does justice come in? What about this red-white-and-blue stuff? Here was a law-enforcement officer, who was supposed to be lookin out for me, tellin me not to testify against criminals. And now I'm wonderin, what am I goin through all this for anyway?

It was as severe a blow to his pride, and his slender hopes, as Joe had yet suffered. And it left him feeling even more confused and anxious and hurt than ever.

I I

'There's a Contract on Your Life'

In June, Joe flew to Louisville, Kentucky, to meet for
his second pretrial preparation with the Atlantic County
prosecutors and Sergeant Khoury. The prosecutor told
him that the trial had been postponed until August at the
request of the defense. Once more they took Joe through
his direct testimony and a brief cross-examination. They
agreed to meet again a few weeks before the trial.

Sergeant Khoury was in touch with Joe's parents, and
he brought Joe the latest news of his family. He told Joe
that his grandmother had died. Joe had been close to her,
and he regretted deeply not having been able to attend
the funeral. Khoury also told him that his in-laws had
placed the house in Brigantine up for sale.

Joe told him about the incident with his in-laws and
the cutoff of subsistence. Khoury offered to do whatever
he could to help, and he gave Joe a private number where
he could be reached in an emergency. He urged Joe to
call any time, collect.

Joe had become close to Sergeant Khoury and had
grown to depend on him. Khoury was a tall, quiet,
reserved man, careful in his manner and uncompromising
about his professionalism. But from the first, his concern
for Joe had been genuine, and Joe had responded to it
gratefully.

A few weeks after the meeting, Joe found a note on the

bulletin board at work asking him to call the Marshal's Service. He did so, from a pay phone, and identified himself.

'What prison are you calling from?' the marshal asked him.

It was not the first time this had happened. Since Joe rarely spoke to the same marshal twice, none of them knew him or his situation. Most protected witnesses were criminals, Joe had learned, and often the marshal with whom he spoke assumed he was calling from jail.

Joe explained that he was not a criminal and was not in prison, but was calling in for a message. The marshal told him he was to call Sergeant Khoury.

Khoury told Joe that they would be meeting with him for preparation in August, but that the trial had again been postponed by the defense.

I asked him what was goin on. He said, 'The word is on the street that there's a contract on your life, for $200,000.' He thought they kept postponin the case to give them time to either break me down or to find me. He wasn't tellin me to worry me, but to make me more careful.

But the news just made things worse. When I was drivin in the truck, I'd look in the rearview mirror constantly. I was livin alone, and at night I'd sleep for an hour, then wake up for an hour. The area I was livin in was so dark I was afraid to go out. I began to think about carryin a gun.

The news from Sergeant Khoury sent Joe into a tail-spin of depression and paranoia. He was now frightened all the time and suspicious of everyone. A few days after the conversation with Khoury, he could stand it no longer. He had to talk to someone, if only to break out of the isolation in which he now felt so trapped and horribly vulnerable. But who could he trust?

In desperation, he went to a Catholic church in Topeka and asked to see a priest. The pastor, Father Henry Schmidt, took him to the rectory.

I talked to him straight; I told him everything, the whole situation. He asked me questions about my kids and how I felt about my wife; he seemed very concerned. Then he said he'd come down to Silcott to visit me. When he saw my place and how I was livin, he said to me, 'What the hell are you staying here for? You come live at the rectory.' I told him I didn't think I'd feel right doin that, but he said, 'You'll feel fine. You can come and go as you please, and you'll feel more secure.' I tried to argue, but he just said, 'You come live with me.'

That weekend, Joe moved from his room in Silcott to the rectory in Topeka. Father Schmidt was a streetwise former army chaplain, and he understood Joe's situation completely. They quickly became close friends, sharing meals and spending the evenings talking. Having someone he could talk to, someone who did not judge him or treat him like a criminal, was a tremendous relief to Joe.

Father Schmidt would not accept money from Joe, so to repay him Joe did maintenance work at the rectory in his spare time and free plumbing work for poor parishioners. For the first time since he had left the house in Jasper, Joe felt comfortable. Though he missed his family keenly, he was relatively at peace.

Nonetheless, the trial was approaching, and Joe was spending more time trying to prepare himself to testify, to face Scarfo and Leonetti, and, perhaps, to be killed in the process.

Then, at the meeting with the prosecutors in August, Joe was told that the trial had been postponed yet again.

One afternoon in October, Joe returned from work to the rectory to find a message asking him to call the Marshals; as usual, he had to assure the marshal who answered that he was not calling from a jail. The marshal informed him that the office had been contacted by the prosecutors. It was time for Joe to go back and testify.

The next morning, a marshal picked Joe up at the rectory and drove him to the airport. He was told he would be flying to Newark, New Jersey, where he would be met by an escort of marshals. He would remain in their custody for the duration of his stay back East.

Joe was met at the airport by a team of five marshals in two unmarked cars. They drove him by a circuitous route to a motel in Trenton, where he was to spend the night. Three armed marshals remained with him at all times. The first thing they did when they settled into the motel room was to remove the mouthpiece from the telephone, to prevent Joe from making any calls.

The next morning, Sergeant Khoury and the prosecutor drove up from the county seat, Mays Landing, to begin Joe's final pretrial preparation. Joe was glad to see them. He knew none of the marshals, and they scarcely spoke to him. He was anxious and worried, and it was good to have someone to talk to.

The preparation went on for five days while Joe waited for his turn to testify. With each day that went by, he became more anxious. At one point, in the hope of calming himself, he asked if he might visit with his mother and father, whom he had not seen or spoken to since leaving the house in Brigantine. The prosecutor had no objection, but the marshals said they would have to think about it.

In the meantime, the Atlantic County Prosecutor's Office received a request from the FBI in Philadelphia to interview Joe. The federal Organized Crime Strike Force was preparing indictments against the Philadelphia mob, and they felt that Joe might be useful to their investigations. The prosecutors agreed, and Joe was driven secretly to FBI headquarters in downtown Philadelphia.

For three hours he was interrogated in a claustrophobic room by two agents. They dragged him again and again through his relations with Scarfo and the murder of Vincent Falcone. The agents made it clear to Joe that they did not believe him, and their intense questioning left him sweating and exhausted.

At last, one of the two agents, a tall, thickset Irishman named Jim Maher, wagged a finger at him. 'You stay where you are,' he ordered. 'We'll be back.'

The agents left the room, closing the door behind them. In a few minutes they returned and stood scowling over Joe. Then, suddenly, Maher extended a hand to him. Joe shook it, puzzled. 'We believe you,' Maher said, smiling. 'You're telling the truth.'

Before he left Philadelphia, Joe was also interviewed by the chief of the Organized Crime Strike Force, a professorial, pipe-smoking US attorney named Joel Friedman. Friedman listened abstractedly to Joe's story, asking a few pointed questions. Then Joe was turned back over to the Marshal's Service.

One of the marshals, Joe had learned, was Italian, and he interceded with this man to arrange a meeting with his parents. At last Joe was told that a short visit would be permitted, but only in the holding room at the courthouse in Mays Landing.

On the morning of his sixth day at the motel, the marshals informed Joe that it was time to go to court. By now he was sick with nerves, and the marshals' methods of moving him did nothing to calm him down.

Before leaving the motel room, Joe was strapped into a bulletproof vest. He was told to walk quickly and to stay close to the marshals at all times. There were two unmarked cars waiting, and Joe was shoved into the back of one of these. Two heavily armed marshals sat in front and two in back, and they ordered Joe to lie down on the floor and stay there.

Out on the highway between Trenton and Mays Landing, the marshals were joined by an escort of New Jersey State Police. Every few miles the marshals' car would pull to the side of the road, and the driver would get out and change the license plate before they went on.

Lying on the floor at the marshals' feet, Joe felt his heart pounding. No-one spoke to him. Indeed, the marshals had never even looked him in the eye. He was being moved like a piece of baggage, he felt, or worse, like some toxic substance.

I was a nervous wreck, and I was thinkin, why don't you guys shoot me? You might as well – I'm half-dead already.

At the county courthouse in Mays Landing, there were more marshals on the roof armed with high-powered rifles. There were also many police, sheriffs, and county detectives, all armed.

'When we get out,' one of the marshals barked to Joe, 'you move fast, understand?' The car doors were thrown open, and the marshals leaped out, brandishing their pistols. More marshals carrying submachine guns surrounded Joe. He was grabbed by the elbows and thrust inside the building.

In a narrow, unlit corridor, two marshals with

sawed-off shotguns stood waiting. Joe was hustled between them toward an elevator. As if by magic, the doors opened as they reached it. Inside were more marshals, carrying riot guns. Joe edged in among them until he was crowded by gun barrels and burly bodies, and the doors slid shut.

They took me down to the holdin room, and there, among all these marshals with guns, were my mother, my father, my sister, and my brother. I hadn't seen them in almost a year. We all started cryin and huggin each other. In a few minutes the marshal came over and said, 'We need Joe now.'

They took me into a little room, and a man was there waitin for me. The marshal said, 'This is Mr Garber, one of the defense lawyers. Do you want me to close the door? It's all right – I searched him.' I asked what this was all about. The marshal said the defense had a right to talk to me before I testified. It was the first I'd heard of it. I asked if I had to do it, and the marshal said no, so I looked at Garber and said, 'I got nothin to say to you.'

Joe was taken to see the other two defense lawyers, Edwin Jacobs and Robert Simone, and again he refused to talk with them. Then he was escorted back to the elevator and up to the courtroom.

Until the judge and jury were seated, Joe was held in a secure area adjacent to the court, surrounded by armed marshals. Despite the preparation, he was nervous now to the point of collapse. In a few moments he would come face to face with Nicky Scarfo, Philip Leonetti, and Lawrence Merlino, men whom he had not seen in nearly a year. And he would have to testify against them, telling the story of the murder yet again – not to the police this time, but to the killers' own faces.

Just before Joe was taken into the courtroom, Sergeant Khoury appeared. He reached into his pocket and handed something to Joe. 'My mother wanted you to have this,' he said.

Joe glanced down. It was a rosary.

'Good luck,' Khoury said.

12

'Tell the Jury What You Saw'

Joe was startled by how small the courtroom was. When he entered, the first person he saw was Scarfo, seated at the defense table not ten feet from the witness stand. Next to Scarfo sat Leonetti and Merlino, each flanked by his lawyer. As Joe took his place on the stand, the three defendants glared at him.

I'd never been in a courtroom before and I was nervous, but when I saw them, I was petrified. I hadn't seen them in over a year, and even though they were on my mind all the time, thinkin about them and facin them were two different things. It was a kind of fear I'd never felt before. It was like I was seein them, but they weren't really there, like in a dream.

The prosecutor stood and asked Joe his name. He asked him if he knew the defendants. Joe replied that he did. He then instructed Joe to come down off the witness stand, approach the defense table, and point out each defendant by name.

Joe walked the few paces to where the three men were seated. He pointed first to Scarfo, naming him, next to Leonetti, and finally to Merlino. Then he returned to the stand.

Joe was then taken through his direct testimony, as he

had prepared it. The prosecutor had him lay out the history of his relations with Scarfo and his group, meticulously leading him through the story step by step, often interrupting to have him identify one or another of the defendants as he referred to him.

There were repeated objections by the defense lawyers, led by Robert Simone. Joe's accounts of the conversations were labeled hearsay, and attempts were made to differentiate among his dealings with Scarfo, Leonetti, and Merlino by their respective attorneys. For the most part the judge overruled these and allowed Joe to continue.

Joe told the story of Nicky's offer to him to become a gangster, and some time was spent on the transfer of the guns. Joe described the luring of Vincent Falcone and the invitation to the Christmas party. And then he was brought to the day of the murder.

The prosecutor began with Joe's trip to Brigantine and his walk with Barbara in the woods, when he had told her he thought someone was going to be killed. By the time they reached the drive to Margate and Phil Disney's apartment, Joe was reliving the event.

For Joe, Nicky was no longer sitting at the defense table, but on Phil Disney's couch, watching a football game. Philip Leonetti was again standing next to Joe, with Lawrence Merlino on the far side of the table. And Vincent was once more fixing drinks in the kitchen.

The prosecutor had Joe stand up and walk them through the next few minutes.

Q. At this point I want you to relate to the jury what happened, what you saw.

A. I had a drink up to my mouth, and Philip Leonetti pulled a gun out of his jacket and shot Vincent

Falcone, extended his arm and shot him in the back of the head.

Q. What did Mr Falcone then do?

A. He turned halfway around and slid down in the corner, and sort of sat with his hands on his stomach.

Q. Did you recognize the gun?

A. Yes.

Q. Whose gun was it?

A. Mine.

Joe then described the second shot, to the chest, and the sudden confrontation by Philip. He recounted the ordeal of tying Falcone and wrapping him in the blanket. The courtroom was still as he spoke.

Q. Did Mr Scarfo say anything right before you tied the head portion of the body?

A. He says, 'I love this, I love this. The big shot is dead.'

Q. Did he do anything with his hands?

A. He picked Vincent Falcone's head up and closed his eyes, and pushed the blanket over his face.

It had been a compelling account, broken only as the prosecutor produced evidence to support the story: Falcone's jacket and shirt, the bloody blanket, photographs of the body.

With Joe's description of the disposal of the clothes and bullets, and of his movements until the time of his meeting with the police, the state rested. The judge took a recess.

Joe had testified for six hours. His throat was dry, and he was sweating and exhausted. Nonetheless, he still had to face cross-examination by the three defense lawyers. Their job would be to break down his story and destroy his credibility. Anything less than that might mean a guilty verdict for their clients.

Simone began amiably enough, asking Joe if he were nervous and upset. Joe admitted that he was. Simone then raised the question of Joe's finances, pointing out that he had declared bankruptcy some months before the murder. He linked Joe's financial troubles to his having moved out of his house, and he suggested that Scarfo and Leonetti had helped to support him at that time by providing him with an apartment and jobs. He suggested that, far from being afraid of them, Joe ought to have been grateful to them. He then turned to Scarfo's invitation to Joe to become a gangster.

Q. You did not tell him that you didn't want to be a gangster?

A. No.

Q. Would you say that when you wrapped the body and put it in the car your conduct was that of a gangster? And when you got the guns, would you say you acted like a gangster?

A. Yes.

Q. You considered yourself to be a law-abiding citizen, is that correct?

A. Correct.

Q. You were a gangster but a law-abiding citizen.

A. If you say that.

Q. I am not saying it; I am asking you. Were you a law-abiding citizen or were you a gangster?

Joe was becoming confused and frustrated. It was not like the pretrial preparation. The questions were coming very fast, and there was no-one there now to help him respond. He was growing restless and resentful; it was as though he were the one on trial.

Simone zeroed in on the moments after the murder. Joe had walked twice to a phone booth. Why had he not fled? Why had he not phoned the police? There was a police car nearby. Why had he not gone to the policeman?

Joe protested that he was afraid because he thought he would be involved. Simone asked him whether he *had*, in fact, been involved. Joe answered lamely that he did not know.

Simone now focused on Joe's statement to the police after the murder, picking out conflicts between that and his testimony. With each inconsistency he forced Joe to admit he had been mistaken, piling up the mistakes until they seemed a hopeless tangle of evasion.

He ridiculed Joe's assertion that he feared Scarfo and the others, pointing, for example, to Joe's account of the ride with Leonetti and Merlino when Joe thought he would be killed.

Q. When did that revelation come to you, sir?

A. When we started riding on those back roads.

Q. Did someone pull a gun out and shoot you?

A. No.

Q. Did someone shoot at you?

A. No.

Q. You stopped and you had dinner?

A. Right.

Q. Did you eat?

A. Yeah.

Q. Well, the fact that you thought you were going to be killed didn't hurt your appetite, did it?

He then turned to the murder itself and the heart of his cross-examination. He asked why, if Joe had suspected that a murder was to be committed, he had not gone to the police.

A. What was I going to tell them – I think somebody's going to be killed? Then what might have happened to me?

Q. It might have helped, sir.

A. I didn't do it.

Q. That is, unless you wanted the person to be killed, and you killed him yourself.

It was the beginning of a brutal assault on Joe's testimony and on his role as a witness, a barrage of innuendo mounting to accusation that would not end until his credibility had been reduced to rubble.

Joe had already been portrayed as a man with domestic and financial troubles. He had been cast as a gangster, and he had admitted to not alerting the police to the murder for fear of implicating himself.

From this point on, for three days, the defense attorneys tried to build a case in the jury's mind that Vincent Falcone had been murdered not by the defendants, but by Joe Salerno.

Simone told Joe that the defense had witnesses who would claim that Scarfo, Leonetti, and Merlino had not been at Phil Disney's house. He defied Joe to name one person who could support his story that the four of them had been there together. Joe replied that he could not.

Simone then pointed out that Joe had already admitted that he himself was there, with Falcone. And he had likewise admitted that it had been his gun that had killed Falcone, and that it was he who had tied up the body.

Simone asked Joe if he had had any motive for killing Falcone. When Joe denied that he had, Simone suggested that Joe owed Falcone money, and that the two had engaged in shady business dealings together. He implied that Joe had avoided prosecution for involvement in the murder by blaming the defendants and cooperating with the police. Then, referring back to Joe's financial troubles, he argued that Joe had done quite well by his cooperation, having his debts dismissed and receiving a new home and subsistence payments from the government.

Joe was becoming more and more angry as the questioning pounded on. He began arguing with Simone; arguments which he invariably lost. Then he started answering haphazardly, even flippantly. He ended by simply capitulating to Simone, agreeing wearily with whatever the lawyer said.

It was the position to which Simone had hoped to reduce him. Focusing on Joe's account of the disposal of the evidence, he now pushed Joe, unresisting, through a damning series of hypothetical questions.

Q. Of course, if you committed this murder yourself, your clothes would be all there was in the bag, isn't that correct?

A. Yes, if you say so.

Q. If I say so?

A. Yes.

Q. And if somebody were trying to set Mr Leonetti up, it wouldn't be a bad idea to drop the bullets in the sewer a block and a half from his house, would it?

A. No, it wouldn't.

Q. Would it be a bad idea, if you were guilty of this murder by yourself, to tell your wife before it happened that somebody's going to get killed, and then afterward say, 'Somebody got killed, and they did it' rather than 'Somebody got killed, and I did it'? That wouldn't be a bad idea, would it?

A. No.

Q. You know, if you didn't say somebody else killed Mr Falcone, you would be a prime suspect yourself. Isn't that so?

A. I would imagine so, yes.

Simone concluded his assault on Joe's testimony by leading him through a scenario in which he had gone alone to the apartment with Falcone, shot him, and disposed of the body by himself.

Weary, confused, disgusted, Joe did not protest.

Q. Now, as a strong fellow, you would have no difficulty dragging that body and rolling it down the steps, wrapped as it was?

A. No.

Q. With your strength, if you really put yourself to it, you could have done that if you had to.

A. Possibly.

Q. Couldn't you have?

A. Yes. Yes.

MR SIMONE. I have no further questions.

The defense dragged on for two more days, with Garber and Jacobs portraying Joe as a violent man, desperate for money, who had killed Falcone and blamed the defendants in order to save himself. The prosecutor's redirect questioning did little to dispel the impression.

After more than thirty hours on the stand, Joe was finally dismissed.

Again he was surrounded by marshals as he left the building. On the way out he was allowed to visit briefly with his parents, and there was another tearful reunion before he was hurried to the airport.

Back in Kansas, Joe entered into an uneasy truce with his wife. He lived at the house for a few days while he waited anxiously for news of the verdict.

Barbara questioned him about his testimony. It was the most conversation they had had in months, and Joe allowed himself to hope that he had been right in thinking that the trial would mark a turning point in their relationship. Now that the testimony was over, perhaps things would get better. Once Scarfo and the others were convicted, perhaps they really could make plans to go home.

Days went by without word from back East. Finally, Joe called Sergeant Khoury at the private number Khoury had given him.

I asked him if the jury had come back with a verdict, and he said they had. Then there was this silence on the phone, and he said, 'Joe, we didn't do it. They were acquitted.' I was bewildered. I didn't know what to think. Then, I remembered what the marshals had said at the very beginning, that I'd never see my home or family again. And I started to cry.

He said to me, 'Believe me, we're more sorry about this than you. We all appreciate what you did. It took guts. You were the first one to face up to these people, and we won't forget it.' I thanked him, and he said, 'Don't worry, Joe, we're going to stay on these guys. We'll get them.'

The verdict had a devastating effect on Joe and on his

tenuous reconciliation with Barbara. When he told her, whatever hope she, too, had harbored was destroyed. In dismay, she threw up her hands and claimed it was no surprise. She declared that the whole case had been rigged, that Scarfo had bought off the police and the prosecutors.

The idea revolted Joe, and he rejected it angrily. 'If that was true,' he shouted at her, 'there wouldn't be any law at all – these people would run the whole country. And they don't. They *don't* run the country.'

The argument lasted the rest of the day.

The family's situation was now more hopeless and more dangerous than ever before. Scarfo and his gang were free, and there was nothing now to stop them from searching Joe out. The Salernos could not stay where they were; they would have to move as far away as they could.

The day after learning the verdict, Joe called the Marshal's Office and told them he was leaving Kansas. They replied that they could not help him relocate but advised him that if he wished to remain in the Witness Program, he should contact the Marshal's Office wherever he settled.

As usual, when he had called, they had asked him what prison he was in.

13

Nicodemo Dominico Scarfo, Boss

Nicky Scarfo celebrated his acquittal in the Falcone murder case with patriotic panache. On the steps of the Mays Landing courthouse, he announced to reporters: 'Thank God for the American jury system. It's the greatest in the world!'

When he returned to 26 North Georgia Avenue, he had a wall at the back of the building painted with a Liberty Bell and the words GOD BLESS AMERICA – IT'S GREAT TO BE AN AMERICAN.

Scarfo had other reasons to celebrate. He was now the acknowledged master of Atlantic City. He was also consigliere of the Philadelphia Family, and his friend Phil Testa was boss. Things were going well.

There were problems, however.

For one thing, casino construction was coming to a close, which meant that the lucrative contracting business was phasing out. Scarfo now had to deepen his penetration of the casinos themselves in order to retain his control.

At the same time, Nicky's influence over the service industry through Local 54 was being challenged by another Atlantic City union figure, John McCullough. McCullough, head of the roofers' union, was organizing independent locals among bar and restaurant workers and security guards. Nicky could not tolerate such rivalry.

Earlier, Scarfo had applied to Bruno to intercede and force McCullough out, but the old Don had refused. Now Bruno was gone, and Scarfo felt he could count on Testa to deal with McCullough or to allow Nicky to do so himself.

In the late summer and fall of 1980, Testa invited McCullough several times to meetings. Perhaps fearing an ambush, McCullough refused, and he began carrying a gun. Angry at the rebuff, Testa turned the matter over to Scarfo to settle in his own way.

In December, 1980 – almost exactly one year after Vincent Falcone had been murdered in Margate – a flower-delivery van pulled up outside the Philadelphia home of John McCullough. One of the two men inside got out and walked up to McCullough's door, carrying a box of poinsettias. Mrs McCullough answered the door and took the flowers.

The delivery man said that he had a larger box for them in the van. John McCullough was in the living room talking on the phone. He told his wife to give the man a big tip, since it was Christmas.

The delivery man returned to the door, carrying the larger box. He stepped inside, pushed Mrs McCullough out of the way, pulled a gun from the box, and shot her husband in the head. McCullough fell to the floor. The gunman stepped to his side and shot him five more times.

Mrs McCullough, screaming, tried to reach the door. The gunman threw her back, ran out, and fled in the van.

By early 1981, Phil Testa seemed to have everything under control. He had inherited a stable, if stagnant, organization from Bruno, and he was carrying out his program for revamping it. Nicky Scarfo had doubled the organization's membership, bringing in new blood, as well as new money from Atlantic City. And Pete Casella, the underboss, was moving aggressively into the speed industry in an effort to monopolize the supply of its basic constituent, P2P. The Family's future seemed more promising and secure than it had even under the Docile Don.

In the early morning hours of 15 March, 1981, Testa returned to his house on Porter Street in South Philadelphia. As he reached for the knob of the screen door, there was a tremendous explosion. A remote-control bomb destroyed the front of the house and shattered windows for blocks around. Parts of Testa's body were blown into the street, others through the smoking house into the kitchen. Flesh and debris were riddled with thousands of finishing nails.

It was not a typical mob hit, and police theorized that the roofers' union had rigged the bomb in retaliation for McCullough's murder.

The slaughter of the new boss shocked not only the neighborhood, but the Family as well. Pete Casella immediately went to New York to apply for authority both to replace Testa and to eliminate what he claimed was a dissident faction that may have cooperated in Testa's assassination. This faction, he told the Commision, was headed by Nicky Scarfo.

Scarfo's friends in the Genovese Family reported Casella's treachery to him, and Nicky quickly pieced together what had happened. Casella, after having spent fifteen years in prison, had not been content with the job of underboss. With Bruno's gambling chief, Frank Narducci, Sr, Casella had planned a coup against the leadership, promising to make Narducci his underboss. Now he was maneuvering to take over the Family and exterminate Scarfo's faction.

Nicky knew he had to move quickly, and he went to New York to negotiate with the Genovese Family for support before the Commission. The outlines of the deal were clear-cut: the Genoveses would back Scarfo for boss and support his right to avenge Testa; Scarfo, in turn, would give them a larger role in Atlantic City. It was an alliance made along ethnic lines. If the deal went through, Calabrians would control both the Atlantic City casinos and Philadelphia.

For the next few days, while the Commission considered the claims of both Casella and Scarfo to the leadership, Nicky surrounded himself with bodyguards and kept out of sight. His seclusion gave rise to speculation that neither he nor Casella would succeed Testa, and attention focused on longtime Bruno associate Frank D'Alfonso. The media was naming D'Alfonso as the new boss, and colleagues were beginning to pay him respect accordingly. D'Alfonso, known as Frankie Flowers, enjoyed the sudden celebrity.

Nicky watched Frankie Flowers' posturing in silence. Until New York ruled, there was nothing he could do about it, but it was not a spectacle he intended to forget.

By the time of Testa's funeral, the Commission had decided in Scarfo's favor. Nicky was given permission to replace Testa and to murder Casella. But Casella, sensing that something had gone wrong, disappeared. His absence from Testa's funeral was as effective a barrier to his succession as his death would have been. Thus, as the cortege made its way to Holy Cross Cemetery, it was Nicky Scarfo who rode in the limousine behind the hearse carrying Phil Testa to his grave.

Nicky Scarfo became boss of the Philadelphia Family in the spring of 1981. He appointed Salvatore Merlino as his underboss and Frank Monte, a Testa gambling capo, as consigliere. His nephew, Philip Leonetti, was made a capo.

Like Phil Testa before him, Scarfo had plans. But Nicky planned to change not merely the Family's direction, but its very character. He was determined to remake the Family in his own image, transforming it into an aggressive gangster operation. To begin with, that meant settling scores and suppressing opposition.

John Calabrese had been a drug dealer associated with the Family for years. He had expanded his distribution network to Atlantic City, but he had not bothered to secure Nicky Scarfo's permission. On 6 October, 1981, Calabrese had dinner at Cous' Little Italy, a popular Family hangout in South Philadelphia. As he stepped on to the sidewalk, two men in ski masks approached him and shot him to death.

Two weeks later, Frank D'Alfonso was dropped off by friends at the same restaurant. Within a few minutes, he was lying unconscious on the pavement, beaten nearly to death with a crowbar. There were no witnesses to the attack, and D'Alfonso himself refused to admit to the police that he had been assaulted. From that night, he never again laid claim to the leadership of the Philadelphia Family.

At around the same time, Frank Narducci, Sr, who had conspired with Casella to kill Testa, was convicted of bribing law-enforcement officials. Then, in January 1982, he went on trial for racketeering. On the evening of 7 January as he got out of his Cadillac half a block from his South Philadelphia home, two men walked up to him and shot him ten times. Narducci died in the gutter next to his car.

Within a few weeks of Narducci's murder, two of his soldiers were found dead. Vincent Panetta and his girl-friend were strangled in Panetta's suburban Philadelphia home. Their bodies were discovered on 4 February.

Three weeks later, in response to a missing person report, Philadelphia police searched a car belonging to Narducci associate Dominic DeVito. DeVito's body was in the trunk. He had been shot in the head three times; his hands had been bound together and then tied to his feet 'cowboy style,' as Nicky liked to call it, and his body had been wrapped in trash bags.

Then, on 15 March – the anniversary of Phil Testa's death – the body of Rocco Marinucci was found in a South Philadelphia parking lot. Marinucci had been an associate of Pete Casella's; it was he who had made and detonated the bomb that killed Testa. When he was found, stuffed into trash bags and covered with a sheet, his hands were tied, and he had been shot a dozen times in the head and chest. Three firecrackers had been thrust into his throat as a symbol of his treachery.

It was a frustrating period for law-enforcement officials, who watched the death toll mount even as they were endeavouring to indict the victims. For, after years of surveillance and wiretaps, federal authorities had felt ready to begin a broad assault on the Philadelphia Family.

In 1980, federal criminal indictments were prepared under the Racketeering Influenced and Corrupt Organizations (RICO) statute. RICO had been created by Congress ten years earlier as a weapon for federal prosecutors to use against organized crime. A broad and complex law, it allowed the government to place before a court not just individual mob crimes, but the entire scope of a Family's criminal activities.

RICO was a hybrid statute, involving a two-part prosecution in which both conspiracy and specific crimes were alleged. The government first had to show that the defendants were members of an enterprise engaged in illegal activities, and then that they had facilitated or participated in the enterprise's crimes. The combination of the two was the core of the statute. It meant that both leadership and soldiers could be prosecuted at once – that the street thugs who committed the crimes and the bosses who ordered those crimes from their offices were equally guilty.

Precisely because of the law's scope, RICO prosecutions involved massive, long-term investigations to gather evidence embracing the whole of a mob Family's business. The federal Organized Crime Strike Force and the FBI in Philadelphia had spent years on just such an investigation. Now they planned to wield RICO to break up the Philadelphia Family.

The indictments named Angelo Bruno, Phil Testa, Frank Narducci, and ten others as members of the Philadelphia *Cosa Nostra*. By the time the indictments were actually executed in early 1982, however, half of those named were dead.

Nothing like this string of mob killings had ever been seen in Philadelphia before. Indeed, not since Chicago during Prohibition had so many mobsters been murdered so quickly. The prosecutors could not update the indictments fast enough to keep up with the killings. Yet they could not know that the 'hard work' of Nicky Scarfo's clan of Calabrese was only just beginning.

14

'You're Taking a Trip, Boy'

After the acquittal of Nicky Scarfo, Joe Salerno decided
to move his family to Alaska. He had never been there,
but he had seen an advertisement in a newspaper offering
skilled workers jobs on the oil pipeline – and besides,
Alaska seemed as far away as he could get.

Barbara agreed to the move, and she encouraged Joe
to go there first and find a job and a house. Then she
and the boys would follow. Joe called the Marshals in
Topeka to let them know of his plans. They gave him
the number of the Marshal's Service in Fairbanks and
advised him to call that office as soon as he got there.

By this time, Joe had gotten a credit card in his new
name, and he used it to pay for his plane ticket and a
motel room. He had read a book about Alaska before
setting out, but it had not prepared him for the Arctic
wilderness in which he now found himself. What was
more, although he arrived at midday, it was dark.

Joe felt completely disoriented. He sat in his motel
room all afternoon waiting for daylight, which did not
come. The next morning when he awoke, it was still dark.
Puzzled, Joe went to a nearby bar for a beer.

*I kept checkin my watch. It was one o'clock in the
afternoon, but it was still dark out. I thought I was losin
my mind. Finally, I called the bartender over and asked*

*him what was goin on, how come it was always dark. He
told me that up there it was night for half the year and
day for half the year. It was December, and I asked him
when it would be daylight again, and he told me, about
April.*

Joe checked in with the Marshals, and as usual had to
explain that he was not calling from jail. He asked for
their help in finding a job. The next day they called him
back with the name of a pipeline contractor.

When Joe called he was told that the owner was on a
hunting trip and could not be reached. Joe waited for a
week for the man to return, in the meantime living off
his credit card. At last he was asked to come in for an
interview. He called Barbara to give her the good news.
The boys got on the phone, too, and he told them about
Alaska, and how they would go hunting and fishing
together when they arrived. Then Joe went for the
interview.

*I rented a car and I drove out to the contractor's office.
The Marshals had referred me to him, so I figured if he
liked me, I'd get the job. It paid twenty-five dollars an
hour, which was more than triple what I'd been makin in
Kansas.*

*I met the owner, and we talked. I told him about my
experience, and it seemed to be goin pretty well. When I
finished he said to me, 'That's all good. That's great. But
I have a rule around here: we don't hire criminals.'*

*I told him I wasn't a criminal, and I asked him what
he knew about me. He said, 'Nothing, except that the
Marshals sent you.' So I asked if the Marshals had told
him about me, and he said, 'No, and I don't want to know.
I'm sorry, but we don't hire criminals.'*

Joe left the office, disappointed and depressed. He started back to town, but in the darkness he lost his way. At last he found himself in a new industrial park that was in the final stages of construction.

The place looked familiar to me, and I realized it looked like New Jersey. I stopped in a parking lot that was still bein striped. The contractor's trailer was right there, and in the window I saw a face I recognized. It was a builder I used to work for in New Jersey, and sure enough, there was his name right on the sign. I used to go huntin with this guy, and he knew my wife and my kids. I thought suddenly, I'd love to talk to him. He looked out the window at me, and I don't know if he recognized me, but I drove away. I knew he had family back in Jersey, and I felt I couldn't take a chance on him gettin involved with me.

Back at the motel, Joe called Barbara to tell her he had not gotten the job. He suggested that they might try somewhere else, and he reminded her that he had a standing offer from his friend in Florida to join him in the plumbing business there. Barbara told him there was no point in going any farther. Things were not going to get better; it would not work out between them.

They argued back and forth on the phone for nearly an hour. At last it was clear to Joe that Barbara had made up her mind. 'What am I supposed to do?' he said finally. 'I've got no money, and I'm up to the limit on the credit card.'

'You can always get a job,' Barbara told him. 'You can find work somewhere.'

It was the end. The trip to Alaska had been a last, forlorn hope. Now it was gone, and with it, evidently, so was their marriage.

Joe packed his things and went to the airport. He had a small suitcase of clothes, a box of plumbing tools, and thirty-four dollars in cash.

He had no idea where he would go. He got a map of the United States from the car-rental agent, glanced at it for a few moments, and picked a town at random: Portland, Oregon. There was no reason to go there, and no reason not to go. He was alone, he had nothing, and there was a price on his head. Yet he had to start over somewhere, and Portland seemed as good a place as any.

When Joe reached Portland, he called the Marshal's Office there and asked for help in finding work and a place to live. 'What jail are you calling from?' the marshal demanded. Joe explained that he was not in prison, but that he needed help.

'We don't even know who you are,' came the response. Joe tried to tell him, but the marshal cut him off. 'We'll see what we can do.'

Joe took a room in the cheapest motel he could find, in a poor section of the city. He bought a newspaper and started applying for plumbing jobs. He needed a job quickly, so he decided to rent a car to get to the interviews. But when he presented his credit card at the same chain from which he had rented the car in Alaska, they confiscated it.

He now could not pay for his motel room, and he could not get credit elsewhere. He tried at several stores, but when they punched his social security number into their computers, the record was blank.

Joe called the Marshal's Office back. Again, he identified himself and asked for assistance. 'Yeah,' the marshal replied, 'we know who you are. You're off subsistence, right?'

Joe started to explain what had happened.

'You broke the rules of the program,' the marshal interrupted. When Joe tried again to protest, the marshal hung up on him.

For a few more days Joe searched for a job, but he was having no luck. Soon he would be thrown out of the motel. He knew no-one, and he had no transportation and almost no money. He was desperate.

At the end of a cold day of walking the Portland streets trying to find work, Joe reached a decision. He could not go back to Kansas, and he could not go on as he was. There was no future for him in the limbo of the Witness Program. He decided that he would go back home, to Philadelphia, and defy Scarfo. If they killed him, so be it. But it would be better to die fighting in his own home than to continue living this way.

It was freezin cold. I went to a telephone booth and made a call to the FBI in Philadelphia. I asked for Jim Maher, the agent who interrogated me and said he believed me. I told him, 'Jim, I can't take this any more. I'm gonna get some money together, I'm buyin a ticket, and I'm goin home.' He asked me what the trouble was, and I explained it to him. I was so angry I was in tears.

Jim said to me, 'Give me the number of the phone booth where you are.' It was the first time I'd ever gone against the Marshals, but I told him where I was. He said, 'You stay where you are – I'll call you right back.' Ten minutes later the phone rang. 'Somebody's coming over to pick you up,' he said. 'Promise me you won't move.'

In a few minutes, a car pulled up at the phone booth, and a stocky man wearing a Stetson hat and cowboy boots got out. He identified himself as Special Agent Williams of the FBI. He had a tough, authoritative manner. 'A good friend of yours just called me,' he told Joe. 'Get in the car.'

Williams drove toward the center of town. He said that Maher had explained Joe's situation to him and that he would take care of it. He took Joe to a bank in downtown Portland and introduced him to one of the officers. Williams told her that Joe was a friend of his and needed a loan.

The officer asked Joe to fill out an application. When he was unable to provide any credit history, references, or employment record, Williams vouched for him, and the officer gave Joe $2,000 in cash.

Williams then mentioned that Joe needed a place to live. The bank officer told Joe that she owned some condominiums in Portland and said that he was welcome to rent one from her. She added that her son was selling his car, an old Chevrolet, and she arranged for Joe to put a down payment on it.

Williams drove Joe to the motel, where he paid his bill and packed his things. They then went to the condominium, a new, airy one-bedroom in a good section of town.

'I'll work out something for you to sleep on until we can get you some furniture,' Williams said.

Joe was overwhelmed. Within an hour he had gotten a place to live, an automobile, and enough money to last until he found a job. After the bureaucratic indifference of the Marshals, this solicitude by the FBI was nearly a miracle.

That evening Williams stopped by with a portable bed. On Saturday, his day off, he drove Joe to a discount furniture outlet and used his own credit to buy him furniture.

Joe did not know how to thank him. Williams shrugged it off; he was glad to do a favor for a fellow FBI agent, he said, and besides, Joe had tried to do them a favor by testifying.

After months of being treated like a criminal by the Marshals, the remark, made so casually, brought tears to Joe's eyes.

Joe applied for a job with a company that owned a chain of plumbing businesses throughout the Portland area. The help of the FBI and the kindness shown him by the bank officer had given his morale a boost, and he was determined to succeed. If he could establish himself, he might bring his sons out to visit him, or even to live with him. He wanted the job badly.

He spoke with the manager and convinced him that while he had no credentials to show, he was a skilled, experienced plumber.

The manager, Larry Jenkins, had been a plumber for thirty-five years. He was soft-spoken and sympathetic. When it was clear to him that Joe was telling the truth, he said he would give him a try. 'If you're a good plumber, that's all I need to know,' he told Joe. 'We'll start you out at seventeen dollars an hour. But,' he added, 'we're a union shop. If it works out, you'll have to join the local.'

During the next few weeks, Joe threw himself into his new job. Since he lived alone and knew no-one, he showed up early and worked late. Unlike the other new men, he had a broad and detailed knowledge of urban plumbing, and he was also able to handle calls in rural areas. He soon established himself as one of the most skilled plumbers in the company. At the end of the sixty-day grace period, Jenkins told him it was time for him to join the local. Joe hesitated.

'I think I'm gonna have trouble gettin into the union,' he told Larry.

'It'll be no problem,' Larry assured him. 'You've been a plumber for a long time. I've seen your work. There've been no complaints.'

Joe had come to like Larry. He was a kindly man, and Joe trusted him. He told Larry he had to talk to him and asked if they could have lunch.

I said I couldn't supply the union with any background. He asked what I meant. I told him I wasn't a criminal, but that I had testified for the government and they'd changed my name and my social security number. I explained about my sons, and how much I needed this job and needed to get into the union.

He heard me out, and he said, 'I understand. I've got kids myself.' He told me he'd speak to the owner, and he promised he wouldn't say anything about what I'd told him. The next day he told me to go to the union hall that night and bring my initiation fee. I was worried about the union, so I called the FBI agent, and he told me the local was all right.

There were five men, all old plumbers. They asked me questions for about two hours, stuff I had learned back East that new plumbers in the West never heard of. At last one of them said to the others, 'What do you think?' and another one said, 'He sure talks like a plumber.' And that was it. I was in the union, workin for scale — thirty-two dollars an hour.

It seemed a turning point in a long chain of disasters and disillusionments. Joe began making friends among the other plumbers, and he soon settled into his new life. He liked Portland. Unlike Topeka, it was reminiscent of the East Coast, and it was big enough that he could feel anonymous and secure.

He contacted Barbara to tell her where he was, and to

ask if she would like to come out and live with him. She told him that she had decided on a divorce.

It was not a surprise to Joe, and he accepted the news calmly. He asked whether one of their older sons could come out to keep him company. Barbara agreed to send Michael, who was then fifteen, for a visit.

Joe and Barbara were divorced that same year, 1982.

Joe had been working in Portland for several months, living with his son Mike, when the Marshal's Service called him. He got the message at work and went to a public phone to call back.

'Looks like you're going to have to take a trip, boy,' the marshal told him.

Joe asked where.

'Some people in Washington want to see you.'

'Why are you contacting me?' Joe wanted to know. 'I thought I was off the program.'

'Don't get into that,' the marshal replied, impatiently. 'That's none of your business. All you need to know is that these people want to see you, and we're going to take you back.'

Joe did not now know whether he was in or out of the Witness Program. Though he remained in contact with the Marshals, he no longer had most of the program's benefits. There was no subsistence, no help with finding work and housing, and his family still had not received their new birth certificates. Yet at any moment a marshal might tap him on the shoulder, disrupt his life, and send him back East to testify.

The point was driven home when a marshal came to Joe's apartment with an airplane ticket for him. 'You're leaving next week,' the marshal told him.

Joe asked how long he would be away. The marshal shrugged. It might be several days, he said.

'I've got a job,' Joe told him, 'and I don't want to lose it. Are you gonna arrange things with my boss?'

'That's not our problem,' the marshal replied. 'We're just giving you a message that they want to see you.'

The next day Joe spoke to Larry Jenkins, who told him that a leave of absence would have to be approved by the owner. Again Joe turned to the FBI. He explained the situation to Special Agent Williams, who offered to call the owner of the plumbing company and arrange things with him. 'If he's got any problems with it,' Williams said, 'I'll go and see him myself.'

Before Joe left for Washington, Larry told him that the leave had been approved and that he would still have his job when he got back. Joe thanked him and offered to work Saturdays to make up the time. Larry assured him that this would not be necessary: a friend of his had arranged everything with the boss.

15

'I Done Five or Six'

Joe had been summoned to appear before the US Senate's Permanent Subcommittee on Investigations, which was conducting hearings on the involvement of organized crime in labor unions. Joe was to testify about Nicky Scarfo's relations with Local 54 of Atlantic City.

A marshal picked him up at his Portland apartment and drove him to the airport. As usual, he was to be the last person off the plane. After leaving the plane in Washington, Joe walked into the arrival lounge at National Airport and looked for the marshal who was to meet him. Nearby was a young black man in a new, expensive-looking suit. He was wearing sandals with sheer socks and, Joe noted with alarm, soft gloves exactly like those that Nicky Scarfo had worn in the house in Margate.

The man approached him. 'Are you Joe?' he asked.

Joe said that he was.

'Come with me,' the man said.

Joe followed him toward the terminal, feeling uneasy. The man had not shown him any credentials and had not identified himself as a marshal. Joe kept a pace back, watching him. He did not like the look of his suit and, especially, of those gloves. The man stopped suddenly outside the entrance to a men's room. He turned to Joe. 'Step in here,' he told him.

Warily, Joe followed him in. The men's room was empty. The man paused and turned his back to Joe, then half-turned again toward him. Seeing that the man was sliding his hand inside his coat, Joe threw down his bag and grabbed him, pinning his arms and shoving him to the floor. He twisted the man's right arm up behind his back, tore open his coat, and took a gun from his belt. Joe stood over him with the gun, demanding to know who he was.

'I'm a marshal,' the man protested. He hurriedly sat up and reached again inside his coat. Joe pointed the gun at him.

'Honest, man, look,' he said, holding out a badge. Joe examined it and threw it back at him.

'Maybe I should have identified myself before,' the man said.

Joe was trembling with rage. 'Maybe you *should* have!' he shouted. 'There are people who wanna kill me!'

The marshal stood up, straightening his suit, and Joe handed him back his gun.

'Please,' he asked Joe, 'don't tell anybody about this.'

Joe spent the night in a cheap motel in Virginia. Two marshals had dinner with him and stayed in an adjoining room. The next day Joe met with the attorneys for the Senate subcommittee, who prepared him for his testimony. He told his story, as he had done so many times in the past, and the lawyers focused in on Nicky's remarks about Local 54. They told Joe they would draw up a statement for him to read to the senators, who would then take turns asking him questions.

A few days later, the marshals drove Joe to Capitol Hill. He was taken through a secure entrance to a small holding room, where Jim Maher, the FBI agent from Philadelphia, was waiting. Joe brought him up to date on his situation and thanked him for his help.

Along with Joe, Jim Maher, and the marshals, there was another man seated at the table in the holding room. He was a fair-complected man in his fifties, with carefully groomed graying hair. Dressed in an impeccably tailored suit, he looked like a jet-setting executive or a prime minister's *porte-parole*.

Jim Maher inclined his head toward the man. 'You know who that is?' he asked Joe. 'That's Charlie Allen.'

'Who's Charlie Allen?' Joe asked.

'His real name's Charlie Palermo. He's in the Witness Program too. He worked for all the big boys. He was Jimmy Hoffa's hit man.'

Maher offered to introduce Joe to Allen and they went over and shook hands. 'So,' Allen drawled, 'you got involved with that little son of a bitch in Jersey, huh?'

Joe admitted that he had.

'Well, he's a fuckin nothin, that guy. In my day, I'da chewed him up.'

They talked for a few minutes and then Allen stood up and gestured toward the marshals. 'You see these roaches?' he said with disgust. 'They don't even know how to keep the place clean. Look at these ashtrays . . .' He picked one up and brandished it under a marshal's nose. 'Fuckin roaches, don't even clean the ashtrays,' he declared. 'Here, *I'll* clean em.'

He then went around the room, emptying the ashtrays and straightening the chairs as he spoke with Joe.

'They payin you good for this?' he asked.

Joe said that he was not being paid at all. He asked if Allen was being paid.

'Fuckin right, they're payin me,' he said. 'I don't testify for nothin; I put a lota guys away for these people.'

He paused, wiping out an ashtray with his handkerchief.

'I get $2500 a month from these people. I'll get it for the rest of my life. That's the deal I made, and they can't break it cause I got it in writing. Fuck the program,' he concluded, replacing the tray. 'No checks, no testimony.'

They chatted until it was time to testify. Allen told Joe that he had a beautiful house in the country, and he invited Joe to visit him. 'I got a vegetable garden you wouldn't believe,' he boasted. He formed his hands into a big bowl. 'I grow tomatoes this big, and I make the best clams and macaroni in the world.'

Joe asked Allen whether he had committed any crimes.

'I done five or six . . .' Allen replied.

'Five or six what?'

'Murders.'

Joe wanted to know if he was ever afraid for his safety. Allen made a disdainful face.

'Whenever I get scared,' he confided, patting his hip pocket, 'I carry the piece.'

The point was not lost on Joe. Here was a professional killer who admitted to half a dozen murders. He, too, was in the program – but he would be earning $2500 a month for life, he owned his own home, and he carried a gun to protect himself. Joe had never committed a crime, but his subsistence payments had been cut off because his in-laws had come for a visit without his knowledge. The conversation with Allen gave Joe some perspective on how poorly he had been treated, and the revelation stung him.

Joe and Charlie Allen testified side by side before the Senate subcommittee, seated behind a curtain that screened them from the public. Joe went first, reading the statement which the attorneys had written for him. Then it was Allen's turn.

Allen announced that he would not read his statement

but would submit it for the record, and he invited the senators to question him. Joe learned later that Allen could neither read nor write.

The chairman, Senator William Roth of Delaware, asked whether Allen had ever killed anyone for Jimmy Hoffa. Allen replied, as he had told Joe, 'Five or six.'

Roth asked what he meant. Had he killed five people, or six people?

'Well, Senator,' Allen replied, 'it was this way. On the sixth guy, the fuckin gun wouldn't work. But since I had the intention to kill him, I say "five or six."'

Allen went on to explain that he had entered the Witness Program after mob boss Tony Provenzano had ordered Hoffa's murder, which Allen felt would touch off a war over control of the Teamsters' Union.

The senators asked what had happened to Hoffa's body. Allen said that the body had been dismembered, ground into pieces, and scattered in the Florida Everglades.

At the close of Allen's testimony, Senator Sam Nunn of Georgia asked him what he thought was the most effective weapon against organized crime. Allen paused for a moment and then nodded toward Joe, seated next to him.

'You could really wipe it out,' he said, 'if you had more people like this man here come forward.'

Joe returned to Portland, and to his job. His son Mike had gone back to stay with Barbara while Joe testified, and now he rejoined his father. Barbara, meanwhile, had moved with the other two boys to Denver, where she hoped to make a new start.

A month after his return, Joe was again contacted by the Marshals. 'You're going to be taking another trip,' he was told. 'They want to see you again back East.'

This time, it was the New Jersey Gaming Commission, which was looking into the Scarfo organization's activities in Atlantic City. Scarfo was then under indictment for illegal possession of a weapon by a felon, a charge that had resulted from the discovery of a derringer in his apartment at the time of the Falcone murder. That, and the murders within the Philadelphia Family, had finally moved the Gaming Commission to investigate Scarfo's relations with the casinos.

Joe did not want to leave his son and his job again. He called Joe Khoury and asked his advice. Khoury told him that there was a good chance that Scarfo would be banned from the casinos, and for that they needed Joe's testimony.

Again Joe arranged to take time off from his job, and the Marshals flew him to Newark. From there he was taken to a motel in Trenton, where he spent the night.

The next day was reminiscent of the day he had testified in the Falcone case. Heavily armed marshals picked Joe up in an unmarked car and drove him to the Gaming Commission offices near Atlantic City. Again there was the bulletproof vest, the State Police escort, and sharpshooters on the roof.

Joe testified for several hours about his knowledge of Scarfo's character and activities. The commissioners asked him pointed questions about Nicky's habits, his friends, and his involvement in the casinos. Then a lawyer representing Scarfo, who was not present, cross-examined Joe. Joe's experience in the Falcone trial had prepared him for this, and this time the lawyer's efforts to intimidate and confuse him did not work.

As a result of the hearings, Nicky Scarfo and his associates were banned from eating, drinking, or gambling in the Atlantic City casinos. In a heavy blow to Nicky, who had been an amateur boxer, they were also forbidden to attend the boxing matches.

The decision gave Joe some measure of satisfaction, but he hoped that this would be his last trip back East to testify. He recalled the words of the marshal in Kansas: *Once you testify, they'll use you for the rest of your life.* Joe was beginning to wonder whether he should have followed that marshal's advice.

16

'Do You Know That You've Been Shot?'

Joe had been back at work in Portland for a few weeks when Larry Jenkins told him that he had a message from the Marshals. 'They said it's important,' he added.

Joe walked to the public phone in dismay. They could not go on interrupting his life to bring him back to testify. If this kept up, he was sure to lose his job. Joe called the Marshal's Office and identified himself.

'What prison are you calling from?' the marshal, a young woman, asked, Joe explained yet again that he was not in jail but had gotten a message to call in.

She told me that the marshal who had called was out of the office. I asked her what the message was, since he'd said it was important. 'Well,' she said, 'I don't know too much about it, but one of our witnesses' father has been shot. But I don't know which one.'

I asked her who it was, but she said, 'I told you, I don't know who. You'll have to wait till he gets back.' And she hung up.

Joe was frantic. It was summer, and he knew that his parents would be at their motel in Wildwood. He called there, and one of his cousins answered the phone.

'Oh, Joseph,' she said, 'Uncle Joe's been shot!'

Wildwood Crest, New Jersey, 9 August, 1982.

Eleven o'clock at night, and the heat had finally relented. Joe Salerno, Sr, and his wife, Juliet, sat outside their motel office by the pool, chatting with one of the guests. She was a nurse from Pennsylvania who came down every summer. Joe excused himself and went inside to make a sandwich. He was a large, powerful man of sixty, with a thick neck and broad shoulders. It had been in the nineties all day, and he was wearing shorts and sandals, with no shirt.

Joe planned to walk the dog, as he did every night. This night, however, the dog cowered under the bed, refusing to come out, frightened of something. At last, Joe gave up and went back downstairs to the office.

A few minutes later his wife joined him, locking the plate-glass door of the office. As she did so, she heard footsteps on the stairs outside. She glanced out and saw a man wearing a gray jogging suit with blue stripes standing impatiently at the door. The hood of his suit was pulled over his head, so that his face was obscured.

Mrs Salerno watched while the man tugged twice at the door, then began pacing back and forth between the door and the window, his hands stuffed into the broad pockets of the sweat-suit. The NO VACANCY sign was lit, and she could not imagine what he wanted.

'Probably wants information,' her husband said from behind her.

Mrs Salerno shook her head. 'I don't like the look of him,' she said. 'What's he doing with that hood on in this heat . . . ?'

Mr Salerno started toward the door.

His wife said again, 'Joe, I don't like the way he looks. Don't open the door.'

The man in the jogging suit hurried back to the door as Joe Salerno reached it. Joe unlocked the door and pushed it *ajar. As he did so, the man pulled his left hand out of his pocket.*

There was an explosion, and a flash that lighted up the office.

Joe dropped to one knee. There was a second explosion, and Mrs Salerno felt a rush of air on her face.

'You son of a bitch!' Joe yelled, and he pulled the door closed and locked it.

Juliet started screaming. 'Joe, are you hit? Are you hit!'

Joe staggered back into the office. 'Yes . . .' he said. 'Yes.'

One hand was to his throat. Blood was pouring between his fingers as he walked, spilling down on to the plastic runner they had laid to protect the new carpet. Joe sat heavily on a film projector by the desk. There was a pile of clean washcloths nearby, and he pressed a handful of them to his neck.

Juliet ran to the phone. She called for the police. She was near hysterics and deafened by the shots. She could not hear herself shouting into the phone.

Their son and daughter, Thomas and Lisa, were on their way home from the movies when they saw the ambulance and police cars and the crowd outside the motel.

'It's Daddy,' Lisa said. 'I know it's Daddy.'

She did not wait for Thomas to stop. She jumped from the moving car and ran to the motel, fighting her way through the crowd. Her father was being wheeled out of the office on a stretcher. There was blood everywhere. Lisa screamed. 'Daddy! Please don't die!'

The lights overhead blinded Joe, Sr. He was fighting shock, trying to remain conscious. Shadows of faces, backlit, bent over him.

'Mr Salerno . . .' one of the shadows said. 'Do you know where you are?'

'Hospital . . .' *Joe replied.*

'Do you know that you've been shot?'

'Yeah . . .'

At his side another voice said: 'We'd better start irrigating this . . .'

The first voice said, 'Just leave the wound alone.' Then, to Joe: 'Do you know who I am?'

'No . . .'

'I'm Dr Brown. I'm your doctor. Do you feel all right?'

'Yeah, I feel all right.'

They were moving him again. The ceiling lights slid by.

'Now, Mr Salerno, we're going to get you out of here and put you into a room where the police can talk to you. Do you understand, Mr Salerno?'

Joe nodded, and closed his eyes.

'Those sons of bitches,' *he said.*

Joe put in an anxious call to the hospital from a phone booth in Portland.

I was thinkin, look at this . . . look what I done. My mother answered the phone. She was cryin. She said they thought he was gonna be OK: the bullet had gone through his neck and come out the back. Then my father got on the phone, and he told me not to worry, that he was all right. And he said to me, 'Son, don't you ever testify against these people ever again.'

Joe was torn with remorse and anger. Once he knew that his father was all right, he put in a call to Joe Khoury in New Jersey. He told Khoury that he was going back home to declare war on Scarfo and his people. Khoury tried to dissuade him, but Joe said he was already on his way.

As soon as Joe hung up, Khoury called Jim Maher at

the FBI office in Philadelphia. He quickly explained the situation to Maher, who at once phoned Agent Williams in Portland.

Joe, meanwhile, had driven to the airport in Portland. He would buy a ticket to Philadelphia, and when he got there, he would buy a gun. As he hurried into the terminal, someone called to him. It was Special Agent Williams.

'What are you going to do, Joe?' he asked.

Joe did not answer.

'Don't worry,' Williams said, 'we'll take care of those people. Just give us time. C'mon, I'll buy you a couple of drinks.'

He took Joe's arm and led him out of the airport.

For the next few days, Joe called his parents continually. Each time, his mother begged him to promise never to testify again, and each time Joe promised.

Then Barbara called from Denver.

She told Joe she had heard about his father, and she had heard something else, too. Her parents were friendly with a man who owned a restaurant in Atlantic City. This man had told them that on a recent trip out West, he had seen Joe in a plumbing truck in the Portland area.

Joe immediately called the Marshal's Office. He was told that they could do nothing about it. Joe asked what he should do. 'Move,' the marshal replied.

It was a frightening situation. Scarfo and his people were after his family, they were certainly after him, and he had been seen.

Joe sent his son Mike back to live with Barbara. He called Larry Jenkins and explained what had happened, and quit his job. He gave up his condominium and sold his furniture. And he went into hiding.

PART THREE

WITNESS FOR THE PROSECUTION, 1982–1988

17

The Little Guy Declares War

Nicky Scarfo had given responsibility for the revenge of
Phil Testa's death to Testa's son, Salvatore. He saw in
Sal Testa a valuable ally, and he elevated him to capo.
But while he entrusted the younger Testa with much of
the 'hard work' of the family, Nicky also watched him
carefully. Sal was much like his own nephew Philip,
Nicky knew, aggressive and ambitious. But there was no
tie of blood to ensure Sal's loyalty.

Scarfo was also making more men for his organization,
young killers like Frank Narducci, Jr, his brother Phil,
Thomas DelGiorno, and Nick Caramandi, all of whom
were eager to earn their membership. Scarfo had now
surrounded himself with a homicidal crew such as the
Philadelphia mob had never known. It was the army that
he had begun planning during his exile in Atlantic City,
and for which he had sought to recruit Joe Salerno. Like
any army, it needed a war to fight.

The war was not long in coming.

Scarfo was aware of the federal government's offensive
against the Family. He was also aware that a member
of the Family had cooperated with the FBI and the
Organized Crime Strike Force.

Harry Riccobene was the grand old man of the mob.
Ancient, diminutive, stooped, he was nicknamed The
Hunchback, and he was one of the few members who

recalled Sabella and the Jewish wars of the late twenties. The most venerated member of the Family, Riccobene had for decades run his own gambling and loan-sharking operations, independent of the bosses' control. He also had a solid, long-standing faction of his own within the Family.

The respect accorded Riccobene, and his independence, would have been sufficient to earn him Scarfo's enmity. But Riccobene also had ambitions to become boss, ambitions that had led him to assist the government's assault on Scarfo's organization. With the deaths of Narducci and his associates, Harry Riccobene posed the greatest threat to Nicky's leadership.

In April 1982, one of Scarfo's soldiers approached Harry Riccobene's half-brother, Sonny. He told Sonny that Harry was to be killed and ordered him to set it up. Sonny reported this to Harry, who determined to strike first.

On the evening of 13 May, Scarfo's consigliere, Frank Monte, stopped at a gas station in Southwest Philadelphia to have his Cadillac serviced. Parked across the street was a darkened camper. Inside were Joe Pedulla and Vic Deluca, two Riccobene soldiers, armed with rifles mounting telescopic sights. As Monte stepped from his car, he was shot five times in the back and face. He died an hour later.

When Scarfo received the news, he flew into a rage. He summoned Philip Leonetti and Sal Testa and told them he was declaring war on the Riccobene faction. The first target was to be The Hunchback himself.

Late one humid June night, three weeks after the murder of Frank Monte, Harry Riccobene went to a phone booth near his home in Southwest Philadelphia. When he finished his call and pushed open the door of the booth, a stocky young man hurried up to him in the darkness, pointed a gun at his head, and fired.

The old man ducked, and the bullet grazed his forehead. He grabbed the gunman around the waist, and five more shots were fired as the two struggled. Riccobene was struck in the elbow, arm, and side, but he stayed on his feet until the gunman fled. Riccobene was taken to a hospital, where he recovered from the wounds.

A few weeks later, young Sal Testa was sitting outside a restaurant in the Italian Market of South Philadelphia. It was rush hour, and Ninth Street, with its awninged food stalls, was busy with pedestrians and traffic. As Testa was finishing a dish of steamed clams, a big Ford sedan slowed down opposite him. From the passenger-side window a sawed-off shotgun poked out, and there was a thudding explosion.

Testa was caught full in the side with a load of buckshot that ripped into his stomach and legs and nearly severed his left arm.

The Ford raced away down Ninth Street, swerving around cars and scattering shoppers the length of the market. A police car that had been behind it gave chase. The two cars careened through the narrow streets at seventy miles an hour, until finally the Ford hit a lamppost, skidded on to the sidewalk, and flipped over.

Vic Deluca and Joe Pedulla, the two Riccobene soldiers who had killed Frank Monte, were pulled from the wreck and arrested. They were released the same day, but this fact was of no consolation to them once they learned that Sal Testa had survived. After a few days of hiding out, they turned themselves in to the police. Tried and convicted of the Testa shooting, both Deluca and Pedulla offered to become government witnesses.

It was the first breakthrough the police had had in the series of mob shootings that had been going on for months. And it was their first indication that there was a war in progress within the Family. The FBI began to refer to it as the Riccobene War. Where it would end, not even The Hunchback's own soldiers could tell them.

Nicky Scarfo took time out from his generalship in the war to settle the matter of the plumber. It had been a thorn in his side ever since his arrest for the Falcone murder nearly three years before. Acquittal was not enough: the plumber had hurt him, and now it was time to hurt the plumber.

In August, Nicky summoned one of his new made men, Phil Narducci. Both Narducci and his older brother, Frank, Jr, were now Scarfo soldiers, despite the fact that the Little Guy had murdered their father. The boys' loyalty to Scarfo was grotesque even by mob standards.

Further, there was the irony that one of the motives for the murder was that Scarfo had originally given the contract on Joe Salerno, Sr, to the elder Narducci. Frank, Sr, had known the Salernos all his life, and evidently bound by the old notions of honor, he had not carried out the order. For Nicky, this was proof that Narducci could not be trusted, and he had ordered him killed.

When Narducci was shot down in the gutter at the end of his street, it was Joe Salerno, Sr, who ran to get Monsignor McLaughlin to give the gangster the last rites. Later, Salerno accompanied the priest to Narducci's house, where they prayed a rosary for his soul and paid their respects to the family, including the two sons.

Now Scarfo ordered one of those sons, Phil, to shadow the elder Salerno and, when the time was right, to kill him.

It was not a difficult assignment. The Narduccis were neighbors of the Salernos in South Philadelphia. Phil knew that they owned a motel in Wildwood, and he learned that Joe, Sr, walked his dog every night around eleven o'clock. The jogging suit was Phil's own idea.

On that August night, Phil waited in a vacant lot across Atlantic Avenue from the motel until Joe, Sr, went inside. Normally he came out again in a few minutes with the dog. This night, however, he did not appear, and his wife went inside and locked the door.

Phil was an impulsive, impatient young man. He hurried over to the motel and tugged at the door, and then paced restlessly back and forth, trying to attract their attention. When Joe, Sr, opened the door, Phil pulled a .38 from his jogging suit and fired, aiming for Joe's head. But there was a step up to the office, and the bullet struck low. Phil fired again, and the door was slammed in his face.

He turned and ran across Atlantic Avenue, throwing the gun down as he did so. He knew that his first shot had hit, but he was not sure about the second.

Nicky seemed pleased, despite the fact that Joe, Sr, had not been killed. The point had been made: the plumber had been punished. For the next few days, Scarfo, Philip Leonetti, and Lawrence Merlino paraded around Atlantic City in jogging suits like the one Phil Narducci had worn during the shooting. At that time Scarfo was out on bail for the weapons offense. The police were so outraged by his behavior that they arrested him for associating with known criminals, a violation of the conditions of his bail.

The outrage was not confined to Atlantic City. No-one in the FBI could recall the mob's ever having retaliated against a witness's family, even during the thirties in Chicago and New York. Such behavior violated even the rules of the underworld.

In response, the Bureau, the Atlantic County Prosecutor's Office, the New Jersey State Police, and the police in Philadelphia, Wildwood Crest, and Atlantic City mounted the most intensive surveillance in the history of the Family. Teams of policemen and FBI agents followed Family members twenty-four hours a day.

No-one was left alone, from the leadership down to the lowest numbers runner. No Family member could leave his house, eat a meal, or buy a newspaper without being shadowed. Scarfo and his lieutenants were stopped by police on the slightest pretense and called in for questioning by a dozen state and federal agencies. The result was that Family business virtually came to a halt.

The surveillance became so oppressive that several of the mobsters went to court seeking injunctions to keep the police away. Meanwhile, reams of reports on their movements were being filed, which later would form a mosaic of the background of the Riccobene War.

On 17 August, a week after the shooting of Joe Salerno, Sr, Nicky Scarfo was sentenced to two years' imprisonment for illegal possession of a handgun by a felon. Two days later he arrived at La Tuna Federal Penitentiary in El Paso, Texas.

On the following day, Joe Salerno, Sr, received a telephone call at his motel in Wildwood. At this time state policemen were living at the motel, and the Salernos were under round-the-clock protection.

Joe picked up the phone, which was bugged, and heard a man's voice. 'Now your whole family is dead,' the caller said, and hung up.

A few weeks later, when the summer tourist season ended, the Salernos moved back to their row house in South Philadelphia. Their neighbors shunned them, and some even warned them that they would be killed.

Several times Joe's sister, Lisa, ran into the Merlinos and Narduccis in restaurants. They always made a point of coming up to her and making suggestive or insulting remarks. Joe's brother, Thomas, who owned a small business in the neighborhood, lost a third of his customers. There were more threatening phone calls at the house, and two or three times a day the phone would ring and there would be only silence at the other end.

The police, who had the house under surveillance, urged the Salernos to leave. The family held a conference around the dining-room table to discuss it. The decision was left to Joe, Sr. 'I'm not moving for nobody,' he declared.

When the police suggested to him that the family enter the Witness Protection Program, he was even more emphatic.

'No fuckin way,' he told them.

Nicky Scarfo was not through. Before entering prison, he gave his nephew Philip a list of seven people he wanted killed. It was a battle plan for the war, and Sal Testa was to run the campaign in Nicky's absence. Testa wasted no time getting started.

Two days after Scarfo started his sentence, Harry Riccobene was assaulted for the second time. He was stopped at a traffic light in South Philadelphia when a man in a jogging suit ran up to him. The jogger pulled a gun and fired four times through the window, threw down the gun, and disappeared. Riccobene was unhurt.

In January 1983, Riccobene was sentenced to nine years in prison for racketeering. With both Scarfo and Riccobene in jail, the war slackened off. Nicky, apparently, was not pleased with the situation. In an angry phone call from prison, he scolded his nephew Philip: 'Are you gonna clean the boat, or am I gonna have to do it?'

It was sufficient prodding. In April, the war resumed, and entered a new and even more ruthless phase.

One of the innovations that Nicky had introduced in Philadelphia was a street tax. Formerly, independent gamblers and drug dealers had to obtain the Family's permission to operate in its territory. Now Nicky demanded payment for the privilege.

The announcement of the change in policy was not subtle. Young thugs were sent into the streets to issue warnings. If the warnings were not heeded or if payments were slow, they were sent back with a more pointed message.

One of these thugs was a new made man named Pasquale Spirito. Known as Pat the Cat, Spirito worked for Scarfo capo Joseph Ciancaglini. On 29 April, 1983, Spirito was driving through South Philadelphia with two other men. When he stopped at a red light, one of his passengers drew a gun and shot him in the head.

Just as the shooting of Joseph Salerno, Sr, had set a precedent for the scope of Family violence, so did the killing of Pat the Cat. For Spirito was murdered not on Riccobene's orders, but on Scarfo's.

Nicky had learned of Sonny Riccobene's treachery in having warned his half-brother Harry that he was to be killed. In response, Scarfo had ordered Spirito to murder Sonny. For weeks, nothing was done, and Nicky began to lose patience with his bright young man. Then he discovered that Pat the Cat was skimming profits from his street-tax collections. That was too much for the Little Guy, and he ordered Spirito killed.

That the head of the Family would murder one of his own made men for what amounted to relatively minor infractions tightened the grip of fear with which Scarfo controlled his group. No-one dared to defy, or even displease, the boss. His wrath was lethal; it could flare up at any moment, and consume anyone.

Meanwhile, the war against the Riccobenes continued. Later that summer, Frank Martinez, a young member of the Riccobene faction, was confronted by half a dozen men on a South Philadelphia street as he got into his truck. Two of the men opened fire with .38s, hitting Martinez several times. Martinez managed to flee in his truck, and survived.

These two shootings touched off an exchange of killings that turned South Philadelphia into a battle-ground.

Three weeks after the Martinez attack, Riccobene soldier Sal Tamburrino was shot four times while he was in his parents' store; the gunmen were Phil Narducci and another young Scarfo killer, Nick Milano. The following week, the bodies of the Sollena brothers, Sal and Matteo, were found in the trunks of their cars. They had run a narcotics ring in South Jersey and had not observed Scarfo's new rules. Both had been shot in the head after their hands had been tied behind their backs.

With Harry the Hunchback in prison, Scarfo's killers turned their attention to his family.

A few weeks before Christmas, Harry's brother, Robert, was coming home from the grocery store with his mother when a car pulled up to the curb nearby. As a man got out, Robert pulled his mother aside and turned to flee. The man fired a shotgun blast into the back of his head, killing him. When Mrs Riccobene started to scream, the gunman walked over to her and struck her over the head with the shotgun.

The killing was particularly shocking in that it had occurred in the presence of the victim's mother. It was a rule of the Family that no violence could be done in front of a member's mother. For that reason, Nicky himself had always had his mother answer the door at 26 North Georgia Avenue. In this war, however, the rules themselves had fallen victim.

The Riccobenes directed their retaliation at Scarfo's field marshal. On 10 December, four days after Robert's murder, Sal Testa was driving through South Philadelphia with three bodyguards. At Eleventh and Catherine streets, another car swerved into his path, blocking him. Four Riccobene soldiers leaped from the car and opened fire. Testa and his men returned the fire, and for several terrifying minutes the intersection was a combat zone. By the time the police arrived, the Riccobene men had driven off. No-one had been hit. Testa and his bodyguards were questioned and released.

By this time, the Riccobenes had their own hit list, which included the leadership of the Scarfo faction and several soldiers. No-one on either side was safe, and no place in the neighborhood was sacred.

Enrico Riccobene, Harry's young nephew, owned a jewelry store in Downtown Philadelphia. He never went to work now without three or four bodyguards, and without a gun in his pocket. Ten days before Christmas, Enrico opened the store, accompanied by his bodyguards. A few minutes later he glanced out the front window and saw Sal Testa, Philip Leonetti, and Lawrence Merlino walk slowly by. Testa paused, tapped on the glass, and smiled at him.

After the months of murders and weeks of fear, the sight of the three men was too much for Enrico. He went into the back room of his shop, took his gun from his pocket, and shot himself in the head. Of the suicide, Sal Testa later remarked: 'I don't have to kill people any more . . . I just show up, and they do the job themselves.'

The Riccobene faction was broken. Harry the Hunchback, now in his late seventies, was serving a long prison term, as was his half-brother, Sonny. His other brother, Robert, and his nephew, Enrico, were both dead. One of his soldiers had been killed and another nearly killed. The others were afraid to operate in the neighborhood.

Scarfo's faction, in contrast, was still strong, and Nicky's leadership was intact. By the time he was released from La Tuna on 20 January, 1984, Nicky knew he had won. Therefore, at the party that was given to welcome him home, he declared an end to the war.

For the next nine months there were no murders in the Family. But when at last the brittle silence was broken, the gunshots sent shock waves from Philadelphia to Atlantic City, and beyond.

18

'If You Run, We'll Find You'

For more than a year, Joe remained in hiding, moving from one small town in Oregon to another. He lived in cheap motels and supported himself by doing odd jobs. At Christmas of 1982 he was in a suburb of Salem, the state capital, working as a handyman in an apartment building in return for a room. The owner of the building was also a plumber, and Joe became friendly with him.

Knowing that Joe had no-one to spend the holidays with, the owner invited him to attend a Christmas concert with him at a local church. The man's girlfriend sang in the choir, and she had a friend, Joanne, whom they suggested that Joe meet.

After the concert, the four of them went to dinner. Joanne was a tall, slender young woman with reddish-blonde hair and small, attractive features. She was intelligent and funny, and Joe enjoyed her company. They began seeing each other regularly.

Joe was beginning to feel comfortable again, and he was making friends in Salem. He decided to stay. He looked for plumbing jobs and applied to the state for a license. As usual, he could produce no credentials, so he decided to confide his true situation to the Contractors' Board inspector who interviewed him.

The inspector was understanding and offered to help if Joe could provide some documentation for his story.

Joe called a US attorney in Philadelphia and asked him to write a letter to the inspector certifying his professional qualifications. The attorney did so. Joe passed the state exam and got his plumbing license.

He bought a van and started a small business. Once again, he sought some stability in his life. He called Barbara and told her where he was, and had her send Mike to live with him again. He also told Joanne who he really was and explained his situation to her. She accepted the news with concern and caring. It was an emotional turning point for Joe. He now had someone in whom he could confide, and the fact was a great relief to him.

He also got back in touch with the Marshal's Service. He needed to do so in order to reestablish his link with his family in Philadelphia, with whom he had not spoken for more than a year. And, indeed, the Marshals told Joe that they had mail for him from his parents.

Among the other news, he learned that both of his grandfathers had died while he was in hiding. Not only had he not been able to attend their funerals, he had not even known of their deaths.

A few days later the Marshals called again.

They told me the [Organized Crime] Strike Force in Camden was goin to prosecute Local 54, and the US attorney wanted me to testify. I said, 'No way – I'm not testifyin any more.' They said I'd have to do it, that I had no choice. 'How about my parents?' I asked them. 'Look what happened last time.' The Marshals said, 'You let us worry about that.'

Joe had sworn to his parents that he would never again be a witness. They, in turn, had warned him that if he broke his promise, they would disown him.

Desperate for advice, Joe called Joe Khoury at the

Atlantic County Prosecutor's Office. Khoury urged him to speak directly with the US attorney in Camden and explain his reasons for not wanting to testify.

Joe did as he suggested and got in touch with the attorney.

He was a very military kind of guy, all rules and regulations. He told me he had a case to try and if I didn't cooperate, he'd subpoena me. I said, 'You won't be able to find me to serve the subpoena.' 'If you run, we'll find you,' he said. 'And when we find you, if you still won't testify, you'll sit in jail until you do.'

Joe called his parents and found that the US attorney had already been in touch with them. Again, they asked Joe to promise not to testify. Joe and his parents began searching for a compromise. They contacted a lawyer, and they asked the parish priest, Monsignor McLaughlin, to mediate.

For weeks they argued back and forth. The US Attorney insisted that Scarfo was menacing Joe's family precisely to prevent Joe from testifying. After he had testified, the attorney said, there would be no more danger. Joe responded that his father had been shot *after* his testimony to the Gaming Commission, in retaliation. The attorney did not understand these people and how they thought, Joe told him. The attorney was adamant: he wanted Joe's testimony, and he would accept nothing less. If Joe refused, he would be arrested.

They had reached an impasse.

'The only way I'm gonna get out of this,' Joe told his father at last, 'is to run. And for that I'll need money.'

Joe's father wired him $2500. Joe sent Mike back again to live with Barbara, abandoned his business and van, and dropped out of sight.

He started south, traveling the length of California to San Diego. There he stayed briefly with a cousin, before moving on through Arizona to Santa Fe, New Mexico. By this time he was running out of money, so he started back for Oregon.

The marshal inspector in Portland, who had driven Joe to the airport for his testimony before Congress and the Gaming Commission, was placed in charge of the search for him. The US attorney had been as good as his word. Joe's photo, old and new names, and new social security number had been distributed to the police, and there was a warrant for his arrest. He was now being hunted not only by the Scarfo mob but by the federal government as well.

When Joe returned to Salem, he contacted Joanne. She told him that she was under police surveillance and that marshals had come to her parents' house, where she lived, to look for him.

Joe needed money, so he asked Joanne to arrange to have his father wire some to her at once. Meanwhile, he took a room at a motel and went into town to hock his only remaining possessions, his plumbing tools.

As Joe was coming out of the pawnshop, a car stopped at a red light opposite him. He glanced at the driver. It was the marshal inspector. He turned and hurried off. The marshal had not recognized him.

Joe met Joanne at the motel, and she handed him the cash his father had sent. It had not been easy. Joe's father had had to use the name of his father-in-law – Adelizzi – and had wired the money to a friend of Joanne's. As time went on, the money-sending procedure became more complicated. At last Monsignor McLaughlin took responsibility for sending the money, which he wired to a variety of sympathetic friends of Joanne's family.

One time, Father McLaughlin wired money to a friend of Joanne's, an old lady who lived alone. When she went to the Western Union office to pick it up, the clerk started questioning her. He asked her who the money was from, and she said, 'My husband.' The clerk was lookin at the wire, and it said 'Monsignor Edward McLaughlin.' The clerk asked what her husband did for a living, and the old lady said he was a truck driver. Now the clerk was really confused. So the old lady went on about how he was always on the road, and she never knew where the money was comin from, and sometimes it wasn't even in his name. Finally, just to get rid of her, he handed it over.

By this time, Joanne was being watched continually. Once, after turning money over to Joe, she found marshals waiting for her when she returned to her parents' house. They grilled her about Joe, claiming they knew she was in touch with him. Joanne denied it. Then, evidently trying to drive a wedge between her and Joe, they told her that he had been spotted in the company of another woman. They warned her about the consequences of aiding a fugitive. Joanne insisted she could not help them, and she asked them to leave.

At Christmastime in 1983, Joe was living in a motel outside of Salem when he developed severe chest pains. He thought he was having a heart attack, and he called Joanne. She hurried to join him. He was in terrible condition: he had been running for six months; his health had deteriorated, and his morale was in tatters. He was out of money once again. As Joanne sat with him in the motel room, Joe came to a decision.

'I can't go on doin this,' I told her. 'There's no way I can keep runnin from these people.' I called Joe Khoury from the motel, and he said, 'Turn yourself in.' He offered to

*put together a conference call with a marshal in Phil-
adelphia, the Italian guy who had arranged the visit with
my parents.*

*I told the marshal I didn't want to be arrested. 'You
know I'm not a criminal,' I said. He assured me I
wouldn't be treated like one; there would be no handcuffs,
none of that. He asked where I was. 'I'm dependin on
you,' I told him, and I gave him the address.*

While Joe waited for the marshals to arrive, he packed
his bag, and he asked Joanne to settle his bill with the
office. Then he unlocked the door and left it ajar.

Two unmarked cars screeched to a halt outside the
motel. In the next minute, the door to Joe's room was
kicked in, and three marshals piled into the room, their
guns drawn.

Two of them threw Joe face-first against the wall.
While one held a gun at his back, the other searched him.
The third marshal opened Joe's bag and scattered the
contents across the bed. Then they twisted his arms
behind his back and handcuffed him.

'You're coming with us,' one of them barked.

Joe tried to protest, telling them that he was not a
criminal, and that he had turned himself in. In reply, one
of the marshals, a woman, warned him to keep his mouth
shut. They dragged him out of the room and pushed him
into a car.

Joanne came back in time to see them driving off. She
went to the room, packed Joe's things, and drove home.
Although she called the Marshal's Office and the local
police repeatedly for the next few days, she was unable
to learn where Joe had been taken.

Joe was in the backseat of the car, cuffed next to the
famale marshal.

'They promised me you wouldn't do this,' he said.

'Shut up,' the marshal said. 'If there's any talking to be done, we'll do it.'

Joe was driven to the county jail, where he was strip-searched, fingerprinted, photographed, and given an orange overall to wear. Carrying a rolled-up mattress and a pillow, he was taken to a holding cell in which there were about thirty other prisoners.

Joe tried to make the marshals understand what a dangerous position he was in. There was still a price on his head, and he had no idea who these prisoners were.

'Keep your fucking mouth shut,' he was told.

Joe spent that night and the next day in the holding cell. Around dinnertime, a marshal came to the cell and called for him. Joe quickly gathered up his mattress and pillow. He assumed that word had finally reached the jail that he was a protected witness, and that he would now be moved to a motel.

He followed the marshal down a corridor to a blank door at the far end. The marshal unlocked the door. Joe was bewildered. It was a padded cell.

'What the hell are you guys doin?' Joe demanded.

The marshal grabbed his arm. 'C'mon, get in,' he said. He shoved Joe inside and locked the door.

Joe began pounding at the door. 'Hey!' he yelled after the marshal. 'Hey, at least put me in a regular cell!'

But the marshal was gone.

The cell was an empty, brown vinyl-covered box, four feet wide by eight feet deep. Joe could touch the ceiling with his hand. There were dozens of fingernail marks where prisoners had tried to scratch their way through the padding, and one corner had been burned black. There were no windows. The only opening to the outside was a narrow slot high in the door.

Joe was seized with a sudden panic. For the first time

in his life, he knew claustrophobia. But what was even worse was the crushing sense of unfairness. Why were they doing this to him? What had he ever done to harm them? How had he deserved this treatment? He leaned against the wall and sank to the floor. If they wanted to drive him crazy, they were succeeding. He had a desperate impulse to kill himself. He heard himself begin to pant, then moan. And then he started to cry.

For seven hours he agonized in the cell, disoriented, broken with despair. The cell was bare and featureless, lacking even a toilet. There was no way to protest nor anyone to talk to. Joe had no idea how long he would be kept in this place.

He felt he was going mad, and to save his sanity he began to pray. He begged God for some relief; just to get him out of that cell would be enough. If not, then he prayed for some way to end his life, for he knew he could not survive there much longer.

The guard shift changed, and Joe pulled himself up to the little slot in the door. A young, stocky, blond-haired guard came through, checking the cells, and Joe called to him.

'Officer,' he said, 'can I say somethin to you?'

'Make it quick,' the young guard replied.

'Can you do me a big favor?' Joe panted out. 'Can you put me in that cell across the way?'

The guard seemed to hesitate.

'I'll tell you somethin,' Joe went on quickly, 'God's gonna put you in heaven for doin this for me.'

The guard shrugged. 'Yeah,' he said. 'OK.'

He unlocked the padded cell and transferred Joe to a normal cell opposite. When the door was locked, Joe turned to him. 'God bless you,' he said.

The new cell was luxurious compared to that awful place. There was air and light, and a toilet and a sink.

Most important of all, Joe could see outside the cell, breaking the horrible sense of isolation he had felt. The urge to kill himself was gone, and he felt that he might survive after all.

He lay down on the iron bedstead, closed his eyes, and passed out.

The next morning Joe was taken from the cell by a pair of marshals and was led to one of two waiting vans. The vans were to take the thirty prisoners into Salem for sentencing, but one would not start. All thirty men were then chained together and packed into the other van. When the doors were closed, the atmosphere was stifling. As they were driven into the city, the men jostled and fell over one another, cursing and complaining.

Joe was chained to a mild-looking middle-aged man. Joe asked what he was in for.

He told me that he'd worked hard for years to support his family, and then he'd been offered the chance to make some real money. It was a drug deal, a one-time thing. He said he'd never done anything like that before, but he couldn't turn down the chance. He'd gotten caught, and today, he said, he was gonna be sentenced. He figured he'd get thirty years, and he'd never see his wife or kids again.

At the jail in Salem, Joe was locked in a holding cell with half of the men. All were convicted criminals, he knew, and he kept carefully apart from them. At last a guard came to the cell door to begin taking them out one by one.

'Joe Salerno!' the guard called out.

Joe was horrified. Any one of these men was liable to know about the contract on his life. Joe fought to control himself and said nothing, sitting with his head bowed, staring at his hands.

'Joe Salerno!' the guard called again.

When there was no response, the guard walked away. A few minutes later he was back with a marshal. The marshal called out Joe's new name, and Joe got up and left the cell.

He was taken to a small conference room and introduced to a public defender. Joe quickly explained his situation to the lawyer, who advised him to refuse extradition to New Jersey. He told Joe that, given time, they could fight back, and perhaps get him released.

'What happens in the meantime?' Joe asked.

The lawyer told him he would have to stay in jail.

Joe shook his head. 'No way,' he said.

Joe was returned to the holding cell. At the end of the day, the prisoners were taken back to the county jail, where Joe was put into a single cell. It was the third day of his incarceration. During that time he had not been charged with a crime, nor had he been allowed to contact anyone. He was being denied even a criminal's rights.

The following morning, two marshals came to take Joe to the airport. As they cuffed him, he asked them: 'They aren't gonna put me in jail when I get back East, are they?'

'Don't worry about a thing,' the marshals said.

The marshals accompanied Joe on the flight to Philadelphia. At the airport, the first person Joe saw was the Italian marshal, Nick. He was relieved.

I said, 'Boy, Nick, am I glad to see you. You don't know the kind of trouble I've had.' They put me in the back of a car, and I said to Nick, 'You wouldn't put me in jail, would you?' He didn't answer, and I started to panic; I was remembering that padded cell. 'Look,' I said to him, 'do anything you want – shoot me in the leg, Nick, put me in the hospital – but I don't wanna go back to jail. I never did anything. I don't deserve it.'

'You'll be OK,' he said. 'Believe me.' That's when I knew they were gonna put me in jail.

'Promise me one thing,' I asked him. 'Promise you won't put me in a padded cell.'

'I'll make sure of that,' he said.

Joe was taken to Lewisburg Penitentiary, a maximum security prison outside Philadelphia. He was locked in a single cell in the highest-security wing, where he spent the week of New Year. At one point he was taken into the city and brought before a judge. It was there that he met the US attorney for the first time.

I apologized to him for all the trouble I had caused, hopin that he'd give me a break. The judge put me on $100,000 bond, and he said I could call my parents and ask them to post it. I told him they could, but the attorney said to me, 'If you do that, if you go out on the street, you're on your own. No protection, nothing.'

I was in a bad spot, and he knew it, so they kept me in jail. I couldn't call my family; nobody knew where I was. But the worst thing was that I had always believed in the system, and now, the way they were treatin me, I didn't know if the system was right or wrong. I was angry, confused – I didn't know what to believe any more. It was like a nightmare.

Joe spent two more days in the state penitentiary. It was an aged, alien place. The heat had been turned up full against the January cold. The cells were stifling, and the overhead pipes dripped condensation day and night.

It was as though it were raining continually inside the prison, and Joe's clothes, his mattress, and the floor were constantly soaked.

In the cells opposite his were violent criminals, the worst of the population. One night, he overheard them discussing Nicky Scarfo and Philip Leonetti. As he listened, he realized to his horror that some of the prisoners were associated with Scarfo's operations. At any moment he was liable to be recognized. If one of the guards used his real name, as they had done in Oregon, he would certainly be killed, for there was still $200,000 on his head.

Because Joe was the only prisoner on the block with a cell to himself, he became the object of the others' curiosity, and they asked him repeatedly what he was in for. At first, he denied having committed a crime, but when it became apparent that they suspected he was an informer, to protect himself he invented a story about his criminal past.

He was vague, and reticent about details. Word soon spread that Joe was the most dangerous prisoner on the block. The other inmates and even the guards began to show him respect, as the rumors about him multiplied.

When a new prisoner was brought in, scarcely more than a boy, the others taunted him by threatening to have him put in the cell with Joe. The boy became so frightened that he broke down in tears. He, too, had heard what a desperate character Joe was.

By now the situation was just unreal. Here I was in the toughest block in the prison, surrounded by all kinds of crazy criminals, and they were all scared of me, and the guards were treatin me like I was some famous gangster, bringin me extra food and givin me privileges. And all the time I was thinkin, this is insane – I'm just a plumber.

Two days before Joe was to testify, a team of marshals took him to a safe house in New York City. It was a strange place, half hotel, half prison. Joe was locked in a one-bedroom apartment that had no windows. There was a closed-circuit television monitor in each room, including the bathroom, and he was watched by marshals twenty-four hours a day. He was dismayed to discover that among the marshals who monitored him were several women.

Again he was totally dependent on the marshals, with whom he communicated through an intercom. They brought him his meals and kept the apartment clean. There was a television, but it showed only videotaped movies, chosen by the marshals. Joe was not allowed out, and there was no phone.

The night before his testimony, Joe was driven to Philadelphia and locked in a cell in the basement of the courthouse. The US attorney spent five hours with him, going over his testimony. Though the attorney prodded and prompted him, Joe had little to contribute. Neither Scarfo nor Leonetti had been indicted, and his knowledge of the Local 54 officials was limited.

The prosecution began its examination of Joe by asking him whether he knew Scarfo and Leonetti. The defense objected. The US attorney pressed on, focusing on Local 54. Again the defense objected, and asked for a conference with the judge.

Joe sat anxiously on the witness stand while the lawyers and judge huddled together. At last, the judge ruled. There was insufficient evidence to support the conspiracy charge about which Joe had been called to testify. Joe was dismissed.

He was shattered as he left the courtroom. All of it – the hiding, the arrest, the padded cell, the penitentiary – had been for nothing. He had been on the stand for no more than ten minutes.

After that day's session, the US attorney came to the cell to sign a form releasing Joe. The release contained the provision that for the following year, Joe would have to report in person once a week to the marshals. The attorney told him that while he did not expect that he would ever be called as a witness again, they wanted to know where he was if they did need him.

When Joe's parents learned that he was in Philadelphia, they asked the US attorney for permission to visit with him. The attorney refused. The Salernos told him that they had not seen their son in nearly five years and had not heard from him in months. The attorney assured them that Joe was all right, and he advised them not to send him any more money.

'He's a big boy,' the attorney drawled. 'It's time he took care of himself.' And besides, he added, he had the Marshals to look after him.

19

'The Feds Want to See You'

Back in Oregon, Joe was destitute. Joanne picked him up at the airport and took him to a motel. He had saved the sixty dollars per diem that the Marshals had given him, but it was all the money he had. He went back to the pawnshop and got his plumbing tools out of hock. Once again, he was forced to start from scratch.

There was a hopeful moment when he checked in with the Marshals, however: he was told he might go back on subsistence. It would take some time, the Marshals said, but they would try to arrange it. Whenever he asked about it after that, he was told to wait. In the end, the promised subsistence never appeared.

Joe's relationship with the Marshals was by now totally perverse. He had to report to them every week, but he received no benefits; he still did not know whether he was even in the Witness Program. The idea that the Marshals had always seemed to hold, that Joe ought to be treated like a criminal, had become a reality. The witness had become the accused; the Protection Program was now a kind of probation.

Joe started plumbing again, and earned enough money to buy a used truck and rent a run-down apartment. As soon as he was settled he sent for his three sons, and they spent that summer with him. It was an important time for Joe. During his months in hiding and on the run, he had had no contact with the boys, and he feared that they had forgotten him. But the reunion was a happy one, and they all enjoyed their time together.

That fall, Joe answered a newspaper ad that had been placed by a plumbing company in a small town in rural Oregon. The company was owned by an elderly man, Stu Matson, and his four sons, all of whom were plumbers. The Matsons had moved to Oregon from the Ozarks and now handled all the plumbing work in that section of the Oregon hills. Joe had never met anyone like them.

Their business was headquartered in a crumbling converted warehouse in the town of Shelbyville. Matson and his wife shared the space, he to run his plumbing business, she to manufacture dolls. A railroad ran nearby. Every few hours, a train would pass through; all of the plumbing supplies would rattle, and hundreds of porcelain dolls would dance on the shelves, their arms and legs waggling among the rusted toilets and lengths of pipe.

When Joe arrived for his interview, he was greeted by the secretary, a husky woman past middle age, wearing a miniskirt. She seemed relieved to see Joe, and she told him that they needed another plumber badly because there was so much work. Joe was puzzled that so busy a shop should seem so derelict and disorganized. The secretary showed Joe into Stu Matson's office.

Every piece of furniture in the office was piled high with plumbing supplies. There were pipes and joints and fittings, most years old and crusted with rust. In the midst of them, behind a desk chest-high in scrap, sat the owner.

Stu Matson was a stout, balding, elderly man in overalls. He had a distracted expression on his face, which was set off by the fact that he wore his glasses askew, half on his forehead, half on his nose.

'Howdy,' he said, as Joe reached over the pile of scrap to take his hand. Joe said hello.

Stu questioned Joe absently about his background, scarcely seeming to take in the answers, while he tinkered with the junk on his desk. At last he pronounced himself satisfied.

'I'll want you to meet my boys, though,' he concluded. 'You can start tomorrow.'

The next morning, Joe was back in Shelbyville for his first day of work. While Stu Matson sat fiddling with the scrap, his eldest son, Eddie, came into the office.

Eddie was a tall, lean man in his thirties, with an untrimmed rug of hair. His cheeks were bulging with sunflower seeds. He was followed closely by a loose-jointed mongrel dog, which, as soon as he stopped walking, began chewing at his leg.

'This is Lady,' Eddie said, as the dog growled and snapped at him. 'She's got wild in her.'

Eddie chatted with Joe, spitting seeds on to the floor while the dog tore at his leg, threatening to knock him over. In a few minutes his brother Fred arrived. He was a huge, bearded man with a thick neck and a carefree expression. He greeted Joe warmly, mumbling past a sandwich wedged in his mouth. He, too, had a dog, Bear, who immediately started a fight with Lady.

As the two dogs snarled and careened around the office, the third son came in. Mattie, in his early twenties, said nothing as his father introduced him to Joe but merely nodded gravely. He was solemn and unsmiling, and so silent that Joe assumed he must be a mute.

The last to arrive was Jake. He came in carrying several bag lunches, which he arranged in a line on the blueprint board. Jake was a short, stocky boy with heavily greased hair. He panted continually from asthma.

When all the brothers were assembled, they began

The Margate beach house where Vincent Falcone was murdered. The stairs down which Joe helped carry the body are in the left foreground.

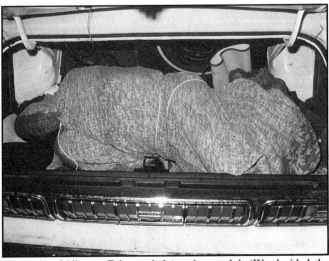

The body of Vincent Falcone tied 'cowboy style'. 'We decided the guy's no good, and we killed him.'

THE MOB IN ATLANTIC CITY

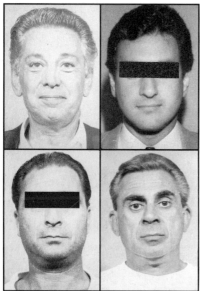

The Mob in exile. Scarfo and his Atlantic City lieutenants: (*from left to right*) Nicky Scarfo, nephew Philip Leonetti, and the Merlino brothers, Lawrence and Salvatore. At the FBI's request, the faces of Philip Leonetti and Lawrence Merlino are partially obscured.

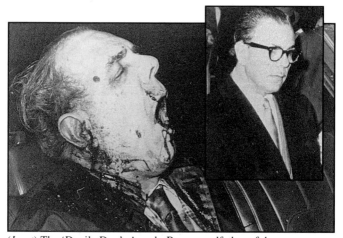

(*Inset*) The 'Docile Don', Angelo Bruno, godfather of the Philadelphia Mafia whose twenty-year rule was remarkable for its lack of violence. His brutal murder on 21 March 1980 (*main picture*) sparked nearly a decade of violence under his successor Phil Testa and, after Testa's murder, Nicky Scarfo.

Sergeant (now Lieutenant) Joseph M. Khoury of the Atlantic County Prosecutor's Office (*right*) taking Sal Merlino into custody. Khoury's close friendship with Joe Salerno was critical to his success as a witness.

(*Right*) Phil Testa, Nicky Scarfo's mentor, Philadelphia's mob boss from March 1980 to March 1981. (*Above*) Aftermath of a coup – the wreckage of Phil Testa's house, 15 March 1981. Testa's murder opened the way for Scarfo to become boss of the Philadelphia Family.

SCARFO'S REIGN OF TERROR

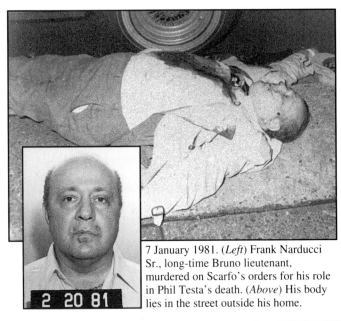

7 January 1981. (*Left*) Frank Narducci Sr., long-time Bruno lieutenant, murdered on Scarfo's orders for his role in Phil Testa's death. (*Above*) His body lies in the street outside his home.

6 October 1981. John Calabrese, shot to death on a South Philadelphia street. A long-time Family drug dealer, he had tried to penetrate Scarfo's Atlantic City operation.

25 February 1982. Dominic DeVito, Narducci soldier, was discovered in the trunk of his car, shot three times in the head. Like Vincent Falcone, he was tied 'cowboy style'.

15 March 1982. The bullet-riddled body of Rocco Marinucci was found stuffed into trash bags in South Philadelphia. For his role in detonating the bomb that killed Phil Testa, firecrackers were thrust into his throat.

SCARFO'S REVENGE ON THE PLUMBER

Hitman Phil Narducci, dispatched to settle Scarfo's score with the Plumber.

Where Joe Salerno Sr. fell – Narducci fled, dropping his gun.

THE TERROR CONTINUES:
THE RICCOBENE WAR MAY 1982 – JANUARY 1984

(*Below*) Harry 'The Hunchback' Riccobene, oldest surviving member of the original Philadelphia Family.

(*Above*) In January 1983 he was jailed for the murder of Frank Monte. With the Hunchback's imprisonment and the decimation of his faction, Scarfo declared victory in the Riccobene War.

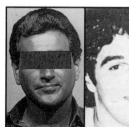
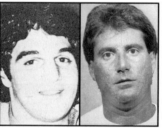

Philip Leonetti (*far left*), Sal Testa (*middle*), field marshals in the Riccobene War and Frank Narducci Jr. (*left*), one of the young soldiers.

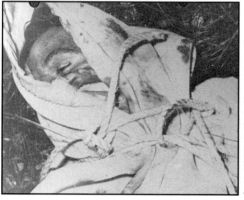

Through his leadership in the Riccobene War, Sal Testa's stature rose to the point where Scarfo felt threatened. After months of stalking him, Nicky's hitmen finally murdered him on 4 September 1984.

Scarfo determined to eliminate the Riccobenes, but the Hunchback struck first. On 13 May 1982, Frank Monte (*right*), Scarfo's *consigliere* was shot to death. Nicky declared all-out war.

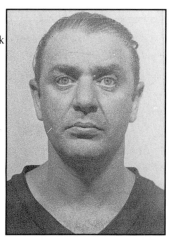

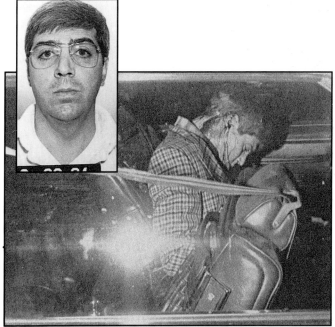

After another attempt on Harry Riccobene, Scarfo soldier Pasquale 'Pat the Cat' Spirito was found shot to death. For years it was believed that Pat the Cat was a victim of the Riccobenes. In fact, he was murdered on Scarfo's orders for hesitating to kill Riccobene's relatives.

SCARFO CONVICTED

In August 1982, Scarfo was sentenced to two years in prison on a weapons charge, but the war went on.

Scarfo appeared in court prior to the RICO trial. Joe Salerno's testimony finally helped convict him and sixteen members of the Philadelphia Family to over six hundred years in prison.

what Joe learned was a daily ritual. Their mother had made lunches for them all, and though the bags were carefully labeled, they began to argue over who would get which one.

The dogs were rolling and twisting over each other on the floor, growling and biting, and the Matsons were engaged in a heated argument over peanut butter versus chicken salad. In the midst of all this, the secretary came in to announce a phone call. Stu answered and asked the customer to wait, and the lunch dispute raged on.

Joe watched it all in wonder.

Then Eddie, the oldest son, takes a chair and throws it over, and he starts yellin at the top of his voice: 'All right, that's it! I'm not takin this any more!' He spits out the seeds, and he points at his brothers one by one, and he says: 'That's it! You're fired, and you're fired, and you're fired!' Then he puts a finger in his father's face and he yells, 'And you're fired, too!' and he points at me and says, 'And you, too! You're fired!'

There's this silence, and we're all standin there lookin at Eddie, and he bursts out laughin. 'I really had you that time, didn't I!' he says. And then they all start laughin. And I'm thinkin, now it makes sense why they can't handle their business even with five plumbers.

Joe spent his first week in Shelbyville living at a motel owned by members of a religious cult. They wore turbans and robes, and they had rings through their noses and jewels on their foreheads. Everything in the motel – rugs, drapes, walls, and bedspreads – was red, and the halls reeked of pungent cooking and incense.

Joe learned that the Matsons were born-again Christians and were kindly, openhanded people. So inoffensive were they that when they decided it was necessary to fire the secretary, neither Stu nor any of his sons could do it. So Stu asked Joe to fire her.

They had decided, Stu said, to replace her with the youngest son, Mattie. The choice puzzled Joe, since he had never heard Mattie speak, but he obliged and gave the secretary her notice. Stu gave her a month's wages as severance pay, and Mattie took over.

With the first phone call, the secret of Mattie's silence was revealed. He had the worst stutter Joe had ever heard. Every call now took twice as long as it should have, and the always tenuous work schedule was now thrown into utter chaos.

They used to trade plumbin jobs for goats and for bodywork on their cars. They were afraid to offend anyone, so they never asked to be paid, and everybody owed them money. One afternoon the phone rang, and Mattie answered: 'M-m-m-m-atson's Plumbing.' There was shoutin on the other end. Then another call and another, same thing.

Then Eddie and the dog walked in. Mattie was all upset: 'Eddie, you b-b-b-ig jerk, did you do these c-c-c-alls today?'

'Yeah,' Eddie said. The dog was chewin on his leg.

'Well, you forg - got to turn the water b - b - back on!'

Eddie was so afraid to go back and face the customers that I had to do it for him.

Joe came to like the Matsons and to value their generosity and good humor, and he set about reorganizing the business for them. He collected back debts, paid the suppliers, and devised a schedule. And though the dogs still fought and the brothers still quarreled over lunches, the business began to prosper.

Stu loaned Joe enough money to rent a house, an old

two-storied single on the edge of town. It was the first house Joe had lived in since leaving Kansas nearly five years earlier. Soon he was settled in Shelbyville, and he sent for his son Mike to come and live with him.

Joanne visited from Salem on weekends. Every Saturday night the Matsons came for dinner, and Joe would make them all a big Italian meal. Eventually Joanne arranged with her employer to be transferred to Shelbyville, and she moved in with Joe and Mike.

Joe worked for the Matsons for a year and a half. He was beginning to feel rooted, and the fear with which he had lived for so long had begun to fade. He had a job and friends and a family again, and it seemed that his life might finally be returning to normal.

Then, in September of 1986, the Marshals called.

'The Feds want to see you,' he was told. 'Looks like you're going back East.'

20

Nicky Builds an Empire

Nineteen eight-four was a busy year for Nicky Scarfo. The Riccobene War had left him more powerful than ever, and he began to flex his muscles. No racket could be run in Philadelphia or Atlantic City without paying him tribute. He enforced his street tax ruthlessly, accumulating more wealth than the Family had ever known. Money was pouring in, from extortion and loan sharking and, especially, from the speed market, which was now monopolized by Scarfo's people.

Nicky himself had grown rich, and he indulged his tastes in cars and clothes liberally. Despite this, however, his official occupation remained custodian at 26 North Georgia Avenue, a job for which he claimed to be making less than $3,000 a year. As a result, he had not filed an income tax return since 1976, a fact which seemed not to trouble the IRS.

Banned from the casinos by the plumber's testimony, Nicky intensified his manipulations of them behind the scenes. One result was that the mayor of Atlantic City was indicted for extortion and corruption on behalf of the Scarfo organization. He pleaded guilty and was sentenced to fifteen years in prison. Scarfo himself remained unindicted.

Scarf, Inc. was doing well, too. In September it received a half-million-dollar contract for concrete work on a state- and county-funded housing project. Then, a few months later, a company owned by Lawrence and Chuckie Merlino was given the iron contract for Resorts International's new high-rise hotel in Atlantic City.

It seemed to make no difference that the contracts were signed at the same time that Philip Leonetti, president of Scarf, Inc. was being indicted along with the mayor on extortion charges, and Lawrence Merlino was being charged with disposing of the body of Sal Sollena, one of the two drug-dealing brothers whose corpses had been found in trash bags in the trunks of their cars.

With his own demesne secure, Nicky started to branch out. He established a residence in Fort Lauderdale, Florida, where he bought a yacht. He named the boat *Usual Suspects* – a reference to the movie *Casablanca* – and he used it to entertain visiting mobsters from around the country. A measure to permit casino gambling was being debated in Florida, and Nicky wanted to be sure he would be in position to take advantage of it if it passed.

He now saw himself as one of the most powerful gangsters in the nation. The Genoveses were solidly behind him in New York, and even the Gambinos, who were Sicilians and had once been hostile to him, were asking him for favors.

A member of the Gambino Family had been assaulted by a New Jersey hoodlum named Frank Stillitano. The Gambinos interceded with Nicky, who dispatched his nephew Philip and Lawrence Merlino to deal with him. Stillitano's trussed, decaying corpse was later found in the trunk of his car at Philadelphia Airport; he had been shot behind the left ear.

With lucrative holdings in the Northeast and Florida, Nicky turned his attention to the West Coast. He made several quick trips to Los Angeles, looking for an opportunity to penetrate the film and video industries. The mob in Southern California was weak, just as it had been in South Jersey. It was suffering from decades of inactivity and from having an aging leadership that spent most of its time in jail. A foothold in Los Angeles would give Nicky a truly national stature.

Despite all this activity, there were also problems. Scarfo's attorney, Robert Simone, who had so devastated the plumber's testimony, was now under indictment for a million dollars in tax evasion. Both of the Merlino brothers were also under indictment, Lawrence for threatening a policeman and Chuckie for trying to bribe one.

But the biggest problem now facing Nicky was one he had foreseen from the start. The Riccobene War had made young Sal Testa one of the most important figures in his organization. Testa had arranged most of the killings and had participated in some of them himself. In the process, he had gathered around him his own group of soldiers, whom the war had wed to him.

With Nicky in prison and then in Florida, Sal Testa had become the most visible leader of the Family. At twenty-eight, he was boyishly handsome, with striking dark good looks and a stylish air of confidence. He was also wealthy: his father had left him an estate worth $800,000 that included a run-down bar in Atlantic City on a site where Donald Trump decided to build a casino. Trump paid Testa $1.1 million for the right to tear the bar down.

Nicky had trusted Testa for his father's sake, and he valued him for his uncompromising ruthlessness. But the fact that there was still no bond of blood to guarantee Testa's loyalty left Scarfo uneasy.

Such a bond seemed to be forming, however, when Testa announced that he was going to marry the daughter of Nicky's underboss, Chuckie Merlino. Maria Merlino was a dark, slender young woman, known in the neighborhood for her beauty. She had nursed Testa back to health after the Italian Market shooting, and they had been inseparable ever since. The wedding was set for April.

Nicky welcomed the news, and he began preparing for a massive, old-fashioned gangster celebration. There would be limousines and vintage champagne, and bosses from around the nation would be invited. It would be the underworld's social event of the year, and a perfect opportunity for Nicky to flaunt his power and largesse.

By March, and his fifty-fifth birthday, Nicky was making plans in earnest. He even drew on his contractor friends to rebuild the Testa home, vacant since the explosion that had killed Phil, as a wedding gift for the newlyweds.

Three weeks before the ceremony, however, Sal Testa suddenly canceled it. The engagement was off. It was a stunning affront both to Nicky and to Chuckie Merlino, and it left Maria in mournful hysterics. A few nights later the family leadership assembled for dinner at a restaurant in South Philadelphia. Scarfo and Testa argued. The argument grew violent, and Nicky ended by throwing Testa out.

Then, in April, the *Wall Street Journal* ran a front-page story characterizing Testa as the rising star of the Philadelphia Family and naming him as the heir to its leadership. Testa, meanwhile, was organizing his own gang, based in the Italian Market.

It was all too much for Nicky. A hit team was put together, led by Thomas DelGiorno and consisting of soldiers Wayne and Joseph Grande, Nick Milano, Charles Iannece, Francis Iannarella, and Nick Caramandi. The hit was to be supervised by Chuckie Merlino.

For five months the team stalked Testa, waiting for an

opportunity to kill him. But Sal Testa was not stupid. He avoided all contact with Scarfo's people, and he never went anywhere without bodyguards. Testa knew he needed time to build a bulwark against Scarfo, just as the Little Guy had once had to build an army against Bruno. But while Scarfo had had the isolation of Atlantic City, Testa was working under Nicky's very nose.

Finally, DelGiorno went to Scarfo and asked permission to enlist Testa's closest friend, Joseph Pungitore, for the hit. Nicky agreed, and he authorized DelGiorno to tell Pungitore that if he refused, he and his entire family would be killed.

Pungitore was anguished at the prospect of delivering Testa to his death, but he knew he had no choice. He asked only that he not be required to fire the shot himself. Nicky consented, and Pungitore sought out his friend.

Pungitore told Testa he needed him to mediate a dispute over money between himself and Wayne Grande. Testa offered to meet the two at a candy store owned by Grande. He arrived dressed in tennis shorts and T-shirt after playing racquetball, and shook hands with Pungitore and Grande.

He was about to sit down when Wayne Grande's brother, Joseph, joined them. Testa turned to shake Joe's hand. At that moment, Wayne stepped up behind him and shot him twice in the back of the head.

The killers left Testa's body in the candy store until late that night, when it was tied, 'cowboy style,' wrapped in a blanket, and thrown into the back of a van. Two of Scarfo's soldiers then drove the van through a rainstorm to South Jersey and dumped Testa's body beside an unlit road.

The murder of Sal Testa made a point that was not lost on the Family. Sal had been the brightest and most promising of Scarfo's lieutenants, and he had carried out his orders with lethal efficiency. But not even he had been spared the punishment for defiance: not even the son of Phil Testa, the man who had made Nicky what he was, had been shown mercy.

Scarfo, it was now clear, demanded total loyalty and would tolerate no rivals. What was more, as Testa's broken engagement showed, Nicky, like Angelo Bruno, wanted to control his colleagues' personal lives. Unlike Bruno, however, Scarfo left no room for negotiation or compromise. The punishment for lack of discipline was death.

A few months after Joe Salerno had been brought to New Jersey in chains for a trial in which his testimony had been ruled irrelevant, Nicky Scarfo was summoned to Washington to testify before the President's Commission on Organized Crime. He refused, and a US district court ruled that he could not be compelled to appear. By the time a federal circuit court had overturned that decision, the President's Commission had gone out of existence. Nicky had not had to testify, even when ordered to do so on the authority of the president of the United States.

By the mid-1980s, Philadelphia had become the methamphetamine capital of the country. Speed and its constituent chemical, P2P, were making money for the city's motorcycle gangs, for Asian and Caribbean mobs, and for the black Mafia as well as for Scarfo's *Cosa Nostra* Family.

The black mob was particularly active in the drug trade and violent in its methods. Police attributed some twenty murders to the mob's internal fighting over the traffic in speed, cocaine, heroin, and PCP. Traditionally, the black mob stayed clear of the *Cosa Nostra*'s territory, and the two groups eyed each other with hostility over the no-man's land between them. Then a curious spectacle occurred.

Frank D'Alfonso, the media-crowned successor of Phil Testa, was seen associating with a number of black drug dealers. Word reached Scarfo that Frankie Flowers was negotiating with the black mob for the right to distribute drugs within the Family's territory. What was more, he was moving in on Nicky's domination of the boxing business in Atlantic City. While the beating he had been given seemed to have cured Frankie of his ambitions to be boss, it had not made him any smarter.

On the night of 23 July, 1985, D'Alfonso went for a walk in the neighborhood to escape the suffocating summer humidity of South Philadelphia. As he stopped to light a cigarette, a black Cadillac pulled up alongside him, and two men got out. One stepped in front of him and the other beside him, and they shot him five times in the head and chest. He was dead before his body hit the pavement.

Nicky Scarfo had given the job to Thomas DelGiorno, who by now had participated in five murders for the Little Guy and had become a capo. For the hit on D'Alfonso, DelGiorno used Phil Narducci – Joe Salerno, Sr's, assailant – and a new recruit, Joe Ligambi. Phil's brother, Frank, drove the car.

Over the next few months, Nicky tightened the reins on the street tax and the drug trade. Frank Forlini, a contentious concrete supplier with a bad temper and a finger in the numbers racket, was found dead in his pickup truck. He had refused to pay tribute to Scarfo and had received a bullet in the brain for his defiance.

Steven Vento, who had a speed operation in South Philly, also failed to pay, and was shot in the head. DelGiorno confiscated fifty gallons of Vento's P2P and sold them for Scarfo at a price of $1.5 million.

These were merely maintenance maneuvers, not expansion. Scarfo had a larger vision, both for himself and for his empire. With the help of an old friend, he moved to realize it.

A former amateur boxer, Scarfo made a point of following the careers of young fighters from South Philly. He took a particular interest in a Jewish club fighter named Lee Beloff. Later, Beloff had gone into politics and had become a member of the Philadelphia City Council. His district covered the old, historic section of town along the Delaware River.

Through the 1970s and into the '80s, this section was being redeveloped at a furious pace. Two-hundred-year-old buildings that had been allowed to deteriorate were being bought up and restored by private developers who were taking advantage of generous tax incentives.

Under the local political etiquette, the city council would not approve any development scheme without the consent of the district councilman. This gentleman's agreement gave Beloff enormous power over the developers. With Nicky's influence in the unions and contracting trades, the two men had a chokehold on Old City redevelopment.

They began modestly to exploit it in early 1985, when they demanded $25,000 from a surgeon-turned-developer who wanted to restore a building in Beloff's district. Beloff's aide, Robert Rego, guaranteed the doctor that Beloff would see that he was awarded the renovation permit and would have no trouble with labor unions or contractors.

The doctor paid, and Beloff backed his application for the job.

A few months later, the doctor wanted to build townhouses in the district. Rego demanded another $25,000, as well as free improvements to Councilman Beloff's home. Again the doctor agreed, and again he received the permits.

Their success with the surgeon moved Beloff and Scarfo to try again. An Old City developer who was seeking a permit to close a street to traffic outside one of his projects was visited by Rego and Scarfo soldier Nick Caramandi.

Rego told the developer that Beloff would back the proposal in return for a luxury apartment in Old City. The developer hesitated. Caramandi then spoke up. He made it clear that the Family would make construction a permanent nightmare for the developer if he refused. Shortly after the meeting, Beloff introduced a bill in Council to close the street, and he then moved his mistress into the rent-free apartment.

It was all the encouragement Beloff and Nicky needed. The time had come for them to make a move more suited to their abilities and ambitions.

Willard G. Rouse III was one of the most successful and powerful real estate developers in Philadelphia. Rouse Associates had led the rebirth of Philadelphia's downtown, developing it from a business backwater into a national financial and commercial center.

In 1986, Rouse was seeking a $10 million grant from the federal government to build a commercial complex along the Delaware River at Penn's Landing. To support his proposal, he needed the backing of the local councilman, Lee Beloff.

In April, Robert Rego and Nick Caramandi met with a representative of Rouse at his Center City office. Rego made it clear that Beloff would support the Rouse plan in return for $1 million. Caramandi added his assurance that there would be no labor or supply problems. The

Rouse aide heard them out and asked for time to talk the matter over with his boss.

When Willard Rouse got the report, he picked up the phone and called the FBI. The Philadelphia office put an agent under cover at Rouse Associates, and Rouse designated the agent to be the negotiator with Beloff. In October, Beloff, Rego, and Caramandi were arrested for extortion.

It was now apparent to Scarfo that the whole Rouse venture was going to fall apart, and that this would probably involve him. He reacted with characteristic rage and ordered that Caramandi be killed. When Caramandi learned that there was a contract on his life, he offered to testify against Scarfo.

Caramandi's defection caused Scarfo to reevaluate the loyalty of his subordinates, and his suspicions focused on his capo and hit man, Tommy DelGiorno. Through a series of bugged conversations, the New Jersey State Police learned that Scarfo had lost confidence in DelGiorno and had decided to have him killed.

Seeing an opening to turn DelGiorno, the State Police passed their information on to him. He refused to believe the report and demanded proof. The State Police then confronted him with the tapes, and DelGiorno heard for himself that he was to be murdered. He accepted the government's offer of protection and agreed to become a witness.

Between the two of them, DelGiorno and Caramandi not only had knowledge of the structure and personnel of the entire Scarfo organization, but they also knew the details of dozens of murders, assaults, extortions, drug deals, and other crimes that had been committed by Nicky and his Family.

In January 1987, Nicky's name was added to the Rouse indictment. Though the Philadelphia Strike Force and the FBI were being circumspect, they made it clear that this was just the beginning.

The question in the prosecutors' minds, however, was whether a jury would accept the word of Mafia turncoats who were also admitted killers. After all, just a few years before, jurors had refused to believe an honest plumber and had set Scarfo free.

21

'If You're Not Part of It, You'll Never Forgive Yourself'

The call from the Marshals came at an especially bad time for Joe. He had built his reputation with the Matsons to the point at which a local entrepreneur had offered to set him up in business in a resort town on the coast. The prospect of owning his own business again, and of living on the coast, was irresistible to Joe. With his little family, it would almost be like his old life on the Jersey shore.

But now they wanted him to testify again, and he had no idea what it was about.

Joe accepted the business offer, and then he called Joe Khoury.

'The FBI wants to talk to you,' Khoury told him.

Joe was angry and impatient. 'About what?' he snapped.

'It's a RICO thing,' Khoury replied.

'What's that?'

'Just let the guy talk to you.'

While Joe waited, Khoury put through a conference call to an FBI office in New Jersey. An agent joined them on the line and introduced himself as Larry Schneider.

He said to me, 'We have a good case against the people you're familiar with. We've been working on it for a lot

*of years, and you can be very important to us.' I said, 'I
don't think so. I'm doin something really good now, and
I'm not interested any more.' He asked me to at least give
him a chance to explain it to me. Then he told me what
RICO was, and that they had hundreds of hours of tapes
of these people. He asked if he could meet with me. He
said the FBI would pay all my expenses and would
reimburse me for the time I'd lose at work.*

*I told him it was all interesting, but that I had a normal
life now and I didn't want to get involved. Then Joe
Khoury said to me, 'Listen to what he's saying. They've
got a strong case. You can't lose anything by talking it
over with them.'*

Joe agreed to a meeting, but with a few things understood in advance. The sole purpose of the meeting would
be to discuss the government's case. Afterward, he would
reserve the right to decide whether or not to testify.
And, most important, under no circumstances must the
Marshals be involved. Schneider agreed to Joe's terms.

Joe left Matson Plumbing after New Year in 1987, and
he, Joanne, and Mike moved to the coast. There they
were joined by Joe's eldest son, Johnny. Joe started his
business, and when he felt it was established, he called
the FBI to arrange the meeting. In March, he flew alone
to Seattle.

Two agents from the Philadelphia office met him at a
motel. They were cordial and low-key. There was no
pressure, and not a word was said about compelling Joe
to testify. As agreed, the agents had come simply to show
Joe the quality of their evidence. And the evidence was
impressive. The agents told him that Tommy DelGiorno
and Nick Caramandi had become witnesses and had
already made statements to the police.

It was all there – the Rouse extortion, Local 54, the

Riccobene War, and, most important to Joe, the shooting of his father and the Vincent Falcone murder. DelGiorno had told the police that Scarfo had once discussed the Falcone killing with him. Though Joe did not know it at the time, DelGiorno's account supported his own completely.

It was gratifying, and it was intriguing, but it was not convincing. Joe had seen Scarfo get off before, and he was not about to volunteer for another losing cause. Besides, he was still bound by his promise to his parents that he would never testify again. He thanked the agents and told them he would think it over.

He returned to his business and his family. He tried to lose himself in his work, building it for the sake of his family's future. Michael and Johnny were now eighteen and nineteen, and they wanted to learn their father's profession. Joe took them into the business, and the three began working together. Joe felt that it really was becoming more and more like his old life – before Vincent Falcone, before Nicky Scarfo – and he instinctively resisted becoming involved again in all that.

A few weeks later, Joe Khoury called. The FBI wanted to meet with Joe again. This time, Khoury said, the prosecutor from the US Organized Crime Strike Force would come along.

Joe discussed the request with Joanne. She had been with him for four years, through some of the worst of it. She was reluctant to advise him, but she knew that he felt there was an unsettled score between him and the Scarfo mob. Joe vented his reservations, his frustrations, his doubts, and some of his anger. In the end, Joanne urged him to go, for one more talk.

Joe flew to Los Angeles for the meeting. With the FBI agents was a slender, prematurely graying man of forty. He had cold blue eyes and a light brown moustache, and the most dispassionate manner Joe had ever encountered. He introduced himself as Arnold Gordon, special attorney for the Organized Crime Strike Force.

It was Gordon who would lead the prosecution against the Scarfo mob. He told Joe that the federal government intended to take out the entire leadership of the organization, putting not only Scarfo, Leonetti, and the Merlinos on trial, but thirteen others as well. If they succeeded, it would be the first time in history that an entire *Cosa Nostra* Family would be dismantled with a single stroke.

The defendants were to be charged with more than thirty crimes, including nearly 200 counts. The Falcone murder was among them, as was the attack on Joe Salerno, Sr. DelGiorno and Caramandi would be pivotal witnesses, but they would be attacked on their credibility. Robert Simone would lead the attack, and Joe knew how effective he could be.

Joe's testimony, Gordon said, would help to support their stories. Because Joe had never been a criminal, he could supply the credibility that the other two lacked. What was more, he was now an experienced witness. With that, and the preparation he would be given, the defense would be unable to break him down.

Joe was at once tempted and alienated by Gordon. The attorney seemed absolutely cold-blooded; he did not smile, did not banter, did not flinch. Such a man might, indeed, be able to bring Scarfo down once and for all. But could Joe work with him?

As they parted, Gordon made it clear to Joe that while his testimony might make a great deal of difference, the prosecutors would not insist on it. He would not be subpoenaed. The decision was his to make.

It was true. Neither the Strike Force nor the FBI knew where Joe was; they had respected his wish not to be contacted through the Marshals, or to have the Marshals transport him. Instead, they had always approached him through Joe Khoury, whom Joe trusted like a brother. At last he was free to do what he wanted with regard to the prosecutors. But what did he want to do?

My mind was goin back and forth like a seesaw. I knew I needed help to make the decision, so I called everybody – the FBI, Joe Khoury – and ended up havin big fights with all of them. My main concern was retaliation against my family, and I kept thinkin, I gotta be nuts to get involved in this again. So I'd decide not to do it, but then somethin in the corner of my mind would say, you've got to do this.

During the next few weeks, Joe tried to get his mind off the question. But in every spare moment of the day, and halfway through the night, it tormented him. Testifying again would mean violating his pledge to his parents. And worse, it might mean subjecting them to more danger.

Yet he did have a score to settle with Scarfo. For Vincent Falcone's sake. For his father's sake. For the sake of what they had done to his family, his kids. For the sake of what they were still doing in Philadelphia and Jersey. And also for his own sake.

They had killed Vincent Falcone, not he. Yet he was the one who had suffered for it. They had put a price on his head and had hunted him. They were on the streets, they were wealthy, they had power. He had had eight years of worry and privation. They were still lording it over his neighborhood, his home, living off its blood and polluting its life. And because of them, he would never see his home again.

Yet how many times had be been deceived and disappointed? He had told the truth about Vincent Falcone, only to have his words twisted in his mouth by Scarfo's lawyers until the jury did not believe him. He had testified before the Senate, only to learn that he had been treated far worse than a professional killer. He had gone before the Gaming Commission, only to see his father shot in retaliation.

And then the last one, the Local 54 case. That had been a real revelation. The prosecutor had dealt with him as if he had been Scarfo himself, issuing a warrant for him, hunting him down, arresting him, and throwing him in prison. The irony was that the whole time, Scarfo had been free; Scarfo was not even made to appear. The prosecutors had never touched Nicky Scarfo. Instead, every time they wanted to make a name for themselves by prosecuting Nicky, they grabbed Joe by the neck and threw him on the stand.

Yet someone had to stop Scarfo. Someone had to stand up, point the finger, and say: '*There* is the source of the evil.' But all of them had failed – the prosecutors, the police, the government commissions. How could it be a job for him? They were power, and he was just a plumber.

By the time Joe Khoury called to arrange the third meeting, Joe was a chaos of doubt. Mechanically, he agreed to fly to Tucson, and he began to prepare for the trip. Joanne drove him to the airport, but when the time came for him to board his flight, he was shaking so violently that he had to put down his bag.

He could not do it, he told her. He had changed his mind.

Joanne drove him home. Joe called the FBI in New Jersey and asked for Larry Schneider.

I said, 'Look, I'm not gonna do this; I'm not gettin in the middle of this again. My father got shot. You understand: my old man caught a bullet. And I'll tell you somethin else: I've been kissin people's asses in this program for eight years, and I've never gotten anything from it but trouble. My family's busted up, my kids are all over the place, and every time I testify, I gotta start my life all over.'

I was beside myself, goin on and on.

Schneider managed to calm Joe down and convince him to take a later flight to Tucson. There, the prosecutors asked him if he would be willing to go before a grand jury in Newark that was considering the government's request to indict Scarfo and his mob.

Joe asked if his parents would have to find out. The prosecutors said no. Joe asked for a few days to think it over.

Back in Oregon, he called Khoury. He wanted to know what Khoury honestly thought about the case and its prospects for success.

'I'll tell you this much,' Khoury replied. 'They've got a good chance of putting these people away. And if they do, and you're not part of it, you'll never forgive yourself.'

For all his doubts, Joe knew that Khoury was right. He could not come all this way without seeing it through. If the finish *was* coming, he had to be there. The question was how to tell his parents. And for that he had no answer.

He called the FBI office in Philadelphia.

'Yeah,' he told them. 'I'll do it . . . I'll go before the grand jury.'

22

From Bad to Worse for the Little Guy

Suddenly, things were no longer going well for Nicky Scarfo. In January 1987, he was arrested in the Rouse extortion case and was denied bail. He would have to remain in Holmesburg Penitentiary until the trial. But that was not the end, or even the worst.

The Rouse indictment was followed in short order by two more. One was for narcotics trafficking, charging that Nicky, Philip Leonetti, and Chuckie Merlino controlled the methamphetamine business in Philadelphia; it cited Nicky's street tax and the sale of Steven Vento's P2P. The other was for the murder of Sal Testa.

It was all because of Tommy DelGiorno, Nicky knew. He was talking about everything, and Nick Caramandi was backing him up. They were the first members in the history of the Family to break the code of silence, and they deserved to be killed. But both were in the custody of the FBI, and, like the plumber, they could not be found.

There were other problems as well. Chuckie Merlino had already been sentenced to four years in prison on the police bribery charge. Scarfo decided to replace him as underboss with his nephew, Philip.

What was more, Scarfo's lawyer, Robert Simone, had been named in the Rouse case as an unindicted co-

conspirator, and he was fighting an indictment for perjury in another case.

Then came the hardest blow of all. After ten years of preparation the federal government was going to indict Scarfo on racketeering charges. It would be the biggest, broadest-ranging indictment of all, and the hardest one to fight.

In his cell on D-block at Holmesburg, Nicky added it all up.

The indications were that the Feds would throw everything at him at once in a sprawling grab bag of charges going back to the Falcone murder. And the charges involved not only him, but the entire backbone of his organization. Everyone would be dragged in: Philip, Chuckie, Lawrence, the Narduccis, all the capos, and half a dozen soldiers.

It would not be like the Falcone case, where the prosecutors had been required to prove that Nicky, Phil, and Lawrence had been in the room and had committed the murder. Under RICO the Feds only had to prove that they belonged to the Family and that the Family had committed crimes. And then they would all go down.

Nicky was not worried about DelGiorno and Caramandi as witnesses. With their records, no-one would believe them; Simone would see to that. But the Rouse thing was a problem, because Beloff and Rego had dealt with an undercover FBI agent. The agent would back Caramandi, and the jury would find him easier to accept.

But in the drug case and the Testa murder case, Tommy and Nick would be on their own, and Simone would destroy them just as he had destroyed the plumber.

This RICO was another matter. If the plumber testified, he would back up Tommy and Nick, and that might cause problems. But the plumber would never do it – not

215

after what had happened to his father. He had already refused to testify once, and even when they had forced him, he had done no harm at all. And that case was nothing, just another labor probe. No, the plumber would never surface for this, because he knew what would happen, if not to him, then to his family.

On 6 May, 1987, Nicky Scarfo was convicted of conspiracy and extortion in the Rouse case. The testimony of Tommy DelGiorno and Nick Caramandi, supported by that of the FBI undercover agent and others, was sufficient to convince the jury. Scarfo was sentenced to fourteen years in prison. He remained at Holmesburg pending appeal of the verdict and commencement of the drug trial.

One week after his conviction in the Rouse case, Nicky was back in court for the preliminary hearing in the Sal Testa murder.

In November, Scarfo, Leonetti, Chuckie Merlino, and soldiers Frank Iannarella and Charlie Iannece appeared in federal court to face the drug charges. During the weeklong trial, DelGiorno and Caramandi were the only witnesses who linked the defendants to the street tax and the P2P monopoly.

Simone, leading for the defense, tore into them. He made them recite a litany of hundreds of crimes that they had committed, including perjury and a score of murders. They admitted that they were facing long prison terms and hoped to gain relief by their testimony. By the time Simone had finished with them, any credibility they might have had was gone.

It took the jury only seven hours to find Scarfo and the others not guilty of involvement in the drug trade.

Nicky could scarcely contain himself. The verdict had

borne out his confidence that no jury would believe Tommy's and Nick's unsupported testimony. When the last 'Not guilty' was pronounced, Scarfo leaped to his feet, flung his arms in the air, and shouted: 'Who lied?' And then he answered himself: 'DelGiorno and Caramandi!'

The prosecutor, disgusted with the scene, shoved his files into his briefcase and told Scarfo to shut up. Nicky wheeled on him.

'You shut the fuck up!' he screeched. 'It's the end of the lies!'

It was not the end of the prosecutions. Nicky spent the holidays in prison, and in February 1988 he went on trial in the Testa case. At the defense table with Scarfo and Simone were Philip Leonetti, Chuckie Merlino, Frank Iannarella, Joe Pungitore, Joe and Wayne Grande, Charlie Iannece, and another young soldier, Sal Scafidi.

Again the government's case was built on DelGiorno and Caramandi, and again Simone assailed them. He called them rats, turncoats, and liars and accused them of having become informants to save themselves.

It was an act that Simone had rehearsed thoroughly, and it had the same impact on this jury as on the last. The jurors took only three hours to find all nine defendants not guilty of Sal Testa's murder. Later, one of the jurors said there had been no choice but to acquit, since there was no evidence to corroborate DelGiorno's and Caramandi's testimony.

Clearly, the word of the two mobsters, unsupported by testimony from a noncriminal, was not going to convince a jury. Nicky had beaten the drug and Testa raps, and even if the Rouse conviction held up, he would spend no more than four and a half years in jail. Philip had not been convicted, so Scarfo could continue to run the Family from prison through him, as he had done during the Riccobene War.

There was only one obstacle left, and that was the RICO prosecution.

Between the drug and Testa trials, the federal grand jury had returned the indictment: thirty-nine charges, specifying nearly 200 counts. Without the plumber, the whole case would be based on DelGiorno and Caramandi. To Nicky, it seemed as though there was nothing to worry about.

And then the last indictment came down. It was a surprise to everyone. The district attorney of Philadelphia had asked the federal Organized Crime Strike Force to sever one charge from its RICO indictment, the murder of Frank D'Alfonso. The Strike Force agreed. The state now charged Nicky, Lawrence and Chuckie Merlino, Iannarella, Joe Ligambi, Phil and Frank Narducci, and soldiers Gino and Nick Milano with the murder. The state attorney general made it clear that he would seek the death penalty.

23

'One More Time: Face to Face'

In September, Joe flew quietly into Newark, where he was met at the airport by three FBI agents, Larry Schneider, Jim Maher, who had been so helpful to him in Portland, and one of Maher's partners, Gary Langan. Langan was a large, genial man in his forties, who was endeavoring to quit smoking by chewing continually on a plastic cigarette holder.

Joe asked where the armed escort was. 'Nobody knows you're coming,' Maher replied, 'so there's no point in attracting any attention.'

They drove together to a motel near the federal building, where they had dinner and chatted. Joe did not miss the Marshals' manic security; he felt safe and comfortable with the FBI agents, and what was more, they treated him like a cooperative citizen, not a criminal.

He was amazed at how smoothly the grand jury testimony went. Arnold Gordon asked him a series of carefully worded questions about Scarfo and Vincent Falcone, to which Joe replied yes or no. In an hour he was finished.

The next day he was back in Oregon, and, as the FBI had promised, he was reimbursed for his wages and his time. His only regret was that he had not spoken to his parents. But that had been his decision, not the FBI's.

Joe was afraid to tell his parents that he had testified

again, though he knew they were bound to find out sooner or later. In fact, they called him shortly after his return to say they had heard on television about the grand jury. His mother asked pointedly whether he was involved.

It was painful, but he lied to them. Again his mother asked him to promise that he would not testify, and again he did so. He hated the situation and hoped there might soon be some way around it. But his parents' safety was at stake, and he felt the burden of his responsibility for it.

Though Gordon and the FBI had promised Joe that he would not be forced to testify, he knew he was now committed. Jim Maher had told him that the prosecutors considered him to be a key witness, essential for corroborating the testimonies of DelGiorno and Caramandi. But after the indictments were announced in January, Joe's doubts turned to dismay.

The newspapers began publishing profiles of the two turncoats, and the portraits were not flattering. Joe read with increasing anxiety about their pasts, the crimes they had committed, and their gruesome details. He was not surprised that juries had refused to believe them: they were Nicky's kind, after all. These were the men to whom Joe was to lend credibility. And yet a jury had not believed *him*, either.

Through the spring and summer, as the trial approached Joe brooded over his situation. He had allowed himself to be sucked into testifying yet again, and he was angry at himself because of it. What would he say to his parents, and more to the point, what would he do about them? If Scarfo and his people were acquitted, they would be more powerful and more arrogant than ever. Once they had beaten the federal government, there would be no stopping them.

Over and over, Joe imagined the consequences. Scarfo and his people would leave the courtroom celebrating, and then they would start settling their scores. They would kill Joe's parents, brother, and sister without a second thought, and they would defy the authorities to do something about it.

It would be like before, when they wore the 'Just Another Case' shirts during the Falcone trial, or when they paraded in jogging suits after his father's shooting. Except this time it would be worse. This time his family would all be dead.

I called Joe Khoury and told him all this, and I said, 'Who's gonna be responsible, Joe? Not the Feds, not you – me.' He said, 'They've got a strong case. We've turned everything over to them – all the files, all the evidence. They'll get them this time.'

I said, 'Suppose they don't. Then what?' He said, 'Joe, you stood up to these people before, when there was no-one else. You're not the only witness this time.'

I said to him: 'What about these guys – what're they gonna say when the defense lawyers ask them, "How did you kill this guy? What did he look like? Where did he bleed from?" What's the jury gonna think then?'

He said, 'Joe, these prosecutors are the best. They can put these people away for good, but they need you. You can do it, Joe. You've got to do it.'

Joe had kept informed of what the Scarfo organization had been doing since the Falcone trial. He knew about the murders, some twenty-five of them; knew that Scarfo had expanded to Florida; and knew about the growing power of the Family. He understood that he had a responsibility to help put a stop to it, and that with the RICO case he could even have an important role to play.

But in the end, as the trial drew near, his decision was essentially a personal one.

> *I didn't care what anybody was sayin to me. I saw what these people did with my own eyes: I'd seen them commit a murder; I knew that killin was no problem for them. So I decided I was gonna do it. I knew I had to get up on that stand and see them one more time, face to face.*

The trial was set for September 1988. Joe spent the summer months building his business, enjoying the company of his sons, and preparing himself mentally for his testimony. In July, Larry Schneider called from New Jersey to arrange Joe's pretrial preparation. They agreed on a meeting in August.

Then Joe received a shock.

He had been following a major federal RICO trial in New Jersey, checking its progress every Sunday in the *New York Times*. It had been the longest federal trial in history and the biggest racketeering prosecution to date. As in the Scarfo case, the government had witnesses and hundreds of tapes of conversations. A conviction would set a precedent and bolster Joe's morale.

The defendants were acquitted on all counts. The news plunged Joe into depression.

In August, Joe flew to Philadelphia for his preparation. Jim Maher and Gary Langan again met him at the airport, and together they went to a hotel. Two prosecutors were waiting – Arnold Gordon, and another Strike Force attorney, Al Wicks.

The preparation was intensive. Gordon had read the transcripts from the Falcone trial, and now he coached Joe on how to avoid the same pitfalls.

'We're going to handle this testimony our way,' he told Joe before they started. 'Not their way – *ours*.'

Gordon then took Joe through his direct examination. Every few minutes he would stop Joe. 'Not "Yeah,"' he would say. 'Say "Yes, sir." And don't answer, "If you say so" – answer the question. Tell the truth.'

Whenever Joe referred to one of the defendants as 'he' or 'him,' Gordon would interrupt and ask him to use the person's full name. When, after four or five or six hours, Joe would become impatient or careless, Gordon would remind him that he could be his own worst enemy on the stand. He was to remain patient and calm, and not play into the defense attorney's hands.

Joe was being molded into an effective, precise witness. There was to be no ambiguity, no hedging. If he knew the answer, he was to state it clearly and completely. If not, he was to say so. If he did not understand a question, he was to ask that it be repeated; if he was still unsure, he was not to answer. The object was clarity, accuracy, and truth.

Gordon then led Joe through the story of Vincent Falcone's murder. Joe's account was flat, matter-of-fact.

'No,' Gordon said. 'That's not the way it was. You've told this so many times, it's like it didn't happen.' He urged Joe to put himself back in the situation, back in Lawrence Merlino's car, back in Phil Disney's apartment.

'When the jury hears it,' he said, 'it's got to be like the first time, exactly the way you lived it.'

They went back through the event moment by moment. As the agents and the prosecutors watched, Joe once again saw the gun brush by his face, saw Philip Leonetti shoot Falcone, then turn to him with that lethal look and say, 'He was a no-good motherfucker, Joe.'

It was frighteningly real and immediate. When Joe stopped talking, he was sweating and trembling.

'When we come to that,' Gordon told him, 'I'm just going to turn you loose.'

There was one other thing, he stressed. Under no circumstances was Joe to mention the Falcone trial. This was not a murder trial, it was a racketeering trial – and besides, they had lost the Falcone case. The government would ask for a motion that all references to the earlier trial be ruled irrelevant, and Joe was not to bring it up.

Gordon then took a seat in one corner of the hotel room, and Al Wicks began taking Joe through the cross-examination. He was every bit as biting and abrasive as Robert Simone had been eight years before. This time, however, Joe was ready, and with Gordon's help, he found the answers to the bullying, intimidating, and suggestive questions. No, he had not shot Vincent Falcone. No, he had not carried the body himself. No, he was not lying for his own sake.

They worked eight hours a day for three days. At the end of it, Joe was feeling exhausted but confident. On the final day, as the prosecutors were getting ready to go, Wicks told him: 'If you do that on the stand, they won't be able to touch you.' To Joe's disappointment, however, Arnold Gordon said nothing.

'He's a cold-blooded son of a bitch, isn't he,' Joe said to the FBI agents after the two attorneys had left.

The federal racketeering trial of the Scarfo organization began on 8 September, 1988.

With Scarfo were sixteen other defendants: there were his nephew and underboss, Philip Leonetti; the Merlino brothers, Lawrence and Chuckie; the Narducci brothers, Frank and Phil; the Grande brothers, Wayne and Joe; capos Joseph Ciancaglini and Frank Iannarella; and soldiers Nick Virgilio, Charles Iannece, Gino Milano, Ralph Staino, Sal Scafidi, and Joseph and Anthony Pungitore.

All were charged with membership in an organization that existed for criminal purposes, the *Cosa Nostra*, and with participation in its illegal acts. The nearly 200 counts included murder, attempted murder, drug trafficking, extortion, loan sharking, and gambling, among other crimes.

Five weeks into the trial, Joe received a call at work from Joe Khoury. Khoury told him it was time to come back East; they would need him to testify in two days.

Joe packed a few things, and Joanne picked up his ticket. He said goodbye to his sons and asked them to look after the business for him. On 17 October, he boarded a plane for Newark.

24

'Whatever Happens, Your Son is a Hero'

Jim Maher, Gary Langan, and Larry Schneider met Joe at the airport and drove him to a hotel in Cherry Hill, New Jersey. He was apprehensive, both about his testimony and about the fact that he still had not told his parents.

The following day, Joe's testimony was postponed. He spent another night at the hotel, becoming more nervous, and more concerned about his parents. His testimony would be reported in the press, and they would learn of it the same day. That idea was intolerable to him. If he was going to break his promise to them and testify, he must tell them so and explain the decision before he took the stand. Only then could he testify with a clear mind.

Again, his testimony was postponed. Joe was quickly becoming a nervous wreck. He spent the evenings with the prosecutors, who tried to calm and reassure him, but afterward he could not eat, and sleep came with difficulty.

Then there was a third delay, and Joe passed another anxious night at the hotel. The confidence and resolve he had gleaned from Joe Khoury and Arnold Gordon were gradually dissolving. Then the testimony was postponed for a fourth day.

The FBI agents took turns guarding him. They were low-key and unobtrusive, unlike the Marshals, but there was at least one armed agent with Joe at all times. By the fourth night, the agents could see how distraught Joe was. At last, Special Agent Charlie Kluge, who was in charge of the detail, called Joe Khoury and asked him to stay with Joe.

Khoury had attended the ongoing prep sessions and was concerned by Joe's condition. Joe was preoccupied not with the trial, but with his parents. He insisted that if he could see them, he could get their support. Khoury had tried to arrange with the prosecutors for Joe to visit with his parents, but there had been no decision on it yet.

Khoury took Joe out for an Italian dinner, and as they chatted it became clear to him that Joe was in no state to testify. Khoury did his best to reassure him and to lift his spirits, but it was no use.

They finished dinner around eleven, and Khoury asked Joe what he would like to do.

'I want to go see my folks,' Joe replied.

Khoury asked if he was kidding.

Joe shook his head. 'I want to do it.'

Khoury reminded him of the danger. It meant driving into South Philadelphia, into the very heart of the Family's territory.

'Listen,' Joe said quickly, 'nobody knows I'm here, and it's late. We can go right now.'

It was the most difficult decision Khoury had ever had to make. Over the years, he had become close to Joe. He had helped him through difficult times, and he had persuaded him to testify now. He knew that without his family's support, Joe could not be an effective witness.

Khoury asked if Joe was sure.

'Look,' Joe said, stretching out his hands, 'just the idea's got me trembling.'

Khoury nodded.

'All right,' he said.

They drove south through New Jersey in Khoury's unmarked car. Khoury himself was a firearms instructor, and he was heavily armed. It was nearly midnight before they came to the entrance to the Walt Whitman Bridge.

That bridge had always been a threshold in Joe's life. He had crossed it as a boy when he had left home to meet new people, and later when he married and moved to Brigantine. He had crossed it to pick up kitchen cabinets for Philip Leonetti, and guns for Nicky Scarfo.

Each of those trips had taken him farther from home. Now he was crossing the Walt Whitman to return to his home.

On the far side was his neighborhood. He had not seen it since Vincent Falcone's murder, and he had not seen his parents in nearly ten years.

Khoury cruised the neighborhood several times. No-one was on the streets. Both he and Joe were tense with anticipation and alert for any sign of danger. They turned into the narrow side street where the Salernos lived. There were still lights on in the house.

Khoury parked the car, got out quickly, and opened the door for Joe. As they hurried up the steps, Khoury shielded Joe from the street with his body. He pressed the doorbell.

Joe heard his father ask, 'Who is it?'

'It's Sergeant Khoury, Mr Salerno.'

The next moment, the door was opened, and Khoury pushed Joe into the living room.

My mother was sittin readin the paper, and my brother was there, too. My sister, Lisa, came running up from the basement — she'd seen me on the steps. 'It's Joseph!' my mother yelled, and everybody started huggin each other and cryin. Even Joe Khoury was on the verge of tears.

We all went into the dining room and sat around the table. I said, 'I'm gonna testify against these people. That's why I'm here – to tell you. I want to get them for what they did to me, and what they did to Daddy. I need you to back me up.'

My father said, 'I knew all the time. I knew they'd need you in this; it's been in the back of my mind. You can't fool me.'

Then Joe Khoury explained to them about it, and said that my testimony was vital to the case. We talked until three o'clock in the morning, and my father finally said: 'You have balls when you get up on that stand, and don't worry about nothing.'

And I said, 'Dad, I'll do my best.'

Joe was scheduled to testify the following day, 25 October. He did not sleep that night. He was gratified by his family's reaction and grateful for their support, but still he was nervous. In the morning, he and Joe Khoury had breakfast at the motel. Afterward, they got as far as Khoury's car, and Joe vomited in the parking lot. He was pale and trembling, and he felt weak as they drove over the bridge to Philadelphia.

They pulled up outside the federal building on Arch Street. Half a dozen FBI agents met Joe at the curb and walked with him into the secure holding area in the basement adjoining the courthouse. There, too, he threw up.

Court was to convene at nine. At a quarter to nine, Arnold Gordon took the elevator down to the holding room and asked to see Joe.

'Good luck,' Gordon said, and shook Joe's hand.

Joe waited in the basement for two hours. Word came

that he would definitely go on that day. There would be no more delays.

At eleven, marshals came down to summon him. Joe Khoury, Larry Schneider, and Gary Langan walked with him toward the long corridor that led to the court building. The corridor was pillared with marshals hefting shotguns. Joe felt his stomach heave again, and he ducked into the men's room. For a few minutes he retched and choked over the basin, but there was nothing left. He splashed cold water on his face, straightened his jacket and tie, and started for the courtroom.

At the end of the corridor was a small elevator. Joe, Khoury, and Langan crowded in with two armed marshals. The elevator itself was a cell, the floor foul with spit and cigarette butts. They rode up to the fourteenth floor.

They came out in a stunted corridor behind courtroom 148. Opposite was a cell that was guarded by another pair of shotgun-carrying marshals. Joe was asked to wait in the cell, but the door was left open. He went around a small screen to a toilet, and retched again.

He was feeling faint as he waited to be called. Khoury and Langan sat with him, telling him that he would be all right, that he would do well. Joe could not imagine it.

All the years, all the anticipation, all the disappointments now came down to this. What would happen when he walked through that door into court? What would happen when he saw them – Scarfo, Leonetti, and the others – for the first time? And later, after he testified, what would happen then?

At last a bailiff stepped into the cell. 'It's time,' he said.

Khoury and Langan shook Joe's hand. Joe took a deep breath and walked into the courtroom.

The witness stand was elevated and was opposite the

door. Joe saw nothing until he sat down. Then, while a state trooper adjusted the microphone in front of him, he looked out.

The courtroom was large and high, and jammed with people. The spectators' area was filled to capacity and ringed with armed marshals. There were sixteen people in the jury box at Joe's right, all with headsets on their laps and thick folders of evidence at their feet. Tables were heaped with audio and video equipment. Cables cluttered in all directions, taped to the carpet and snaking up the legs of tables and chairs.

At the high bench sat Judge Franklin Van Antwerpen; beneath him were two court clerks, wired with headphones and busy at computer terminals. In front of Joe, at two narrow tables, sat the four prosecutors. But most of the well of the court was crammed with defendants.

There were seventeen of them, and seventeen attorneys – thirty-four people jammed into a space normally occupied by ten. Each defendant had his own table, and each table was piled high with evidence books, documents, briefcases, and audio equipment.

Among the faces, Joe picked out the Merlinos, the Narduccis, Philip Leonetti, and – not five paces to Joe's left – Nicky Scarfo. Scarfo, seated next to Simone, was so close that Joe could have leaned over and touched him.

The sight of Scarfo had an effect on Joe that he could not have anticipated. All his anxiety fell away, and he felt suddenly calm. It was as if something had resolved itself inside him, some determination, some balance. He had wanted to be face to face with Scarfo again, and now that he was, he was actually relieved.

There was no fear; I wasn't nervous. Part of that was because I was more afraid of Arnie Gordon than of Scarfo and his people. Every other time I had testified I was a

nervous wreck, but this time, not at all. It was like Nicky
was there at my disposal, and I was gonna take retaliation
on him, givin back what they gave me and my family.

When I looked at Nicky, he'd put his head down or
turn away. I couldn't wait until the cross-examination:
I was ready for them. Ten years had prepared me for it.

Arnold Gordon stood up to begin the direct examination, and the courtroom fell silent. He took Joe through
the preliminaries in his detached, efficient way. His
questions were worded with great precision, structured
to elicit the story and to preclude obfuscation by the
defense.

Gordon asked Joe to stand and identify the defendants.
Joe did so, pointing first at Scarfo, then at Philip
Leonetti, Lawrence Merlino, and Lawrence's brother,
Chuckie. Following Gordon's crisp questions, Joe de-
tailed his relations with the defendants, feeling more
confident and sure of himself with every answer.

Then Gordon came to the day of the murder.

There was the walk in the frozen woods and the
conversation with Barbara, followed by the drive to Phil
Disney's apartment.

'What happened next?' Gordon asked, and he stepped
aside.

All eyes were now on Joe as he began the story of
Vincent Falcone's last minutes on earth. No-one moved.
No-one made a sound.

It was all before his eyes again, and in his clear,
unwavering voice. The walk up the steps with Vincent,
the open door, Nicky sitting on the sofa. Then the drinks,
the drink to his lips, and Philip's sudden movement.

As Joe spoke, getting deeper into the crime, the
defendants' faces darkened. Philip Leonetti looked
straight at Joe and made a gesture toward his throat. Joe

returned the stare and pushed on, hearing the explosion in his mind.

'And Philip Leonetti pulled a gun out of his jacket, reached over, and shot Vincent Falcone in the head!' he declared in a pounding voice.

The jury was silent and still. Joe took them moment by moment through the second shot, the trussing of the body, and the struggle down the steps to the trunk of the car. When he had finished, he sat back, sweating. He was not drained, not frightened, but fulfilled.

Joe had testified all day, and the judge called an adjournment. Marshals led Joe out of the courtroom into the holding-cell corridor. As he passed through the door, a husky state trooper whispered to him, 'Good job.'

Outside, Joe was joined by Gary Langan and Joe Khoury. Langan was laughing.

'That was great!' he told Joe. 'Terrific!'

Joe snatched the cigarette from Langan's lips. 'I need this more than you,' he told him.

Khoury put an arm around Joe's shoulders. 'You were fantastic,' he said.

Cross-examination began the next morning. On the way to the court, Joe was composed. This time there was no throwing up, no shaking. The only point that concerned him was Gordon's warning not to refer to the Falcone trial. Gordon had obtained the ruling to exclude testimony about it, and he had exphasized that Joe must avoid mentioning it at all costs.

Simone began the cross, and Joe was ready for him from the first ingratiating question. After a series of insinuations about his character, Simone asked Joe if he had ever lied on the stand, under oath.

Joe knew what was coming, and he determined to stop it here and now.

'You're a lawyer,' he shot back at Simone, 'and I'm just a plumber. Last time you twisted my words around, and these people were acquitted of murder. For nine years they walked. I'm here today testifying, and it's not gonna be like last time. You're not gonna make a liar out of me.'

The effect on the jury was unmistakable. Even Simone was thrown off balance, unable to find a rejoinder. What Joe had been warned would be a mistake proved to be the most powerful moment of his testimony. From that point on, though five lawyers took turns at him, no-one could shake Joe Salerno.

With the passage of nine years, everything that had compromised him at the first trial had disappeared. When Simone suggested that Joe stood to gain by entering the Witness Protection Program, Joe shook his head. 'Mr Simone,' he replied, 'it is the worst thing that anybody could ever go through, being on the Federal Witness Protection Program. It's the worst thing in the world. I wouldn't recommend it to anybody.'

When Edwin Jacobs, Chuckie Merlino's lawyer, defied Joe to name one person who could corroborate his story that the defendants were in Phil Disney's apartment, Joe pointed at Scarfo, Leonetti, and Merlino.

'They know what happened that day,' he replied. 'Ask them. They'll corroborate my story.'

Jacobs was at a loss, so he returned to Simone's old tactic of accusing Joe of the murder. Didn't Joe realize that he himself was the prime suspect, he demanded.

Joe laughed at him. 'That's ridiculous, sir,' he said. 'Mr Jacobs, no way.'

'Mr Jacobs, no way?' the lawyer repeated helplessly.

'No,' Joe assured him. 'No way.'

Leonetti's lawyer, Oscar Goodman, wanted to know what kind of deal Joe had made to testify, and how much he was being paid.

'They paid me nothing,' Joe stated. 'I made no deal to be up here. I'm here on my own. Nobody forced me. And nobody's paying me.'

Goodman scoffed at this and demanded to know how Joe had survived for nine years.

Joe looked him straight in the eye. 'I worked,' he said. 'That's how I survived.'

Simone came at him again, ticking off the same accusations he had made nine years earlier. Wouldn't it have been a good idea to plant evidence near Scarf, Inc.? Couldn't he have tied the body by himself? Wasn't he strong enough to have carried it to the car alone?

In each case, Joe conceded the possibility, but quickly canceled it: it could have happened that way, but it didn't. He hadn't done those things. He had not killed Vincent Falcone.

Frustrated, Simone tried to slip the charge past Joe to the jury. He pointed out that Joe had not gone to pay his respects to Vincent Falcone's widow.

'You didn't go to see her, did you?' he began, then added, 'After, after you shot her husband, did you go to see her?'

Joe picked it up instantly. 'I did not shoot her husband,' he fired back at him. 'Come on, Mr Simone.'

Simone was flailing for something to grasp on to, unwilling to relinquish the tactic that had worked nine years before.

'And you're saying not only that you didn't kill him,' he pursued, 'but you're saying that you didn't have a motive to kill him?'

Joe stared him down. 'I didn't kill him,' he replied.

'And you didn't have a motive to kill him?'

'My answer to that question is, I did not kill Vincent Falcone.'

'I heard you say that,' Simone grunted.

'And I didn't have a motive to kill Vincent Falcone,' Joe pushed on. 'That's the answer to the question, sir.'

'I know that's your answer,' was all Simone could say.

Suddenly the relation between witness and defense attorney was reversed. Where nine years before Simone had bullied Joe into submissive agreement, now it was Simone who could do nothing but concede.

By the time Simone had finished for the defense, Joe knew he had won. Whatever now happened, he had faced Scarfo, his associates, and his attorneys, he had told the truth, and he had not been intimidated.

On redirect examination, Arnold Gordon finally laid to rest the defense's challenge, stretching over nine years, to Joe's credibility.

Gordon began by saying that the defense had pointed to some inconsistencies in Joe's statements, and then he asked Joe whether he was in any doubt on the essential story of the murder.

'Not at all, sir, no,' Joe affirmed.

'Is there any question in your mind who it was that shot Vincent Falcone in the back of the head?' Gordon asked.

'No, not at all,' Joe answered.

'Who was that?'

'Philip Leonetti.'

'Are you having any difficulty at all remembering who it was that talked about giving him another one?'

'Not at all.'

'Who was that?'

'Mr Scarfo.'

'Is there any difficulty remembering who it was that shot Vincent Falcone in the chest?'

'No, sir.'

'Who was that?'

'Philip Leonetti.'

'Do you have any difficulty remembering who it was that helped you carry Vincent Falcone's body down those steps?'

'No, sir.'

'Who was that?'

'Lawrence Merlino.'

'And why is it,' Gordon concluded, 'that your memory of those events is so good when you've forgotten other facts?'

Joe folded his hands in front of him, squeezed his lips together a moment, and looked down.

'That's just something I'll never forget for the rest of my life,' he said.

Joe was taken from the courtroom back through the tunnel to FBI headquarters. Instead of the little holding room, however, he was brought upstairs to the office, a sprawling, congested center of activity. Agents gathered around him to shake his hand and slap him on the back. Many of them had been in court for his testimony, and the others had already heard about it.

Klaus Roher, the big, bearlike special agent in charge, called Joe into his office. On his wall was an organizational chart of the Scarfo mob, with X's drawn through the faces of Nicky, Philip, and the others. Roher congratulated Joe in rollicking, vulgar language and told him that they had arranged for him to visit with his parents that evening. As he was giving Joe the details, the phone rang.

'He's right here,' Joe heard him say, and Roher handed him the phone.

It was Arnold Gordon.

Gordon thanked Joe for his testimony. Joe apologized for his reference to the earlier trial. Gordon laughed good-naturedly. 'I knew that would happen,' he said.

'There's something else I wanted to say,' he went on. 'You're a good citizen, Joe. We know it, and I hope that soon everybody else will know it. If there was a medal we could give you, you'd deserve it. It took courage to do what you did. I want to congratulate you.'

It took a moment for Joe to speak. When he did, it was to ask a favor.

'I'm goin back to the motel,' he said. 'I'd appreciate it if you could call there and talk to my parents.'

Gordon promised that he would.

That evening Joe's family joined him, Gary Langan, Jim Maher, and Joe Khoury for a celebration that was to last for three days. At five o'clock Arnold Gordon called, as he had promised. He spoke first to Joe's father, then to his mother.

'Mrs Salerno,' he said in his grave, quiet voice, 'I want you to know, whatever happens, your son is a hero.'

Joe had been away from Oregon for ten days. When he got back, he had a lot of plumbing jobs to catch up on. Meanwhile, the trial continued. DelGiorno had testified just before Joe, and Caramandi followed. Together they were on the stand for fourteen days.

At one point, one of the defense lawyers asked Del-Giorno why he had become a witness. He replied that he had learned he was next to be killed. The lawyer scoffed at him, asking if Nicky Scarfo were really all that terrible. DelGiorno assured him that he was.

'He loves to kill people,' he said. 'He just loves it.'

It was an echo, almost word for word, of what Nicky had said to Joe ten years earlier over the corpse of Vincent Falcone.

In all, nearly 150 witnesses testified. The jury heard 250 tape-recorded conversations, saw 20 videotapes, and looked at more than 700 photographs and pieces of evidence. Joe Salerno, meanwhile, was in an agony of expectation.

Waitin for the verdict was just as bad as waitin to testify. I went around like in a daydream; I couldn't get my thoughts together. I was still wonderin if I should have done it, and thinkin that even if they were convicted, they'd still be looking for retaliation. I was scared about what would happen. I was so used to my mind bein beat up, all I could do was worry.

Every day, Joe called the FBI for word of the verdict. He prodded them for encouragement, but though they assured him it looked good, they added that it was all up to the jury.

The jury retired to deliberate on 17 November, after two months of trial. All that day and the next, Joe was anxious and preoccupied. He called the FBI, the prosecutors, Joe Khoury, and his parents several times a day for news. Meanwhile, his emotions were on a roller coaster.

The jury was takin so long, I was sure they were gonna be acquitted. Then I'd tell myself, no, that can't be. I'd be up all night thinkin about it, then all day; it was like a year, waitin for the verdict. One minute I'd swear they'd be acquitted, then the next I'd say it wasn't possible. And I'd go back and forth like that, convincin myself of both sides.

It was the weekend before Thanksgiving, and Joanne had planned to go to her parents' house for the day. Mike and Johnny had gone to their mother's home in Denver, so Joe was alone.

On Saturday, 19 November, Joe learned that the jury

had announced on the way to dinner that they had reached a verdict. After dinner, court would be called back into session to hear it.

For the next few hours, Joe was frantic with anticipation. At last he could stand it no longer, and he called his parents.

'Joseph!' his mother shouted into the phone the instant she heard his voice, 'Joseph, they're guilty!'

Joe was speechless.

'Guilty on every count!' his mother went on shouting. 'My God, I don't believe it!'

Then, bang, the other line begins ringin. It's Jim Maher. 'Congratulations, buddy,' he says. 'The bastards are done. I can't talk to you right now – I want to go down and see the sons of bitches loaded up.'

My mother's still on the line, and I can hear my sister screamin in the background, and my father's so excited he's talkin Italian.

Then Gary Langan calls on the other line. 'Did you hear?' he says. 'We got them! And you played a big part in it.' He thanked me, and I thanked him. It felt so good, and yet I had come so close so many times to not doin it.

For the next hour, people were calling Joe to share the good news. Joe Khoury called, and more FBI agents, and the prosecutors from Philadelphia. With each call the knowledge became more real to Joe, and with that knowledge came the hope that, at last, it might really be over.

When the verdict came, it took all fear away from me. I never felt like that during the whole ten years, like I was doin hard time in jail and been released outa all that purgatory. I wanted to cry for happiness.

Joe wanted to celebrate, but there was nobody there. Then the doorbell rang. It was a homeless man named Bill whom Joe employed occasionally to dig ditches or to clean up job sites, and to whom he had given money and food. Joe felt especially sorry for him because he himself had been alone, anonymous and adrift.

Bill came in, his clothes ragged and his hair and beard gnarled around his wrinkled face. He asked Joe if he could borrow ten dollars.

I gave it to him, and then I said, 'Bill, I'm gonna have a beer with you.' I got two beers, and we sat at the table and we talked. I didn't hear one word he was sayin. All I could think was, if he only knew what I just heard, what I been through. And then I thought, if I tried to tell him, he wouldn't understand . . . I wouldn't even know where to begin.

Epilogue

On 19 November, 1988, Nicky Scarfo, Philip Leonetti, and fifteen members of their organization were found guilty in federal court of some 200 counts, including conspiracy to commit murder, attempted murder, racketeering, drug trafficking, extortion, loan sharking, illegal gambling, and other offenses.

Sentencing began on 1 May, 1989. Scarfo received fifty-five years' imprisonment; Leonetti, forty-five years; and Chuckie Merlino, forty-five years. Philip Narducci, who had shot Joe Salerno, Sr, was sentenced to forty years; his brother, Frank, received thirty-five. The others were given sentences ranging from thirty to forty-five years each.

The judge recommended that Scarfo, Leonetti, and Philip Narducci be imprisoned in a Level 6 penitentiary. There is only one such institution in the United States, in Marion, Illinois. That prison has the reputation of being the most severe in the country. The judge recommended that most of the others be confined in Level 5 institutions.

The verdict and sentencing were the culmination of the largest successful federal organized-crime prosecution in history. With one trial, the entire Scarfo organization was wiped out, and the Philadelphia *Cosa Nostra* virtually ceased to exist.

Nicky Scarfo's three sons represented a range of response to their father's business.

When the indictments began coming down in 1986, Scarfo's eldest son, Chris, gradually estranged himself from his father.

The youngest son, Mark, seventeen, was torn with uncertainty over his father's guilt. He was taunted at school and in the neighborhood by his peers, and he found it difficult to endure the ordeal of the trials. Then, in the fifth week of the federal RICO trial, Mark Scarfo hanged himself in the bathroom at 26 North Georgia Avenue. He was cut down by his mother, and though he survived the suicide attempt, he lapsed into a profound, perhaps irreversible, coma.

The middle son, Nicky, Jr, twenty-three, identified closely with his father and was the most like him of the three. He attended all of the trials, often in the company of neighborhood friends who shared his ambition to carry on the Family business.

Three days after his brother's suicide attempt, Nicky, Jr, went to visit him in the hospital. On the way out, he got into a quarrel on the elevator with a middle-aged woman. The young Scarfo punched the woman in the face, knocking her to the floor. When the elevator doors opened, a hospital security guard saw him kicking the woman and restrained him. The police were called, and he was arrested.

The incident was reminiscent of the time twenty-five years earlier, when his father had knifed a man in a quarrel over a seat in a diner. Except in the case of the son, the attack was even more unprovoked and pathetic.

In February, 1989, Scarfo, the Merlinos, the Narducci brothers, and Milano brothers, Joe Ligambi, and Francis Iannerella went on trial in Philadelphia for the killing of Frank 'Frankie Flowers' D'Alfonso. The state charged the defendants with murder in the first degree and declared its intention to ask for the death penalty.

The witnesses against those charged included Thomas DelGiorno, as well as one of the defendants themselves, Gino Milano. Milano had become a government witness in return for pleading guilty to third-degree murder. He was unable to convince his brother, Nick, to join with him, and in the end he had to testify against him.

On 5 April, 1989, Scarfo and the others were convicted of murder in the first degree. Convinced that the jury would vote for the death penalty, the defense lawyers, led by Robert Simone, argued on technical grounds that the sentence should be determined by the judge. The judge agreed and dismissed the jury, an action that resulted in an automatic life sentence for the defendants. Speaking on their behalf, Simone declared, 'I feel like I've been pulled out of the grave.'

Under the terms of the sentencing, those defendants who had previously been convicted in the RICO case were required to serve their life sentences first. Following that, their federal sentences would begin. This virtually assured that Scarfo, Leonetti, and the others would die in prison.

The sentences prompted more, and potentially explosive, defections. Lawrence Merlino agreed to cooperate with the government almost at once. The prosecutors accepted, and Merlino began talking to the FBI about several unsolved murders.

Then, in a stunning turnabout, Scarfo's nephew and underboss, Philip Leonetti, offered to become a witness, the highest-ranking Mafioso ever to do so. Immediately, Leonetti was spirited from jail to a secure location, and grilled for weeks by FBI agents. His revelations reportedly reached both high and deep into the whole structure of organized crime on the East Coast. His cooperation may prove to be a turning point in the entire history of the mob in America.

Early in his statements, Leonetti discussed the murder of Vincent Falcone. He confirmed Joe Salerno's version of the killing in detail, and confessed to having pulled the trigger. He also told the FBI where he had hidden Joe's gun ten years before, and a search was launched to recover it.

On the subject of Joe Salerno, Philip, reportedly, was categorical. Joe's RICO testimony, he said, was devastating to the Scarfo organization. Had it not been for the Plumber, Leonetti told the FBI agents, Scarfo and his people were confident that they would have gone free.

Leonetti, Lawrence Merlino, Tommy DelGiorno, and Nick Caramandi, together responsible for a dozen murders, have all made deals with the government. They and their families are in the Witness Protection Program, and are receiving or have been promised financial support and protection for the rest of their lives in return for their cooperation.

Joe Salerno, meanwhile, has moved to yet another town in yet another state. He lives in a modest one-bedroom apartment and earns his living doing plumbing jobs out of the back of Joanne's Volkswagen.

Though Joe has petitioned the government for reimbursement of the wages he lost during his ten years in the Witness Program, he has so far received no response. He has, however, been asked to return to New Jersey to testify in another racketeering trial and, given the defections from the Scarfo mob, will undoubtedly be called as a witness many more times.

Joe feels more secure now that Scarfo and the others are in federal custody, and he hopes one day to return to South Philadelphia, to visit in his parents' home, and vacation at the Jersey shore. His parents share that hope, but the FBI has told them it may be too early for such a trip. Scarfo still has contacts in the neighborhood, and the contract on Joe's life may never be cancelled.

The Salerno family occasionally meets around the dining-room table to discuss the events of the past ten years. The discussions can go on for hours – there is so much to remember, so much to understand. But in the end, Joe's mother sums it up best.

'I am waiting,' she says, 'for my son to come home.'

Appendix A: The Philadelphia La Cosa Nostra, 1911–1988

Salvatore Sabella was founder of the Philadelphia Family and boss through the 1920s.

John Avena succeeded Sabella in 1930 and was murdered in 1936.

Joseph Bruno, 1936–1946, was the first Philadelphia boss to be appointed by the Mob's New York Commission.

Joe Ida was appointed boss in 1946 and retired in 1957. He was succeeded briefly by Antonio Pollina.

Angelo Bruno, the 'Docile Don,' ousted Pollina with New York's backing and ruled the Family until his murder in 1980.

Antonio 'Tony Bananas' Caponegro, Angelo Bruno's consigliere, orchestrated Bruno's murder.

Frank Narducci, Sr, a Bruno capo, collaborated with Caponegro in the Don's assassination.

Nicodemo 'Little Nicky' Scarfo joined the Family in the late 1950s, but was exiled to Atlantic City in 1963. He returned to Philadelphia as consigliere in 1980 and became boss in 1981.

Philip Leonetti, Scarfo's nephew, was Scarfo's right-hand man in Atlantic City and in 1986 became under-boss.

Lawrence and Salvatore Merlino, along with Scarfo and Leonetti, formed the nucleus of Scarfo's Atlantic City organization. Salvatore became Scarfo's underboss in 1981.

Phil Testa became boss in 1980 and appointed Scarfo consigliere.

Pete Casella, Testa's underboss, was Scarfo's rival for Family leadership.

Frank Monte was appointed Scarfo's consigliere in 1981.

Salvatore Testa, Phil Testa's son, became a capo under Scarfo.

Frank Narducci, Jr, was a Scarfo soldier and hitman.

Phil Narducci became a Scarfo soldier with his brother, Frank.

Thomas DelGiorno was a leading Scarfo capo and hitman.

Nick Caramandi was a Scarfo soldier and strongarm man.

Frank 'Frankie Flowers' D'Alfonso, a long-time Family figure, was murdered by Scarfo in 1985.

Pasquale 'Pat the Cat' Spirito
Joe Ligambi
Francis Iannerella
Nick Milano
Gino Milano — Scarfo soldiers
Joseph and Wayne Grande
Joesph Pungitore

Harry 'the Hunchback' Riccobene — From 1982–1984, Scarfo waged a war of extermination against the Riccobene faction of the Family.
Sonny Riccobene
Enrico Riccobene
Robert Riccobene

Sentences handed down in the RICO case:*
Frank Narducci, Jr, 4 May, 1989, 35 years.
Phil Narducci, 4 May, 1989, 40 years

Salvatore Merlino, 10 May, 1989, 45 years.

Lawrence Merlino, sentence deferred in return for co-operation.

Philip Leonetti, 11 May, 1989, 45 years.

Nicodemo Scarfo, 11 May, 1989, 55 years.

*The sentences of Nicky Scarfo, Salvatore Merlino, and Frank and Phil Narducci run consecutively with life sentences from the Frankie Flowers murder case.

Appendix B: Excerpts of Jury Trial, United States of America v. Nicodemo Scarfo, et al.

IN THE UNITED STATES DISTRICT COURT FOR THE EASTERN DISTRICT OF PENNSYLVANIA

UNITED STATES OF AMERICA	: *CRIMINAL NO. 88-003*
	:
v.	: *Philadelphia, Pennsylvania*
	: *October 25, 1988*
NICODEMO SCARFO, et al.	: *Witness: Joseph Salerno, Jr.*

EXCERPT OF JURY TRIAL BEFORE THE HONORABLE FRANKLIN S. VAN ANTWERPEN, J. UNITED STATES DISTRICT JUDGE

APPEARANCES:
For the Government: LOUIS PICHINI, ESQ.
DAVID FRITCHEY, ESQ.
JOSEPH PETERS, ESQ.
ARNOLD GORDON, ESQ.
Strike Force
615 Chestnut Street

Suite 700
Philadelphia, PA 19106

For the Defendant   ROBERT F. SIMONE, ESQ.
Nicodemo Scarfo: 1919 Walnut Street
Philadelphia, PA 19103

For the Defendant   OSCAR B. GOODMAN, ESQ.
Philip Leonetti: Goodman, Stein & Chesnoff
520 South 4th Street
Las Vegas, Nevada 89101-6593

For the Defendant   EDWIN J. JACOBS, JR, ESQ.
Salvatore Merlino: 1125 Pacific Avenue
Atlantic City, NJ 08401

For the Defendant   EDWARD REIF, ESQ.
Lawrence Merlino: Suite 1100
1760 Market Street
Philadelphia, PA 19103

**JOSEPH SALERNO, JR, Government Witness,
Sworn.**

DIRECT EXAMINATION

BY MR GORDON:

Q. Mr Salerno, do you know some of the defendants in this case, in particular the defendant Nicodemo Scarfo, the defendant Philip Leonetti, the defendant Lawrence Merlino and the defendant Salvatore 'Chuckie' Merlino.

A. Yes, I do, sir.

Q. All right, would you look around the courtroom, stand up if necessary, take a good look around the courtroom and tell the court and jury if you're able to pick out those defendants and point to them if you can see them.

A. I'll do that. Mr Scarfo, Mr Leonetti.
Q. What color top does—

> MR SIMONE: I'll stipulate.
> THE WITNESS: Green top, Leonetti; Mr Scarfo, gray hair, next to Mr Simone; I'm looking for Lawrence Merlino. Lawrence Merlino—

BY MR GORDON:
Q. What is Mr Merlino wearing?
A. He's wearing a striped top.

> MR REIF: We'll stipulate he's at the table, we'll stipulate to that.
> THE WITNESS: And I'm looking for Chuck Merlino. Chuck Merlino's sitting back there.
> MR GORDON: Your Honor, may the record reflect that this witness has correctly identified the four defendants whose names I've mentioned?
> THE COURT: Yes, the record may so reflect.
> MR GORDON: Thank you.

BY MR GORDON:
Q. Mr Salerno, approximately when did you first meet Philip Leonetti?
A. Around, I believe, early 70s; '71, '72.
Q. And approximately when did you first meet Nicodemo Scarfo?
A. Approximately at that time, also.
Q. And when did you first meet Lawrence Merlino?
A. Around 1978.
Q. Now, directing your attention back to the year 1978 where were you living in the early part of that year?
A. I was living in Brigantine, 10 Ocean Drive West.
Q. And is that in New Jersey?
A. Yes, it is.
Q. Where is Brigantine in relation to Atlantic City, New Jersey?

A. You have to go over a bridge, I'd say about ten minutes away; it's ten, fifteen minutes away.

Q. Is it next to Atlantic City, New Jersey?

A. Yes, it is.

Q. And who did you live in Brigantine with at that time?

A. Myself, my wife and my three children.

Q. What business were you in at that time?

A. I was in the plumbing business.

Q. And were you in it on your own or did you work for somebody or did you have partners at that time in 1978?

A. I was in the business on my own.

Q. Was your business in trouble or experiencing financial difficulties back in 1978?

A. Yes, it was, sir.

Q. Did there come a time when you wanted to borrow some money because of your business' difficulties?

A. Yes, I did.

Q. Were you able to borrow money from a bank at that time?

A. No, could not do that.

Q. Why is that?

A. I had bad credit and I had no collateral to borrow money.

Q. Now what if anything did you do in an attempt to borrow money?

A. I first spoke to a Mr Biancari, Vincent, Mr Biancari, and he says, 'Why don't you ask Philip Leonetti.'

MR GOODMAN: Objection, hearsay; move to strike.
MR GORDON: I can rephrase the question, your Honor.
THE COURT: All right.

BY MR GORDON:

Q. First of all, who was Vincent Biancari?

A. He was a friend of myself and Philip Leonetti.

Q. And after you had a conversation with Mr Biancari, without telling us what he said, what did you next do with regard to attempting to borrow money?

A. I went to Philip Leonetti and asked him if I could borrow $10,000.

Q. And where did that take place, that conversation?

A. Took place in Atlantic City.

Q. And approximately when was this? And by that I mean the year and the time of the year if you can recall?

A. It was middle 1978, I believe.

Q. And would you describe the conversation you had with Philip Leonetti on that day when you first went to him?

A. He says, yeah, he says, 'I'll give you the money,' he says, 'I can get it,' he says, and 'what I'll have to do is,' he says, 'I'll have to talk to you tomorrow about it.'

Q. And on that next day did you again have another conversation with Mr Leonetti?

A. Yes, it was at a job site.

Q. Where was the job site?

A. In Brigantine.

Q. And would you describe that conversation that you had?

A. I went to Phil and I asked him if he could get me the $10,000, and I needed, I needed it fast; I was desperate for the money. So he says, 'Yes,' he says, 'I can get it for you,' he says, 'I'll have to go to Cherry Hill to get it for you though.'

Q. Now, approximately how far was Cherry Hill from Brigantine?

A. I'd say an hour to an hour and a half maybe.

Q. By automobile?

A. By automobile.

Q. Is Cherry Hill also located in New Jersey?

A. Yes, it is.

Q. And what happened after you had that conversation about getting the money from Cherry Hill?

A. I was on this particular job site and about between 20 minutes and a half hour Philip was back with his truck and I thought, well, he probably didn't get the money for me. And he called me over to the truck and he did have the money, the $10,000.

Q. Now, how far is or was the job site in Brigantine from North Georgia Avenue in Atlantic City, New Jersey, approximately?

A. Ten to fifteen minutes.

Q. By automobile?

A. Yes, sir.

Q. Would that be in each direction?

A. That would be one way.

Q. About ten or fifteen minutes one way. Now, will you describe what happened when Mr Leonetti returned with the money; what did he do and say and what did you say?

A. He gave me the money and he said, 'What we usually do is borrow $10,000, interest on $10,000 would be $500.' He says, 'Being that you're a friend of mine, I'll make it $250 per week interest,' and the money had to be paid only in cash money.

Q. And how would the principal be paid back?

A. When I get a whole lump sum of money I could pay the principal back.

Q. And when you say that Mr Leonetti gave you the $10,000, what form of money was the $10,000 in at the time, was it a check or was it cash?

A. It was cash money.

Q. And did you start to pay the $250 a week interest on that $10,000?

A. Yes, I did.

Q. Did there come a time when you fell behind in the weekly interest payments?

A. Yes.

Q. And what caused you to fall behind?

A. I had gotten sick, went into the hospital and got back in my payments.

Q. And how far back on the payments had you fallen?

A. I was a thousand dollars back on interest payments.

Q. Was that four weeks approximately?

A. Four weeks.

Q. And what happened after you got out of the hospital with regard to those back payments?

A. I had gotten home in Brigantine and was going to a job site with my truck and I met Philip, he had his uncle's car. And I got in the car with Philip and he asked me, he says, 'You know, you're a thousand dollars behind on payments.' So I says, 'Well,' I says, 'I'm going to have to get it in a day or so.' So he says, 'You know,' he says, 'people that I got this money from gets kind of rough sometimes so try to get it, if you can, as fast as you can.'

Q. What did you undersatnd Mr Leonetti to mean when he said the people can get rough sometimes?

A. I understood that something could happen physically to me or my family.

Q. Did you make that thousand dollar payment of back interest?

A. Yes, I did.

Q. Who did you make it to?

A. Philip Leonetti.

Q. And did you continue to make the interest payments of $250 a week?

A. Yes, I did.

Q. For what period of time did those payments continue?

A. From June, I guess about the whole total time was about maybe 13 or 14 months.

Q. From 1978 into 1979?

A. Yes, sir.

Q. And who did you make those weekly $250 payments to during that entire time?

A. Philip Leonetti.

Q. Did there come a time when you paid back part of the principal of that loan?

A. Yes, I did.

Q. Why did you decide to pay it all off or pay it back at that time?

A. I couldn't pay any more, it was too much; I just couldn't do it and I had to get the money to pay it back, this $250 a week was killing me.

Q. Where did you get the money from to pay it back?

A. I called my father up and I told him I needed money, I needed $10,000. So I talked him into giving it to me and he gave me the $10,000.

Q. And after you got the $10,000 from your father what did you do with it?

A. I tried to track down Philip and he was at Rick Casale's house that day, I recall – that's in Margate – and I seen him and I gave him $9,000. I gave him $8,000 in principal in cash and $1,000 back interest payments.

Q. And how much principal did you still owe at that time?

A. I owed still $2,000 yet.

Q. And did you ever pay any more of the principal after that?

A. Yes, I paid one more thousand dollars.

Q. Who did you pay that to?

A. To Philip.

Q. And after you paid that additional thousand dollars did you still owe some principal?

A. Yes, I did.

Q. And what was the balance that you owed at that time?

A. A thousand dollars.

Q. And what conversation if any did you have with Philip Leonetti at the time that you gave him that thousand dollars?

A. I asked him, I says, 'Does your Uncle Nick know about this money?' So he says, 'Where do you think I got it from.'

Q. And when you were talking to Philip about his Uncle Nick, who were you referring to?

A. Nicky Scarfo.

Q. Was there any conversation at that time about the remaining balance of a thousand dollars that you still owed?

A. Yeah, he told me, he says, 'Forget about that for now; don't worry about it.'

Q. Did you ever pay that remaining $1,000

A. No, I did not.

Q. So you paid back a total of $9,000 in principal?

A. Yes.

Q. Plus $250 a week interest for a period of more than a year?

A. Yes, I did.

Q. Sometime in the year 1979 did you separate from your wife and move to another location?

A. Yes, I did.

Q. Where did you first move when you left your wife in Brigantine?

A. I moved to Chuck Merlino's house in – on Haverford Avenue in Margate.

Q. And how did you happen to move into that particular house?

A. He needed some plumbing work done and we were going

258

to trade off some rent for some plumbing and I moved in there, in their house.

Q. When you say trade rent for plumbing, were you going to live there without paying rent and do some work in return?

A. Well, I was going to do some work for him in return and staying there in the house.

Q. Did you stay there for a period of time?

A. Yes, I did.

Q. Did you eventually move out?

A. Yes, I did.

Q. And did you move to another location after that?

A. Yes.

Q. Where was that?

A. I moved to Ventnor for a couple, few weeks.

Q. And after you moved out of that – did there come a time when you moved out of the Ventnor location?

A. Yes.

Q. And where did you move to next?

A. I moved to Georgia Avenue.

Q. And when you say 'Georgia Avenue,' specifically where on Georgia Avenue did you move?

A. I moved right up above Nicky Scarfo's apartment, I believe it's either 26 or 28 North Georgia Avenue; I'm not sure of the address.

Q. And that's Atlantic City, New Jersey?

A. Yes, it is.

Q. Who owned that apartment building?

A. Mrs Katherine Scarfo, Nick – Nick Scarfo's mother.

Q. Now, at that time approximately when was that that you moved into the apartments on North Georgia Avenue?

A. It was September of '79 until sometime in December, I moved out.

Q. And what was your relationship with Philip Leonetti at the time that you moved into the apartments on Georgia Avenue?

A. We were friends.

Q. And what was your relationship with Nicodemo Scarfo at that time?

A. We were friends.

Q. And what was your relationship with Lawrence Merlino at that time?

A. We were friends.

Q. When you say you were friends did you socialize with those three individuals on various occasions?

A. Yes, I did.

Q. By socializing, I mean did you go out occasionally drinking with them?

A. Yes, sir.

Q. Did you sometimes to go restaurants with them?

A. Yes, sir.

Q. At some time did you have a conversation with Philip Leonetti about a man named Eddie Cipresso?

A. Yes.

Q. Approximately when if you can recall did that conversation take place?

A. Probably in the latter part of 1978 or maybe 1979; I'm not really sure of the dates.

Q. And where did the conversation take place?

A. Well, it was myself and Philip, we were in the truck together.

Q. What truck were you in?

A. In the Scarf, Inc. truck.

Q. Who was driving?

A. Philip was driving the truck

Q. Anybody else in the truck besides you and Philip Leonetti?

A. No, sir.

Q. What did you say to him and what if anything did he say to you?

A. I asked him, I says, 'I know a guy named Eddie Cipresso and he used to be a racketeer or whatever in the city of Philadelphia.' So he says, 'No,' he says, 'He ain't nothing.' So I says, 'Well, what do you guys do?' So he had a magazine and he showed me the magazine.

Q. Do you remember what magazine it was?

A. Yes, I do.

Q. What was the name of it?

A. It was the Philadelphia Magazine.

Q. And who showed you the magazine?

A. Philip did.

Q. Did he show you the whole magazine or a specific part of it?

A. A specific part.

> MR GORDON: Your Honor, at this time I ask the witness to look at what has been marked for identification as Government Exhibit 19.

BY MR GORDON:

Q. Do you recognize that copy of the magazine article from June of 1978?

A. Yeah, I do.

Q. Is that the magazine article that Philip Leonetti showed to you?

A. Yes.

Q. Can you find the specific part of the article that Mr Leonetti showed you?

A. Yeah, it's right here.

Q. When he showed it to you what if anything did he do or say?

A. He says, 'This is who we are, this is what we do and this is what we get away with.'

Q. And what was he doing at the time that he said, 'This is who we are;' how did you know what part of the article he was referring to?

A. He pointed to it.

Q. And would you read the heading over the part of the article that Mr Leonetti pointed to?

A. It says 'Contract killings.'

Q. Now, would you read just the first line under 'Contract killings'?

A. 'The police working the Helfant murder.'

> MR GORDON: Your Honor, this time I'd ask that what has been marked as Government Exhibit 19L be displayed to the jury.
>
> THE COURT: Very well.

MR SIMONE: Objected to; no reason.

He read it to the jury. I mean, what's the reason now?

THE COURT: Let me see that article.

MR GORDON: Would the Court wish me to point to the specific part of it?

THE COURT: I'll permit the exhibit to be shown over the objection. Note that the article appears to be a number of pages in length.

BY MR GORDON:

Q. Was that the title of the article in reference, Mr Salerno?

A. Yes.

Q. And what part of the article did Mr Leonetti point to?

A. 'Contract killings.'

Q. And what's the first line say?

A. 'The police working the Helfant murder case.'

Q. All right, that's sufficient. Now you can put the pointer down and the article can be removed, the exhibit.

THE COURT: What was the number on that?

MR GORDON: That was Government Exhibit 19L, your Honor.

THE COURT: All right.

BY MR GORDON:

Q. Did you ever have any discussions with Philip Leonetti involving his uncle, Nicodemo Scarfo?

A. Yes, I did.

Q. Do you recall what if anything was said during that or those discussions?

MR GOODMAN: Could we have foundation, your Honor?

THE COURT: Yes.

BY MR GORDON:

Q. Approximately when did you have the discussion or discussions with Philip Leonetti about his uncle?

A. We were out to dinner one night, myself and Philip.

Q. Now, what year are you talking about?

A. 1979.

Q. Was anybody else present during this particular—

A. No.

Q. —discussion?

A. No . . .

Q. Did you ever have any conversation with Philip Leonetti regarding his uncle and Atlantic City?

A. Yes, sir.

Q. What if anything did Mr Leonetti say to you about his uncle and Atlantic City?

A. He said, 'My uncle is going to be number one, he's going to own Atlantic City someday.'

Q. At some time after you moved into the apartments on North Georgia Avenue did you ever have a discussion with Nicodemo Scarfo during which the term 'gangsters' was discussed?

A. Yes, I did.

Q. Could you describe first of all how that conversation began and where it began and who was present?

A. It was only myself and Nicky Scarfo and he asked me if I knew what a Gangster was.

Q. And where did that take place?

A. In Scarf, Inc.'s office.

Q. And what did you say at that time?

A. I says, 'I don't know what you mean by that.'

Q. Then what happened?

A. He says, 'We'll talk about it later.'

Q. Did you later have a follow up discussion?

A. Yes, I did.

Q. About how much later?

A. Maybe a week later.

Q. And where did the next discussion take place?

A. At the Brajole Café, Atlantic City.

Q. And who was present for that discussion?

A. Myself and Nick Scarfo.

Q. And what was said during the course of that discussion?

A. He says, 'Remember when I asked you if you wanted to be a gangster or what gangsters were?' I says, 'Yeah,' I says,

'I remember.' And he says, 'Well,' he says, 'let me tell you. There's gangsters, there's racketeers and there's junkies.' And he said, 'We're the gangsters,' he said, 'we do our own things.' He says, 'You know what I mean?'

Q. Well, when you say, 'He said, "You know what I mean" ' you made some sign with your hand. Is that a sign that you're making now or is that a sign that was used during the course of that conversation?

A. It was used during the course of the conversation.

Q. And who made that hand sign or signal?

A. Mr Scarfo.

Q. And would you do it again and—

A. He went like that.

Q. And what did you understand that to mean?

A. Being a gun.

Q. And what else did Mr Scarfo say during that conversation if anything?

A. He asked me if I ever seen anything in my life, he said, if I could stand up to it.

Q. And what did you say?

A. I said, 'Yes, I can.'

Q. What did you understand him to mean when he said, 'If you ever seen anything could you stand up to it'?

A. If I ever seen anybody killed if I could stand up to it and keep my mouth shut, that's what I meant it to be.

Q. Now, at some point during the same period of time after you moved into the apartments on North Georgia Avenue did you ever have a discussion with Mr Scarfo concerning your family's blood lines?

A. Yes.

Q. And would you describe that conversation, please?

A. He asked me where my family heritage came from.

Q. Who asked you that?

A. Mr Scarfo.

Q. And who was present during the conversation?

A. Just me and him, that's it. And he said, I told him, I says, 'My dad was Calabrese and my mother was Napolitan, Brutsese (ph.), that kind of thing. And he says, 'You have no Sicilians in your family,' I says, 'No.' And he said, 'That's good,' he says, 'because the Calabrese people are the real people.' He says, 'We're the real ones, we're the real gangsters and we do our stuff.'

Q. And when you say you told him that your father was Calabrese, what were you referring to?

A. Where my father came from, a part of Italy.

Q. And were you also referring to the part of Italy that your mother's family came from?

A. Yes, same thing.

Q. Was anything else said to you or asked of you during that same conversation?

A. Yes. He asked me if there's anybody in law enforcement in my family and so I says, 'No.' And he said, 'That's good,' he said, 'because law enforcement in families in our business is no good.'

Q. Now, during that period of time when you were living on North Georgia Avenue how frequently would you see Mr Scarfo and Mr Leonetti?

A. Mostly every day.

Q. And would you socialize with them frequently?

A. Yes.

Q. Did you like being in the company of Nicodemo Scarfo and Philip Leonetti and Lawrence Merlino?

A. Yes, I did.

Q. Why did you like being in their company?

A. I held a lot of respect, I was proud to be out with them; they just carried a lot of clout when you went to places and things.

Q. Well, what do you mean when you say it carried a lot of clout and you were proud to be out with them?

A. Well, if you went somewhere with them people would just cater to them, look up to them, and it was a good feeling for me to be with them to have that, to have that gratis from other people.

Q. And why did you understand people were doing that?

A. It's because they were scared to death of him.

Q. Sometime in the latter part of the year 1979, near the end

265

of the year, did Nicodemo Scarfo travel on a trip or a vacation
to Italy?

A. Yes, he did.

Q. Who did he go there with?

A. He went with Chuck Merlino.

MR SIMONE: Excuse me, what was the date of that?

MR GORDON: The latter part of 1979.

BY MR GORDON:

Q. And after Nicodemo Scarfo returned from Italy did you
have a conversation with him concerning guns?

A. Yes, I did.

Q. All right, where did that conversation take place?

A. It took place in a restaurant in Philadelphia, Virgilio's
Restaurant.

Q. And who was present during that conversation?

A. Myself, Philip Leonetti, Lawrence Merlino, Chuck Merlino
and Nick Scarfo.

Q. And what was said during the conversation?

A. Nicky Scarfo asked me, he says, 'Do you have any guns,
Joe,' so I says, 'Yeah, I got some guns.' And he asked me what
kind they were and I described these guns to him that I had.

Q. What guns did you describe to Nicodemo Scarfo at that
time?

A. I had an old .32 handgun and I had a 30 aught 6 rifle.

Q. And after you described those guns to Nicodemo Scarfo
what if anything else was said?

A. He said, 'Somebody,' he says, 'bring them things around,'
he says, 'I want to look at them.'

Q. And what did you say?

A. I says, 'OK, I will; I'll do that.'

Q. Now, at that time where were those guns being kept?

A. They were at my father's house in Philadelphia.

Q. Why were they at his house as opposed to either at the house
you had been in in Brigantine or some place that you were
living?

A. I was in and out my wife's house and I had three children and my parents came down one Sunday to talk to my wife and myself to try to get back together and all that stuff and I said I don't know if we could or not, so my father said, he says, 'Being that you're going to be in and out of the house,' he said, 'why don't I take these guns for safekeeping and bring them back to Philadelphia.'

Q. Where had you gotten the .32 caliber handgun from?

A. I got it from my father.

Q. And do you know where he got it from?

A. He got it from his grandfather.

Q. And where had you gotten the 30 aught 6 rifle?

A. I got it from a friend of mine that I did a job for, we traded off the rifle for the plumbing job I did for him.

Q. Now, after you had that first conversation with Nicodemo Scarfo in Virgilio's about guns, did there come a time when you were going to travel to Philadelphia to pick up some kitchen cabinets?

A. Yes.

Q. And before leaving on that trip to Philadelphia did you have a conversation with Nicodemo Scarfo?

A. Yes, I did.

Q. What was said during the course of that conversation?

A. He said, 'While you guys are going to go to Philadelphia to pick up the cabinets, pick those chandeliers up and bring them back to Atlantic City.'

Q. And where did that conversation take place?

A. At Nicky Scarfo's apartment.

Q. On Georgia Avenue?

A. On Georgia Avenue.

Q. And who was he referring to when he said 'you guys'?

A. Myself and Philip were gonna go to Philadelphia.

Q. And when he said, 'pick those chandeliers up,' what did you understand Nick Scarfo to be referring to when he used the term 'chandeliers'?

A. Guns.

Q. And were you in fact supposed to pick up any chandeliers or light fixtures of any kind?

A. No, I was not.

Q. Do you know why Mr Scarfo used the term 'chandeliers' instead of calling them guns?

A. Yes, because he always thought there was listening devices in his apartment, office, all over the place; that's why he described the guns as chandeliers.

Q. And did you have a further discussion with Nicodemo Scarfo before you left for Philadelphia about picking up the guns or not picking them up?

A. Yes. I told him I didn't want to get the guns. So I told him, I says, 'If I pick the guns up in Philly and come back to Philadelphia or whatever with Scarf, Inc.'s, truck, if we get caught with the guns in the truck, we might have problems.' So he said, 'Forget about it. Don't pick them up now.'

Q. Did there come another occasion when you eventually did pick up the guns?

A. Yes, sir.

Q. Was that during another trip to Philadelphia?

A. Another trip to Philadelphia, yeah.

Q. What was the reason for taking that trip to Philadelphia?

A. Chuckie Merlino's car broke down in Atlantic City and he needed a ride – he lived in Philadelphia – he needed a ride back to Philadelphia. So I was asked to take him back, I says, 'sure'——

Q. Who asked you to take Chuck Merlino to Philadelphia?

A. I don't recall; it was either Philip or Nicky or somebody asked me, so I says yes, I would. So he says, on the way back he says, 'Pick up those things on the way back after you drop Chuckie off at his house.'

Q. Who said that to you?

A. Mr Scarfo.

Q. And what did you understand him to mean by 'those things'?

A. Guns that he asked me for that he wanted to see.

Q. And did you take Chuck Merlino to Philadelphia?

A. Yes, I did.

Q. After you dropped him off did you pick up the guns?

A. Yes, I did.

Q. What guns did you pick up?

A. .32 caliber revolver handgun and a 30 aught 6 rifle.

Q. And where did you take those guns after you picked them up in Philadelphia?

A. Back to Scarf, Incorporated, on Georgia Avenue.

Q. And when you arrived back at Georgia Avenue was it day or nighttime?

A. Nighttime.

Q. And who was there, if anyone?

A. Philip Leonetti, Nicky Scarfo, Lawrence Merlino and myself.

Q. And what if anything was said about the guns or done with the guns?

A. They were passed around the room, they looked at them, they said they were nice, back and forth, and Nicky says, 'Well, what we're gonna do is we're going to stash these guns for you.'

Q. And did you leave the guns with Nicodemo Scarfo at that time?

A. Yes.

Q. Now, was there anything distinctive about that .32 caliber handgun?

A. Yes. It was very old, I had it reconditioned and it had white pearl handles on it and the kind of bullets, it's a longer size bullet than the average regular .32 caliber bullet.

Q. Who was Vincent Falcone?

A. He was a cement contractor and a friend of Nicky Scarfo's, Philip, Lawrence, Chuck Merlino's, myself, he was a friend of mine, also.

Q. And did you socialize with him on various occasions?

A. Yes, I did.

Q. And did Mr Falcone also socialize with Nicodemo Scarfo, Philip Leonetti and Lawrence Merlino?

A. Yes, sir.

Q. Were you all equally friendly or was Mr Falcone more friendly with Scarfo, Merlino and Leonetti than he was with you or less friendly with them than he was with you?

A. All equally friendly.

Q. Was he, do you know if he was a better friend of theirs than yours or—

A. He was probably a better friend of theirs than mine.

Q. Now, did Vincent Falcone remain very friendly or friendly with Nicodemo Scarfo and Philip Leonetti and Lawrence Merlino all throughout the time that you knew him or did that relationship ever change?

A. It started to change.

Q. Do you recall approximately when you noticed that it started to change?

A. It started to change around say in the beginning of November of '79.

Q. What did you notice which led you to believe things changed?

A. I just didn't see him any more, he never used to stop around.

Q. Around where?

A. Around Scarf, Inc.'s office.

Q. Before that time how frequently or how often would Vincent Falcone stop around to Scarf, Inc.?

A. He was there all the time; every day he'd stop there practically.

Q. Did you ever have any conversation or overhear or hear any conversation regarding Vincent Falcone with Nicodemo Scarfo at the time that he stopped coming around as often?

A. Yes.

Q. Would you describe what you saw or heard?

A. Well, first I had a conversation with Vincent Falcone myself.

Q. And without telling us the contents of that, after that conversation did you ever have any conversations with Nick Scarfo or hear any conversations regarding Vincent Falcone?

A. Yes.

Q. What did you hear?

A. Nicky Scarfo got me one day, he told me he wanted me to hang around with Philip. And he says, 'Whatever we say between us, you don't say anything to anybody; just between us.' And he said, 'Hang around with Philip,' he said, 'and especially tomorrow,' he says, 'whatever you do, don't tell Vincent Falcone about this conversation.'

Q. Now, do you recall what day of the week that was, that conversation?

A. That was on December 15th.

Q. And was that—

A. 1979.

Q. And was that the day before Vincent Falcone was killed?

A. Yes, it was.

Q. And after you had that conversation with Nicodemo Scarfo did you go someplace later that day or did you take a walk later that day?

A. Yes, I did.

Q. And what happened?

A. Myself and Lawrence, Lawrence says, 'Take a walk with me, Joe.' So he had a paper bag in his hand; I didn't know what was in the paper bag. We took a walk up Georgia Avenue and he put this paper bag underneath the front seat of the driver's, driver's side of the car, and it was Lawrence's car, and that was the first thing.

Q. Now, when you say Lawrence are you referring to Lawrence Merlino?

A. Yes.

Q. What kind of car was that?

A. It was a Ford Thunderbird.

Q. After that what occurred later that day?

A. And later on that day we all took a ride in the car. Well, not all of us, there was myself, Philip Leonetti and Lawrence Merlino.

Q. Where did you go?

A. Took a ride down some back dark roads someplace they took us. And I was sitting in the back seat and I don't know, I was just paranoid and I kept hunched up on the front seat because I knew there was something stuck underneath the seat of the car in that bag and I knew I gave him the guns and things I heard and stuff, and I didn't know, I was just paranoid. And we took the ride and Philip just telling me, 'Sit back in the seat and relax, sit back in the seat and relax.' But anyway, nothing happened and we went back to Georgia Avenue and we went into some restaurant or something and we had some food to eat.

Q. Now, on the next day, on Sunday, December 16th, 1979, where did you go in the morning?

A. I went to Brigantine, to my house.

Q. The house that your wife and children were living in?

A. Yes, sir.

Q. What was your purpose in going there?

A. I wanted to see the kids and it was around Christmastime and she had said they were going to go cut firewood with the kids and I says, 'I want to come over with you and go with you.'

Q. When you say 'she,' are you talking about your wife?

A. Yes.

Q. Did you go over to see your wife and children?

A. Yes, I did.

Q. And did you go to cut firewood?

A. Yes, I did.

Q. And what conversation, if any, did you have with your wife when you were out at the location where the firewood was being cut?

ME SIMONE: Objection.

THE COURT: I would think it would be sustained unless it's some exception.

BY MR GORDON:

Q. Well, don't tell us what your wife said, just tell us what you said to her?

A. I said to her, I told her I was afraid, 'They want to go someplace today.' I says, 'I don't want to go because I don't know, I think someone's gonna be killed,' I said. I says, 'It could be Vincent,' I says, 'I don't know.' I said, 'I have no idea.' But I says, 'If anything happens to me, I want you to know who I'm with that day.'

Q. And who did you tell her you were going to be with?

A. With Leonetti, Scarfo and Lawrence Merlino.

Q. And after that conversation did you return to the home in Brigantine that your wife and children were living in at that time?

A. Yes, I did.

Q. And what happened after your return?

A. I had bought a tree that day and we started fooling around with the tree, getting the tree ready to decorate and the phone rang and Lawrence says, 'He wants you over here now.'

Q. And when you say 'Lawrence,' you mean Lawrence Merlino?

A. Yes.

Q. And when Lawrence Merlino said, 'He wants you over here now,' who was the 'he' that you understood him to be talking about?

A. Nicky Scarfo.

Q. And where did you go after you received that call?

A. I got in my car and went over to Scarf, Inc.'s office on Georgia Avenue with my car.

Q. Approximately what time was it you received the phone call?

A. It was approximately 2:00, quarter after 2:00.

Q. And how long did it take you to travel from your house in Brigantine to North Georgia Avenue?

A. Ten minutes.

Q. And when you arrived at North Georgia Avenue who if anybody was there?

A. Vincent Falcone, Philip Leonetti, Lawrence Merlino and myself.

Q. And where were you going to go?

A. We were going to go out and have some Christmas drinks at the Ivory Tavern down in Margate or Longport; I'm not sure where it's at. That's what I was told.

Q. Now, what did you do after being told that?

A. I told Philip, I says, 'I don't want to go.' I says, 'I want to go home and decorate my tree with my kids.' And he says 'No,' he says, 'Come on, come on, come on.' So I went. We got in the car, Lawrence's car.

Q. Who else got in that car with you?

A. It was Philip Leonetti, he was on the passenger side in the front seat; Lawrence was driving, he was the driver; I was sitting in back of Lawrence and Vincent Falcone was sitting on the right to me in the back seat.

Q. And in which direction did the car proceed to drive?

A. We went down Atlantic Avenue toward Margate.

Q. And was there any conversation in the car at that time?

A. Yes, there was.

Q. Who was the conversation between?

A. Leonetti was talking about old times to Vincent Falcone, about the good times they used to have together, in the car. And they were talking back and forth and all of a sudden, Philip says that, 'We've got to stop, we've got to pick my uncle up at Phil Disney's house.' This is a house along the coast in Margate.

Q. Is Philip Disney also known as Phil McFillin?

A. Yes, sir.

Q. Had you been to his house on another occasion or two?

A. Yes, I had.

Q. Who had you been to Phil Disney's house with before that date?

A. I was there once with Chuck Merlino and once with Vince Falcone.

Q. And did you know Phil Disney well?

A. No, I did not.

Q. Did you have a key to his house?

A. No, sir.

Q. And after you were told that you had to stop at Phil Disney's house to pick up Philip's uncle, what happened next?

A. We drove, turned off of Atlantic Avenue, went down Decatur Avenue and the four of us got out of the car. And this was a second floor apartment by the beach. So we went up the steps, Nicky Scarfo was sitting there on the couch, had a paper in his hand, eyeglasses on and there was a football game on. And he says, 'Look,' he says – everybody shook hands with him, and he says, 'Look,' he says, 'Make some drinks.' He says, 'Phil will be back in about, in a little while. I have to wait until he gets back before we leave.' So he says, 'Vincent,' he says, 'Go ahead, make some drinks.' So Vincent went into the refrigerator, whatever he did, he got some ice out, got some drinks, put them on the kitchen table, a couple of them. I got one in my hand, Lawrence got one in his hand, and Philip Leonetti was standing next to me on my right-hand side and Scarfo was facing the TV that day.

And Philip Leonetti pulled a gun out of his jacket, reached

over and shot Vincent Falcone in his head is what he did. And then after he did that he turned and looked at me immediately and he said, 'Joe,' he said, 'this guy was a no good mother-fucker.' That's what he said to me. Then he got up, Nicky Scarfo got up and asked me if I was OK, so I says, 'Yeah,' I says, 'I'm fine.' So he went up to the body, got down on the floor and put his ear up to the body, on the chest, opened his jacket up.

Q. Who put his ear to the chest?

A. Nicky Scarfo. And he said, 'I think I'll give him another one.' So Philip says, 'No,' he says, 'I'll give it to him.' So Philip got the gun, put it up against his chest and pulled off another shot into Vincent's chest. Then what happened after that, Nicky Scarfo got the keys out of Vincent Falcone's pocket of his car, gave the keys to Lawrence, told Philip to take the gun, wrap it up in a towel, OK, and told them both to leave the apartment, so they left.

Q. When you say, 'they left,' who are you talking about?

A. Lawrence Merlino and Phil Leonetti left the premises.

Q. And who was left in the apartment at that time?

A. Myself, Nick Scarfo and Vincent Falcone, but he was dead.

Q. Now, approximately how long had it taken you to get from North Georgia Avenue to the house on Decatur Street?

A. Fifteen minutes maybe.

Q. At the time that Philip Leonetti pulled a gun out of his pants, approximately how far was he standing from Vincent Falcone?

A. Six to seven feet.

Q. And at the time that Mr Leonetti reached out and shot Vincent Falcone in the back of the head, about how far was the muzzle of the gun from Vincent Falcone's head?

A. No more than three feet.

Q. What gun did Phil Leonetti use to shoot Vincent Falcone?

A. It was the gun that I brought over to Scarf, Inc.'s, the .32 revolver; he used that.

Q. And at the time that Philip Leonetti shot Vincent Falcone a second time in the chest approximately how far was the muzzle of the gun from Vincent Falcone's chest?

A. Twelve inches or less.

Q. When Nicodemo Scarfo said to you, 'Joe, are you all right' and you said, 'Yes,' were you all right?

A. I was scared to death.

Q. What were you scared of?

A. Being next, getting killed right on the spot.

Q. Why did you say you were all right if you weren't all right?

A. I was afraid not to say I was OK.

Q. Whose car keys had Nicodemo Scarfo taken from Vincent Falcone's pants pocket?

A. Vincent Falcone's car keys to his car, his own personal car.

Q. And who did he give the keys to?

A. Lawrence Merlino.

Q. And do you know what automobile Lawrence Merlino and Philip Leonetti left those premises in?

A. Lawrence Merlino's car, the car that we drove there with.

Q. Now at the time that that car left was there any other car present on that scene?

A. Yes, Nicky Scarfo's car.

Q. What kind of car was that?

A. It was a black four-door Cadillac.

Q. And where was it parked?

A. It was parked at the driveway of the house, the duplex there.

Q. Was it visible on the street?

A. Yes.

Q. And after Lawrence Merlino and Philip Leonetti left – well, let me back up. First of all, how much time had gone by approximately from the time that the four of you entered that house until the time Merlino and Philip Leonetti left?

A. No more than fifteen minutes.

Q. And after Lawrence Merlino and Philip Leonetti left, what if anything did Nicodemo Scarfo say?

A. He came up to me and he said, grabbed me by the shoulders and said to me, 'You're one of us now.' He says, 'Philip's the best, he'll always be the best.' He says, 'I'll be responsible for anything that happens,' and he says, 'I'm going to be number one next to Phil.'

Q. What Phil did you understand Scarfo to be referring to at that time?

A. Phil Testa from Philadelphia.

Q. And after Nicodemo Scarfo said that, what was done next?

A. He said, 'OK,' he said, 'I need your help, I need your strength.' So we moved the kitchen table out of the kitchen and we laid the body down on the floor, Vincent Falcone's body, and he had a box with a blanket in it and ropes, twine.

Q. Who had that box?

A. He had it, he had the box.

Q. 'He' meaning Nicodemo Scarfo?

A. Nicky Scarfo, yeah. He had the box. And he took the blanket out of the box and he says, 'Here's what I want you to do. I want you to tie him up like a cowboy. Tie his hands behind him, tie his feet behind him, wrap him up in this blanket,' he said, 'and tie this blanket around him.' And I did that. And as the body was laying there the head was only showing, just the head.

And he looked down at the head and said that, 'I love this,' he said, 'I love this.' That's what he said. Then he says, 'Go ahead,' and covered the top, he says, 'Tie the head up.' And I tied the head of the body up.

Q. Who was it that bent down and said, 'I love this, I love it'?

A. Nicky Scarfo.

Q. After the body was tied up and completely covered, did there come a time when you made a phone call?

A. Yes.

Q. And what happened which caused you to make a call?

A. We were waiting for Lawrence to get back with Vincent Falcone's car and there was time going by. And Nicky says, 'Well, let's call him up.' I wanted to use the phone in the house, he says, 'No, don't use the phone in the house. Go down to the pay phone on the corner and call them from there.'

So he gave me change, I went down to the pay phone and what I did was I called my wife up, she wasn't available. I got my son on the phone, Michael, and says, 'Tell your mother that I am OK,' because I had told her what was going to happen or what would happen that day or whatever, and, 'Tell your mom

I'm OK,' that's what I said. And then I called Lawrence Merlino and I says, 'What's keeping you?' He says, 'I got tied up for a while,' he says, 'I'll be over.' So then I left the telephone booth and went back to the apartment again, came upstairs into the apartment and about a couple minutes later a police car pulled up by the bulkhead. And I watched the police officer, he was having coffee or something from the thermos. And—

Q. Did you make that observation from inside the house?

A. I could see it, yeah, I could see it from inside the house.

Q. What happened after the police officer came up?

A. So Nicky says, 'Uh-oh,' he says, 'You've got to get back to the phone and call Lawrence off not to get back here with the car.' And so I went back to the telephone booth again and before I got to the booth, the cop car left, took off. And I called Lawrence and he says, 'Well,' he says 'I'm on my way.'

Q. What did you do after that?

A. I went back to the apartment and Lawrence finally showed up with Vincent Falcone's car.

Q. Lawrence Merlino was driving Vincent Falcone's car when he returned?

A. Yes, sir.

Q. What kind of car was it?

A. It was a white Cougar with a blue top.

Q. Is a Cougar a Mercury?

A. Yes.

Q. Did Philip Leonetti ever return to the house while you were there?

A. No, sir.

Q. Now, after Lawrence Merlino came back inside, what happened then?

A. He said, 'OK,' he says, 'take the body down the steps whatever, and put it in the trunk of Vincent Falcone's car.' So—

Q. Who said that?

A. Nicky Scarfo told Lawrence and myself. So we picked the body up and we brought it toward the top of the steps and he says, 'Wait a minute.' He says, 'I always wanted something out of that car,' this is Vincent Falcone's car.

Q. Who said that?

A. Nicky Scarfo. So Lawrence went down and I don't know what he wanted or whatever, he took whatever out of the car and I guess he put it into Nicky's car, I don't know whatever. So we took the body down the steps, I had the bottom part of the body, Lawrence had the top part of the body. And midway or whatever down the steps the body had dropped, we picked it back up again and we put it in the trunk of the car.

Q. The trunk of whose car?

A. Vincent Falcone's car.

Q. At that time was it light or dark outside?

A. Dark.

Q. Approximately how large a man did Vincent Falcone appear to be to you?

A. He was, I'd say, 185 pounds or maybe even 200 pounds.

Q. Do you recall approximately how tall he was?

A. Five ten and a half, maybe.

Q. How much did you weigh at that time?

A. 175, 170.

MR GORDON: Your Honor, at this time I would ask the members of the jury to look at Book 1 and turn to the photograph behind Tab No. 18. And at this time, and that photograph is marked as Government Exhibit 423 and I ask that the enlargement – you don't have to do that yet, Mr Salerno – I ask that the enlargement which is marked as Government Exhibit 423L be displayed to the jury.

BY MR. GORDON:

Q. Mr Salerno, would you look to your right, please? Do you recognize the scene shown in that photograph?

A. Yes, I do.

Q. And what is shown?

A. This is where Nicky Scarfo was sitting when the murder took place, right here.

Q. And which direction was Mr Scarfo looking?

A. He was looking toward – toward you.

Q. And is that the room or the two rooms that you, Mr Scarfo,

Mr Falcone, Mr Leonetti, Mr Merlino were in at the time of the shooting?

A. That's correct.

Q. And where approximately on that photograph, if it appears, was Mr Falcone standing at the time that he was shot?

A. From here to here this is a corner in the kitchen, this kitchen comes like that to this corner, and he was standing in this corner right here.

Q. And which direction was he facing?

A. He had his back turned toward this area.

Q. And where was Philip Leonetti standing at the time that he pulled the gun out of his waist?

A. He was standing here, right in this area.

Q. And you're pointing to an area near the linoleum or the tile floor and the rug?

A. Just about – about between the linoleum and the carpeting, right about in here.

Q. And where were you standing at that time?

A. I was standing right here.

Q. Indicating to Mr Leonetti's left?

A. Correct.

Q. And where was Lawrence Merlino standing at that time?

A. You can't see it in this picture, he was standing on the side of this table here, the table's round. He was standing right there.

Q. So you're indicating a point that would be off the right portion of the photograph on the other side of the table?

A. Correct.

Q. In the kitchen?

A. In the kitchen.

Q. And where did Mr Falcone fall after being shot in the back of the head?

A. He was facing backwards and when he got shot in the back of the head he twisted and faced forward and crouched down to his knees and he was just sitting, just crouched down right in the corner of this kitchen right here.

Q. Thank you, you can put that pointer down and that photograph may be taken down.

I ask you now, Mr Salerno—

MR GORDON: And members of the jury—

BY MR GORDON:

Q. —to turn in that same Book 1 to the photograph behind Tab No. 23 which is marked for identification as Government Exhibit 425. Would you open up Book No. 1 and turn to Tab 23, please?

Do you recognize what's shown in that photograph, Mr Salerno?

A. The other house.

Q. Which house is that?

A. The house on – on Decatur Avenue; that's where the murder took place.

Q. And are these steps that you took Vincent Falcone's body down with Lawrence Merlino visible in that photograph?

A. Yes, they are.

Q. And there is steps that appear to lead into the sand in the left—

A. Yes, there are.

Q. —foreground.

And I ask you finally to turn in that same book to the photograph behind Tab No 27, which is marked for identification as Government Exhibit 420. That's Tab No. 27. Do you recognize what's shown in that photograph?

A. Vincent Falcone's body in the trunk, is that the photograph you're talking about?

Q. Is that the one you have in front of you behind 27?

A. Yes, it is.

Q. Yes, is that what you recognize it to be, Vincent Falcone's body?

A. Yes, yes, sir.

Q. In the trunk of his automobile?

A. Yes.

Q. Who placed him in that trunk?

A. Myself and Lawrence Merlino.

Q. Who told you to put him in the trunk?

A. Mr Scarfo.

Q. All right, you may close that book now.

After Vincent Falcone's body was placed in the trunk of his automobile what happened next?

A. Nicky says, 'OK,' he says, 'I want you and Lawrence to follow me. I'm driving Vincent's car, stay behind me a block or two.' So myself and Lawrence proceeded to get into Nicky Scarfo's Cadillac and Nicky got into Vincent Falcone's car with the body in the trunk and we followed Nicky with the Cadillac not maybe five minutes away and he parked the car in an area and we wait—

Q. Are you familiar with the area that the car was parked in?

A. Yes.

Q. Was it still in that Margate area?

A. Yes.

Q. And why were you familiar with that particular area where the car was parked?

A. I was going to do a plumbing job in the neighborhood and also there is a Rick Casale that lives right closeby to that area.

Q. Who was Rick Casale?

A. He was a roofer and – and kind of a friend to everybody, you know, Nicky and Philip and everybody else.

Q. Now, when the car was left in that area, Vicent Falcone's car, what happened next?

A. Nicky walked up, walked up the street, got in the driver's – got in the Cadillac, and we were gonna head back to Georgia Avenue. And he said, 'We forgot something.' He said, 'We got'—

Q. Who said, 'we forgot something'?

A. Nicky. Nicky said, 'We forgot something. We have to go back to the apartment and we've got to clean up.' So we went back to the apartment. We went into the house, up the steps, and he told me to take a rag or a cloth or something and wet it with cold water, clean the floor up, clean the cabinets up, 'Anywhere you think anything could be,' he says, 'clean it up.' So I did.

Q. Who told you to clean up everything?

A. Nicky Scarfo.

Q. And after you did that, cleaned up, what happened next?

A. We left that apartment, got into the car, the Cadillac car and we headed down Georgia Avenue.

Q. Now, when you had returned to Phil Disney or Phil McFillin's house, how did you get into the house?

A. Nicky Scarfo had a key to get in.

Q. And when you left the house and you returned towards Georgia Avenue, did you eventually go back to North Georgia Avenue?

A. Yes.

Q. Had Phil Disney or Phil McFillin been at that house any time that day while you and Nicodemo Scarfo, Philip Leonetti, and Lawrence Merlino were there?

A. No, sir.

Q. Was he there at any time while you were there that day?

A. No, sir.

Q. When you went back to North Georgia Avenue what happened?

A. I was told to just take all my clothes that I had on off myself, go upstairs, get cleaned up and you know, 'Take a bag, take the clothes downstairs and I want all the clothes off you that you wore that day.'

So I took whatever stuff I had on, put them in a plastic bag, got cleaned up, put other clothes on, went downstairs into Nicky Scarfo's apartment.

Q. Who told you to take all your clothes off and put them in a bag?

A. Nicky Scarfo.

Q. And when you went back to Nicky Scarfo's apartment with your clothes in a bag, what did you do with those clothes at that time?

A. Repeat the question for me, please?

Q. When you went back down to the apartment did you take your clothes with you?

A. Yes, I did.

Q. And were they in a plastic bag?

A. Yes.

Q. And what did you do with that plastic bag?

A. I put it in another plastic bag.

Q. Do you know what was in the other plastic bag?

A. No.

Q. Do you know what happened to Lawrence Merlino or—

MR REIF: Objection as being leading, your Honor. It's obvious from the first question.

THE COURT: Why not ask do you know what happened to Lawrence Merlino?

MR REIF: Well, the Court will recall the question that was asked before that, this is obviously a leading question.

MR GORDON: Well, I'll rephrase it so it can't possibly be leading.

THE COURT: All right.

MR REIF: It's already told.

BY MR GORDON:

Q. Did you ever again see the clothes that Lawrence Merlino or Philip Leonetti had worn during the time when Vincent Falcone was shot?

A. No, sir.

Q. When you put your clothes into a plastic bag was there anything else in that, in the larger plastic bag?

A. Yes.

Q. Do you know what it was that was in the larger plastic bag?

A. I'm not sure, no.

Q. OK. Now, after doing that what did you do in Nicodemo Scarfo's apartment?

A. We started to have dinner out on the table, you know, and—

Q. Who cooked the dinner?

A. Nicky Scarfo's wife.

Q. And what happened at dinner?

A. I asked, I says, I didn't know why Vincent Falcone.

Q. Who did you ask that to?

A. I asked it to either Philip or Nicky Scarfo.

Q. Who was present at the table at that time?

A. Myself, Nicky Scarfo, Chuck Merlino, Lawrence Merlino and Philip Leonetti.

Q. And where was Nicodemo Scarfo's wife who had cooked the dinner?

A. I didn't see her; I only seen her briefly, then she left.

Q. Now, when you said what you did about Vincent, what was the reply that you received, if any?

A. The answer I got was that Vincent Falcone—

Q. Now, who said this?

A. I believe it was Philip Leonetti or Nicky Scarfo, I'm not sure.

Q. And what was the reply?

A. That Vincent Falcone told Chuck Merlino that Philip Leonetti shouldn't be in the concrete business and that his Uncle Nicky was crazy. So when Chuck Merlino and Scarfo went to Italy, Chuck Merlino relayed this message on to Nicky Scarfo about Vincent and Nicky Scarfo's reply was, 'When we get back,' he says, 'I'm gonna kill him.' That was the answer that I got.

Q. Did you eat dinner in Nicky Scarfo's apartment that night?

A. Yes, sir.

Q. And after dinner did you take a ride someplace?

A. Yes.

Q. Where did you go?

A. Philip asked me to take a ride with him. We took the bag of clothes out from the living room and we went into Nicky Scarfo's car, both of us.

Q. When you say both of you, who do you mean?

A. Philip Leonetti and myself. And we went down toward the Brajole Café, which is closeby to Georgia Avenue, and he dumped the bag, the plastic bag that my clothes were in, in a dumpster.

Q. Who put them in the dumpster?

A. Philip put them in the dumpster.

Q. Then what happened?

A. Then we drove up toward Mississippi Avenue and we stopped at a corner and he handed me a box. And I threw it, he says, 'Get rid of this box,' and I threw the box out the window. He says, 'No, no, no, no,' he says, 'get out of the car and take the box and throw it down the sewer, there's a manhole cover there.' So I picked the box up and threw it down inside the sewer.

Q. Now, when you picked the box up did you see what it was?

A. Yes, I did.

Q. What was it?

A. There were bullets in the box.

Q. What caliber bullet?

A. .32 caliber bullets.

Q. Now, about how far from North Georgia Avenue where the apartments were located was this sewer that the bullets were thrown down?

A. Two to three minutes.

Q. Now, you testified earlier that the gun that was used to shoot Vincent Falcone was the gun that you had given to Nicodemo Scarfo. Did you ever see that gun again after Philip Leonetti left the Decatur Street house with it after the shooting?

A. No, sir.

Q. After throwing the bullets down the sewer did you later go out that evening?

A. Yes.

Q. Where did you go?

A. I went to Caesar's in Atlantic City.

Q. Is that the casino?

A. Yes, it's the casino.

Q. And who did you go there with?

A. Myself and Lawrence, we had some girls with us, and we met Philip there and he had a girlfriend with him also.

Q. At any time that evening did you have a discussion with Philip Leonetti concerning Vincent Falcone?

A. Yes, I did.

Q. Would you describe, first of all, who was present during the conversation?

A. Just myself and Philip. We moved away from the group of people that we were with, we went to another table. And I says why or whatever Vincent. He said, he says, 'I'll tell you something. If I could bring the MF back to life again,' he says, 'I'd kill him again.' That's what he told me. So he says, 'Forget about it and don't ask me anything more about it.'

Q. Who was it that said if he could bring him back again he'd kill him again?

A. Philip Leonetti.

Q. Now, later that night did you return to your house that your wife was living in in Brigantine, New Jersey?

A. Yes, sir.

Q. And what if anything did you tell your wife at that time?

A. I told her what took place and I told her I was scared, I didn't know what to do. And she said she's afraid that I'm even going to be there in the house with the kids, she didn't know about these people what to do and stuff and so I left the house.

Q. When you say you told your wife what happened that day, are you talking about describing the shooting?

A. Yes. I told her that Vincent—

Q. Well, you don't have to go through the whole thing but you told her that Vincent Falcone had been shot?

A. Yes.

Q. And who had done it?

A. Yes.

Q. And after you left your wife's house where did you go later that night?

A. I went to Georgia Avenue.

Q. Is that the place where you had your apartment?

A. Yes.

Q. Nicodemo Scarfo's house?

A. Yes.

Q. And did you stay there that night?

A. Yes, I did.

Q. And the next day was anything special or unusual planned between you and Nicodemo Scarfo and Philip Leonetti and Lawrence Merlino?

A. Yes, there was a plan to go celebrate in Philadelphia, they were going to go to the Camac Baths in Philadelphia. And they told me to go to my house, where I lived in Philadelphia, and they would call me when they'd be ready for me in Philly. So they were supposed to call at 10 o'clock in the morning and I didn't get a call, I got a call late, late in the afternoon, that it was cancelled and his uncle was sick.

Q. Well, what did you do after you got that call?

A. I was told to come on back to Georgia Avenue and I drove from Philadelphia back to Atlantic City to Georgia Avenue.

Q. Now, when you got back to Georgia Avenue, when you came back to Georgia Avenue who, if anybody, was there?

A. There was Sal Testa there, a guy named Vince Salsto (ph.), Philip Leonetti, Lawrence Merlino, one of the Narduccis, I don't know which one, either Philip or Frank; I don't know, I forgot.

Q. One of the Narducci sons?

A. Yes.

Q. And at that time did you want to continue to live in the apartment on North Georgia Avenue?

A. No, sir.

Q. Why not?

A. I was afraid for my life, that's why.

Q. Did you have any discussion with Nicodemo Scarfo about leaving your apartment and moving out?

A. Yes, I did.

Q. What was said during that discussion?

A. I told him what I'd like to do is spend time – it was around Christmastime – I'd like to spend some time with my family. So he says, 'That would be a good idea,' he said, 'because there's going to be a lot of heat around here soon.'

Q. Who said that?

A. Nicky Scarfo.

Q. And did you return to the location in Brigantine where your wife and family lived?

A. Yes, I did.

Q. Did you attempt to contact Nicodemo Scarfo later that same week.

A. Yes, I did.

Q. What did you do?

A. I called Scarf, Inc.'s office from Brigantine and I wanted to know where Nicky was or Philip and I talked to Philip's mother and she said they were at Scanuccio's Restaurant. So I went to the restaurant and I was worried about the gun, because the gun was an old style gun and eventually this man's body was going to be found with bullets in it. And I don't know – didn't know too much about guns, this and that and the other thing, and I was afraid if my father read this thing in the paper, OK, he would get suspicious and I was worried about it and I needed answers.

So I went down there and talked to Nicky about it. He said, 'Just don't even ask me anything about that.'

Q. You talked to Nicky about what?

A. About the gun.

Q. Who was present during that conversation?

A. Philip Leonetti and Nicky Scarfo.

Q. And when Nicky Scarfo said, 'Don't ask me anything about it,' what happened after that?

A. After that Nicky left, OK? And I eventually got to talk to Philip by myself and he said, 'You should have never asked my uncle that, you got him worried.'

Q. What was Philip referring to when he said, 'You never should have asked my uncle that'? What was he talking about?

A. My trust any more, he was worried about my trust probably.

Q. And what did he mean that you should not have asked about?

A. The gun, 'You never should have asked him about the gun.'

Q. Do you know who owns Scanuccio's Restaurant?

A. Yes, I do.

Q. Who?

A. Vince Salsto.

Q. Who is he in relation to Nicodemo Scarfo?

A. He was a friend, he was a friend of Nicky Scarfo's.

Q. After that conversation did you return to Brigantine?

A. Yes, I did.

Q. That same week did you have any further conversations with Nicodemo Scarfo?

A. Yes. He called my house up and he said, 'They found our friend.' He says, 'Come over, I want to talk to you.'

Q. When Nicodemo Scarfo said, 'They found our friend,' who did you understand him to be talking about?

A. Vincent Falcone.

Q. And did you go back over to Scarf, Inc. on Georgia Avenue?

A. Yes, I did.

Q. What happened when you arrived there?

A. Nicky happened to be outside and came to my car and said

to me, he says, 'Stay away for a while, there's going to be a lot of heat around here.' So I says OK and that was it.

Q. And did you return home after that?

A. Yes, I did.

Q. On approximately December 22nd, 1979, did members of the Atlantic County Prosecutor's Office come to your house in Brigantine?

A. Yes, sir.

Q. And what did they ask you or say to you at that time?

> MR SIMONE: Is there a date on that, a date?
> MR GORDON: December 22nd.
> THE WITNESS: They asked me if I knew anything about the homicide of Vincent Falcone.

BY MR GORDON:

Q. And what did you say?

A. I says, 'I don't want to talk about it here in my house.' So they asked me if I wanted to come down to the Prosecutor's Office, and I went down to the Prosecutor's Office.

Q. Now, when they asked you that did they tell you that you had to come with them at that time?

A. No, sir.

Q. And how did you get from your house to the Prosecutor's Office?

A. I drove my car.

Q. Were you with anybody in your car?

A. No.

Q. You drove your car by yourself to the Prosecutor's Office?

A. Yes.

Q. What happened when you arrived at the Atlantic County Prosecutor's Office?

A. I was introduced to a Tony Porcelli, was a detective, he was a detective, excuse me, and he showed me a couple of pictures of Vincent Falcone and asked me if I knew him. So I says, 'Yes, I know him.' So he says, 'You know he's dead' and he says, 'You know you're going to be next,' that's what he told me.

So I says, 'Well,' I says, 'I'll tell you something.' I says,

'I know the whole thing,' I told him. And I says, 'I'm not going to tell you anything,' I said, 'I don't care if you lock me up, I don't care what you do to me. Before I tell you anything,' I says, 'I want someone to get my wife and my kids out of my house and I want them protected immediately,' I says, 'because I'm scared.'

Q. And did the Prosecutor's Office do something with regard to your wife and children?

A. Yes, they did.

Q. Did they take them out of your house?

A. Yes, sir.

Q. And did they take them someplace else?

A. Yes.

Q. And did you become aware of the fact, in other words did it become known to you that your wife and children were out of your house and that they were being protected?

A. Became aware to me, yes.

Q. And after you became aware of that did you give a statement to the Atlantic County Prosecutor's Office?

A. Yes, I gave a statement.

Q. And did you tell them what had happened with regard to the killing of Vincent Falcone?

A. Yes, sir.

Q. And who did you tell the Prosecutors had killed Vincent Falcone?

A. Philip Leonetti.

Q. And who else did you tell them was present during the time of that shooting?

A. Nick Scarfo and Lawrence Merlino and myself.

Q. After you gave that statement to the Prosecutor's Office did you and your family begin to receive protection around the clock from the Prosecutor's Office?

A. Yes, sir.

Q. Sometime after giving that statement did you receive a phone call from Vince Salsto?

A. Yes, I did.

Q. Where were you when you got that phone call?

A. At my home in Brigantine.

Q. And is this the same Vince Salsto that you referred to earlier as the owner of Scanuccio's and a friend of Mr Scarfo's?

A. Yes.

Q. And what did Mr Salsto want when he made that phone call?

> MR SIMONE: Objected to. I think he can ask him what he said, not what he wanted.

BY MR GORDON:

Q. All right, what did he say?

> MR GOODMAN: I object as to what he said.
>
> MR GORDON: Your Honor, this is being offered not for the truth of it but for the reaction on the part of this witness and what he did as a result of it?
>
> THE COURT: Well, all right, I have to hear it to know fully. I'll permit him to answer.

BY MR GORDON:

Q. What did he say?

A. He said he had an emergency for me to do, emergency plumbing job.

Q. And did he describe the plumbing job?

A. He described the plumbing job to me.

Q. And what was your reaction after hearing the description of the plumbing job?

A. There was no way he had anything wrong with the plumbing, the way he described it to me at all. Said he had a bad leak and there couldn't be a possible leak where he was telling me. I didn't believe him and I didn't go.

Q. Why didn't you go?

A. I thought it was a setup.

Q. On approximately December 27th of 1979 did you and your family leave the Atlantic City, Brigantine, New Jersey area?

A. Yes, we did.

Q. And in whose company were you at that time?

A. The Atlantic County Prosecutor's.

Q. And did you stay in their company or protection for approximately a three-week period?

A. Yes.

Q. During that period did you move to various locations around the country?

A. Yes, we did.

Q. At the end of that three-week period, what happened with regard to you and your family?

A. We then met with the United States Federal marshals and we went on the Federal Witness Protection Program.

Q. And did that involve being relocated for you and your family?

A. Yes.

Q. And a name change?

A. Yes.

Q. Now, during the time that you were initially, during that period you were with the Atlantic County Prosecutor's Office, did they give you some money?

A. Yes, they did.

Q. What was the money for?

A. Living expenses.

Q. Did they also pay some bills for you while you were under their protection?

A. Yes, they did.

Q. Did they pay a month's rent, to the best of your recollection?

A. I believe so, yes.

Q. And did they pay some electric and phone bills?

A. Yes, sir.

Q. Did they also pay a traffic ticket for you?

A. Yes, sir.

Q. And did they make good on one check that you had written that had bounced because of not having sufficient funds in the bank to cover it?

A. Yes, they did.

Q. Was that a check to a person named Lester Roberts for about $200?

A. Yes, sir.

Q. During the three-week period that you were in the protection of the Atlantic County Prosecutor's Office were you able to work and make any money?

A. No.

Q. At some time later after that were you given an additional thousand dollars cash by the Atlantic County Prosecutor's Office?

A. Yes.

Q. And on a couple of occasions when they wanted to talk to you after that period of time did they also reimburse you for lost wages for the time that you spent talking to them?

A. I think so, yeah.

Q. Now, after you went into the Marshal's Program, into the Witness Protection Program, were you given a subsistence allowance, a monthly allowance by the Marshals?

A. Yes.

Q. Do you recall approximately how much that was?

A. It was $1,200 a month.

Q. How long did that last?

A. Six months.

Q. And were you also working during that time period?

A. Yes, I was.

Q. At the end of that six-month period did you stop receiving that assistance?

A. I stopped.

Q. Did you work full time after that?

A. Yes.

Q. Have you been working ever since and supporting yourself?

A. Yes, I have.

Q. On several occasions when you met with the FBI and Federal Prosecutors have you been reimbursed for lost wages?

A. Sometimes and sometimes not.

Q. Now in 1979 with the help and advice of an attorney did you file a petition in bankruptcy?

A. Yes, I did.

Q. In that petition did you list all the assets that you own?

A. No, I didn't list any assets.

Q. What did you fail to list in there?

A. I had a rifle that was worth probably about a thousand bucks and some jewelry worth maybe about seven or eight hundred dollars; that was it.

Q. Why didn't you list those items?

A. First of all, I didn't have the rifle, I never thought about the rifle, and the jewelry I just never thought about it, and I just never listed them down.

Q. Where was the rifle at the time that the petition was filed?

A. That was at my dad's house in Philadelphia.

Q. Have you ever written, in addition to the one check we talked about to Lester Roberts, have you written any additional checks which were returned to you because there weren't sufficient funds in the bank to cover them?

A. Yes, I did.

Q. Was one of those checks to a person named Joe Gettis for approximately $1,500?

A. Yes.

Q. Was that check made good by you?

A. It was made good by me, yes.

Q. Did you also write a check which bounced for insufficient funds for $450 to Vince Salsto who was also your insurance agent?

A. Yes, I did.

Q. And as a result of that were your insurance policies cancelled?

A. Yes, they were.

Q. In the summer of 1982 did you testify before the New Jersey Division of Gaming Enforcement?

A. Yes, I did.

Q. Did some of that testimony concern Nicodemo Scarfo?

A. Yes, it did.

Q. Were you also scheduled to testify later that summer in another proceeding involving Nicodemo Scarfo and—

A. That's correct.

Q. —concerning Local 54 Bartenders Union?

A. Yes, sir.

Q. Between your first testimony and that second time when you were scheduled to testify did something happen to your father?

295

A. Yes.

Q. What happened to him?

A. My father was shot.

Q. And where was he shot?

A. Through the neck.

Q. And what location did the shooting occur in?

A. In Wildwood, New Jersey.

Q. Where in Wildwood?

A. Wildwood Crest, it's a place of business, it's a motel my mom and dad has.

Q. Is that the El Reno Motel?

A. Yes, it is.

Q. Is your father's name Joseph Salerno?

A. Yes, sir.

Q. How old are you, Mr Salerno?

A. I'm 44.

Q. Have you ever been convicted of any crime?

A. No, sir.

Q. Have you ever been arrested for any crime?

A. No, sir.

MR GORDON: I have no further questions of this witness, your Honor.

* * *

(The following excerpted testimony occurred in open court:)

JOSEPH SALERNO, JR, Government Witness, previously sworn.

CROSS-EXAMINATION

BY MR JACOBS:

Q. Good evening.

A. Good evening.

Q. Mr Salerno, what you're basically telling us is that back in December of 1979 you were hanging around with someone you considered to be a famous personality, at least locally in Atlantic City, and that's Mr Scarfo, is that right?

A. That's correct.

Q. You described that he got a great deal of catering when he went into public establishments, people knew him; right?

A. I don't know in all establishments; some of them.

Q. And you also told us that you became aware one way or another that there was some publicity about him being a member of organized crime, so you knew all this in December of 1979, didn't you?

A. Yes, sir.

Q. And you also knew, because you've told us, that Mr Scarfo was very fearful of surveillance, didn't you tell us that?

A. Yes, I did.

Q. You said he used a code word, chandeliers, for weapons, right?

A. Correct.

Q. That exhibits a fear for surveillance, right?

A. Yes.

Q. Is that the way you understood it?

A. Yes, yes, I did.

Q. Now, as you tell this story, sir, you would have yourself, Mr Scarfo, Mr Leonetti and Vincent Falcone emerging from Georgia Avenue at 2:20 to 3:15 p.m. in the afternoon on a Sunday in December; is that right? . . .

A. Yeah.

Q. On Sunday, December 16, 1979?

A. Mm-hmm.

Q. Is that time about right? If it's not, change it.

A. Uh, we left Georgia Avenue around 2:30 and we got there about 20, I guess, quarter to 3:00 probably.

Q. When you walked out of Georgia Avenue were the four of you together?

A. Yes, sir.

Q. Did you make any efforts to conceal yourselves?

A. No, sir.

Q. You didn't wear any disguises or anything?

A. No.

Q. The four of you walked out in broad daylight?

A. Yes, we did.

Q. To a car?

A. Mm-hmm.

Q. Lawrence Merlino's car?

A. Yes, sir.

Q. Not a rented car, not a stolen car, Lawrence Merlino's car?

A. That's correct.

Q. Now, sir, isn't Georgia Avenue pretty much in the center of Atlantic City?

A. Yes, it is.

Q. And isn't the Scarfo residence maybe six doors off the main street in Atlantic Avenue?

A. Yes, it is.

Q. And this was in broad daylight, wasn't it?

A. It was broad daylight.

Q. And it was nine days before Christmas?

A. Yes.

Q. And you were in a very dense residential area, weren't you?

A. Yes.

Q. And were you aware at that point of the constant surveillance under which Mr Scarfo was put?

A. No.

Q. Sir, we've seen hundreds and hundreds of photographs in this case and I don't know if you've seen some or all of them. Have you ever seen a photograph—

A. I haven't seen any photographs, sir, at all.

Q. Well, let me finish the question because I'm concerned about a specific photograph. Have you seen any photograph of you and Mr Scarfo and Mr Leonetti and Mr Falcone taken on December 16, 1979?

A. I'm not aware of it . . .

Q. OK. Now, sir, when you spoke with the Atlantic County Prosecutor's Office on December 22, 1979, did they treat you as a suspect?

A. I wouldn't know, sir.

Q. Well, you understand what the word 'suspect' means?

A. Yes, but I wouldn't – I don't know if they treated me like a suspect.

Q. Well, let me rephrase the question and make it easier. Did they tell you you were a suspect?

A. No.

Q. Well, sir, I'm looking at Page 3 of the transcript of the tape-recorded statement they took from you and it says right near the bottom, one, two, three, four, fifth line from the bottom, 'You're a suspect in this matter.' Didn't they tell you that?

A. I don't recall it, I really don't.

Q. Well, do you want me to show it to you or do you want to take my word that it says that?

A. Well, I'll take your word for it.

Q. OK.

A. But I don't recall it.

Q. Fine. Now, they also gave you the rights that any criminal suspect gets, your Fifth Amendment rights, they told you about those rights, didn't they?

A. Yes, they did.

Q. So now it's clear, you were a suspect, right?

A. No.

Q. Sir, you claim that they told you Vincent Falcone has been killed and you're next. You don't see anything like that in this statement that you gave them on December 22nd, will we?

A. I don't think so, but that's what was said to me.

Q. Although it's not in the statement?

A. I don't know if it's in the statement or not, but that's what was said to me.

Q. One of the attorneys asked you, sir, if you provided any bullets or shells for these guns you claim you gave Mr Scarfo or Mr Leonetti or Mr Merlino. What did you say?

A. I said I did supply bullets to .32 caliber gun and I supplied some bullets to the rifle, also.

Q. So you at least admit that the murder weapon was yours and the bullets were yours?

A. No, sir.

Q. You say the bullets are not yours?

A. The bullets that killed Vincent Falcone were not mine.

Q. Your bullets were different?

A. Yes.

Q. Because you say they're different?

A. Because I know they were different

Q. Well, sir, have you had both types of bullets in your life?

A. Did I have—

Q. Sure.

A. Did I have both types of bullets in my life?

Q. Sure.

A. No.

Q. I mean, the difference is—

A. Not for that particular weapon.

Q. Well, for any weapon, sir, let's not worry about that one. The difference between the two is a .32 long and a .32 short, right?

A. That's correct.

Q. And you know there's a .32 long, a .32 short, you've seen a .32 long and a .32 short, haven't you?

A. Correct.

Q. So you'd have no problem getting the other type of bullet, would you?

A. No, but I didn't.

Q. You could but you say you didn't?

A. I did not.

Q. Sir, did I hear you say on your direct testimony that it was you who tied up the body of Mr Falcone?

A. Yes, sir.

Q. You didn't mention anybody else doing that, did you?

A. No, I did not.

Q. When you made your statement on December 22nd, you told the police that you helped tie up the body of Vincent Falcone, didn't you?

A. I don't recall that.

Q. Well, again do you want me to show it to you or do you just want to believe me?

A. Let me see it.

Q. This time you want to check?

A. Yes.

Q. OK.

(*Pause*)

Q. OK, I'll put this right in front of you, sir, we can both see it. We're looking at Page 12 of the statement taken on the 22nd and I'm looking at the final attribution to you, your answer, and I'm looking at the fifth line down, and I'm quoting the words 'And I helped to tie Vincent up.' Did you say that?

A. Yes, it does say that.

Q. You'll agree that's different than what you said on direct examination?

A. Yes, I do agree.

Q. Now, sir, you told the jury on direct examination that after the first shot into Vincent Falcone Mr Scarfo did something. I think you said that he – you said something like, 'We should shoot him again, oh, do it,' and Mr Leonetti said, 'No, allow me,' or something like that. Is that basically what you said?

A. Yes, sir.

Q. OK. Now, how long after the first shot did that happen? How much time do you say went by?

A. 15, 20 seconds.

Q. Why did you tell the police it was between one and five minutes later? Is there a reason for that?

A. I don't know if there's – no, there's no reasons for it but I know there was a second shot fired into Vincent Falcone. The time I'm not really sure of.

Q. Why did you tell the police that Nick Scarfo told Philip Leonetti to fire that second shot? . . .

A. I don't recall saying that at the time. I don't know. That's nine years ago, I don't remember.

Q. Well, sir, before you came to testify you certainly reviewed your prior statements and testimony to other juries, didn't you?

A. No, I did not.

Q. The US Attorneys did not ask you to do that?

A. No.

Q. Sir, who did you tell this jury took the keys from – took Vincent Falcone's keys?

A. I told that Nicky Scarfo took the keys out of his pocket.

Q. And did you tell the police that Lawrence Merlino took the keys, saying, quote, 'Lawrence then took the keys of the car, of the Cougar, Vince Falcone's car.' Did you?

A. But not out of Vince's pocket.

Q. Did you say where Lawrence took them from when you spoke to the police?

A. He took them out of Nicky Scarfo's hands.

Q. Did you tell that to the police?

A. I don't recall that.

Q. If I tell you it's not in there, would you agree?

A. I don't recall. I don't remember.

Q. Sir, you didn't have any trouble telling this jury that Lawrence Merlino and Philip Leonetti left the Decatur Avenue apartment together, I mean, you said that bluntly, didn't you?

A. I did say that.

Q. And you said they left at the instruction of Mr Scarfo?

A. Yes, sir.

Q. Well, sir, one week or six days after this episode, namely on the 22nd when you're talking to the police, didn't you say to the police, 'I think that Philip left with Lawrence'?

A. I know that Philip left with Lawrence.

Q. Well, that's what you're saying now.

A. Well, if I says—

Q. My question is—

A. If I says I think—

Q. —six days after you say this happened, didn't you say to the police, 'I think that Philip left with Lawrence'?

A. OK, if I – regardless, I don't care what I said then. What I'm saying right now—

Q. Well, see, we do though.

MR GORDON: Objection. Your Honor, the witness should be entitled to answer the question.

MR JACOBS: Fine . . .

THE COURT: Very well. Let him answer first.

Do you have more you want to say?

THE WITNESS: When I gave that statement to the police, OK, I just witnessed a murder, I didn't know what to do,

OK? It may be a little different than what I'm saying now, but the thing is that I know is what I seen, I witnessed the murder, OK? That's the main thing. That's why I'm here today . . .

BY MR JACOBS:

Q. Now, sir, tell me if I got this right. Didn't you say this afternoon that you had a conversation with Mr Scarfo in his office and he said, 'Hey, Joe, you want to be a gangster?' You said that, didn't you?

A. Yes.

Q. OK, and that's, he said, 'Hey, Joe, you want to be a gangster,' simple as that?

A. Yes, sir.

Q. And then he said, 'We'll talk about it later,' right?

A. Right.

Q. Didn't you also say that at the Brajole Café, which is a bar and restaurant in Atlantic City—

A. Hm-hmm.

Q. —you had this later conversation and talked about gangsters, racketeers and junkies?

A. Yes, sir.

Q. So I got it right so far, number one was, 'Hey, Joe, do you want to be a gangster,' number two is, 'Gangsters, racketeers and junkies,' and didn't you say number three, third in sequence, third in time, at Virgilio's Restaurant, Mr Scarfo enquired about some guns; did you say that?

A. Yes, I did.

Q. OK. So I got the one, two, three basically right, don't I?

A. Yes.

Q. You told the police on December 22nd, 1979, six days after this episode, that Mr Scarfo already had your guns, already had your guns when he talked to you about becoming a gangster, didn't you?

A. Yes, I did.

Q. That's different, isn't it? It's different than what you told this jury, isn't it?

A. No, no. Repeat that again.

303

Q. On Page 7, for Counsel's reference, right in the center of the page, didn't you say, didn't you say this, sir, quote, 'Yes, and in the meantime I was approached by the uncle. He asked me if I could ever be or want to be a gangster. Now, being they had possessions of my weapons at the time, I could not ask them for it back because of the situation, if you could understand the situation, I was, I started to be afraid a little bit of these people, so I went along with their game,' et cetera. You clearly said to the police that at the time you were approached about being a gangster, Mr Scarfo already had your guns, the exact opposite of what you told this jury, basically, is that right?

A. I don't recall that testimony, sir, I really don't.

Q. Well—

A. I don't recall it. I told you I was confused at the time, that's a police statement. I was nervous, maybe I got some words twisted around, but the truth is I told the jury the truth today. That's what I'm saying, that's it . . .

Q. Sir, didn't you catch on pretty quickly that these investigators were part of the 'Get Scarfo Squad,' that they were very interested in Mr Scarfo and Mr Leonetti?

A. No, sir.

Q. Do you recognize some of them who even came to court today? Mr Corey came to court today from the prosecutor's office, Mr Allegaro came to court from the prosecutor's office, Mr Garafolo (ph.) came to court from the prosecutor's office; do you recognize those guys?

A. The only one I recognize here today is Joe Corey.

Q. Joe Corey, he's – where is he? There he is. Let's identify somebody other than a defendant for once. This is Joe Corey?

A. Stand up, Mr Corey.

Q. Right?

A. Yes, sir.

Q. He's one of the guys you dealt – sit down. He's one of the guys you dealt with nine years ago in the Atlantic County Prosecutor's Office and he's here today?

A. That's correct.

Q. Didn't you catch on pretty quickly that all these folks were very interested, intensely interested in Mr Scarfo, Mr

Leonetti, it was part of the 'Get Scarfo Squad,' wasn't it?

MR GORDON: Objection, your Honor, there is no such thing as a 'Get Scarfo Squad.'

MR JACOBS: There's not?

MR GORDON: Mr Jacobs knows that.

THE COURT: Objection is sustained.

BY MR JACOBS:

Q. Well, sir, it wasn't hard for you to read between the lines and figure out who they were interested in, was it?

A. I wasn't reading between any lines, sir, at all.

Q. OK. Sir, I want to ask you one more thing about this statement you gave on the 22nd. You told us about a conversation with Mr Scarfo where he said, 'Stay close to Philip Leonetti between 4:00 and 6:00 p.m.,' or words to that effect, right?

A. What date was that?

Q. I didn't give you a date. I just said you told us about a conversation.

A. I thought you said the 22nd, you said.

Q. Well, if I put the 22nd in that it was an error on my part. You told us about a conversation with Mr Scarfo where you say he told you, 'Stay close to Philip Leonetti between 4:00 and 6:00 p.m.' Do you remember saying that?

A. Yes.

Q. And you placed that conversation around the 15th of December, do you remember saying that?

A. Yes.

Q. And you told us that he cautioned you not to let anybody know about that, in particular Vince Falcone; do you remember saying that?

A. Yes, I do.

Q. Now, you also – let's put that aside for a moment. You also told the jury that you had some suspicions but you didn't know that Vince Falcone was going to get killed; do you remember saying that?

A. I remember saying that.

Q. OK. So now you agree with both those things. When you talked to the police, did you tell the police this, and this is again

Page 7, referring to that conversation, did you say that your conversation with Mr Scarfo went as follows: 'Yes, that I – would I be afraid if something happened in front of me so at the time I was afraid to say no, I didn't say no, OK, I says no, I says I wouldn't be afraid, right. Now, he told me not to tell a certain person that he told me this.' Are those your words?

A. Back then? What date was it, when?

Q. That was December 22nd, 1979, sir.

A. I don't recall, sir, I really don't.

Q. Sir, I just read from your own tape-recorded statement, these are words out of your mouth. Didn't you say right here in this little sequence something quite different, namely that Mr Scarfo asked you, 'Are you going to be afraid if something happens in front of you,' and you say, 'No,' falsely, and then he says, 'OK, don't tell Vince Falcone.' Isn't that a little summary of what I just read here?

A. I don't know what you're getting at though, I don't know what question you're asking.

Q. Well, here's what I'm getting at, that's a whole lot different than him saying to you—

MR GORDON: Objection to that kind of —
THE COURT: Now, just a minute.

BY MR JACOBS:

Q. That's a heck of a lot different than him saying to you, 'Stay close to Mr Leonetti between 4:00 and 6:00.' It's quite different, isn't it? It's a lot different?

A. I still don't know what the question is. I don't know what you're saying to me.

Q. Question one, did you say this as I just read it?

A. Read it again.

Q. 'Yes, that I, would be afraid if something happens'—

A. Slow down, please. Please, can you slow down?

Q. Yes, I can. 'Yes, that I, would I be afraid if something happened in front of me, so at the time I was afraid to say no. I didn't say no. OK, I says no, I says I wouldn't be afraid, right? Now he told me not to tell a certain person that he told me this.' Did you say that?

A. Yes, but I—

Q. Question: 'Who was that certain person?' Answer: 'Vince Falcone. OK.' Did you say that?

A. Yes.

Q. So you told the police that Mr Scarfo was in effect asking you if you would be afraid if Vince Falcone got killed in front of you? Isn't that what you told the police?

A. No, sir. No.

> MR GORDON: Objection.

BY MR JACOBS:

Q. That's not it?

A. No, that's not it. That's the way it's worded, that's what it is. That's not that.

Q. Well, who worded it? Who worded it, did I word it?

A. No.

Q. Did the police word it?

A. I have no idea.

Q. Well, you have an idea, you worded it, you said that, didn't you?

> MR GORDON: Objection. Your Honor, Counsel has placed his interpretation on the witness' words and asked him isn't it true that that's what he said. The words are one thing, the words may be his.
>
> MR JACOBS: Judge, I—
>
> MR GORDON: It's just counsel's.
>
> MR JACOBS: Judge, I think that's a matter for redirect.
>
> THE COURT: Well, it is cross-examination, but at the same time – I'm going to let that go, it's cross-examination.
>
> MR JACOBS: Thank you . . .

BY MR JACOBS:

Q. During December 1979 do you admit going out and drinking?

A. Yes.

Q. Sometimes were you with Mr Falcone?

A. Very rarely.

Q. That's a yes, some you were, right?

A. I don't remember drinking with Vincent Falcone, no.

Q. OK. How about with Mr Scarfo or Mr Leonetti or Mr Lawrence Merlino?

A. Mostly with either – well, me and Lawrence used to drink together, you know.

Q. Well, who were you with on the nights that you had ten to twenty drinks in one sitting?

A. I never had no ten to twenty drinks.

Q. You didn't? Did you ever testify under oath that you did?

A. Yeah, I probably did because I probably got disgusted with the way you guys questioned me and confused me and twisted the words around.

Q. Well, sir, did this twist any words: Question: 'How many drinks did you have that night?' Answer: 'I don't know, ten or twenty.' Did somebody torture you into that answer? Was Mr Simone up there with a vise-grip on your neck to make you say that?

MR GORDON: Objection
THE COURT: The objection is overruled.

BY MR JACOBS:

Q. You said that, didn't you?

A. Yes, but I didn't kill anybody.

Q. When you were first asked, the first two times you were asked by counsel for the Government whether you were equally friendly with Vince Falcone as were Mr Scarfo, Mr Leonetti and Mr Merlino, the first two times your answer was, 'Yes, we were all equally friendly, yes, we were all equally friendly.' But on the third go round, you finally said that perhaps they were more friendly with Mr Falcone than you were. Do you recall that sequence? It was right in the beginning of your testimony.

A. OK.

Q. Now, the reason you came around the third time is you

previously admitted under oath that the friendship earned between Mr Scarfo and Mr Leonetti and Mr Lawrence Merlino was much stronger with Mr Falcone than with you, you've admitted that under oath, haven't you?

A. Yes, I did.

Q. He was their friend, not your friend?

A. I wouldn't say that, no.

Q. You had admitted that he was much friendlier with them than he was with you; you have said that?

A. But I did not say he wasn't my friend.

Q. OK. Well, now we have a new question on the table: You have admitted he was much more friendly with them than with you, haven't you?

A. Yes.

Q. OK. In fact, he had just had a christening for his kid, invited them and not invited you?

A. I don't know.

Q. Did you know that one of them was the godparent for his child?

A. No.

Q. Mr Scarfo was made the godparent for Vince Falcone's child just a couple weeks earlier?

> MR GORDON: Objection. He just said he doesn't know and counsel is asking him the same question again.
> MR JACOBS: Refreshing his recollection by providing the name. First I said one of them, now I've provided—
> THE COURT: Well, all right, then I'll permit it.
> MR JACOBS: —I should have in the first place, the name.

BY MR JACOBS:

Q. OK. We'll go on what you said then. Now here's what I'm getting at, sir. There's some sworn testimony from you which is a little old, but it's closer to 1979 and you said that you and Mr Falcone were at the Scarfo residence. Now, I remember you saying on direct examination that the friendship between Mr Falcone and Mr Scarfo, Mr Leonetti, and Mr Merlino sort of petered out, became not so strong in November 1979. Do you remember saying that?

A. Yes, sir.

Q. You said that Mr Falcone stopped coming around the Scarfo residence, do you remember that?

A. Yes.

Q. Sir, Mr Falcone was at the Scarfo residence in the afternoon of December 15, 1979, the day before you say this killing occurred, wasn't he?

A. December 15th, Vincent Falcone was there. No, I don't remember it.

Q. Well, is it no or is it I don't remember?

A. I don't remember.

Q. Well, I'll tell you where I got that information. I got it from you. Don't you remember previously testifying to what I've just said, that on December 15th around 6:00 p.m. Vince Falcone came over to North Georgia Avenue, and do you remember characterizing that as a normal occurrence?

A. Then I said that in 1979, 1980?

Q. Yes. Page 107. Well, let me just read your words. This is the prosecutor asking you questions, this is your responses. Question: 'I call your attention now again to December 15. This is after the bag was placed in the car and you returned back to North Georgia Avenue. At that time around 6:00 p.m. did Vincent Falcone come over to North Georgia Avenue?' And you answered the prosecutor, you said, 'Yes, he did.'

So the prosecutor said, 'Was that a normal occurrence?' And you said, 'Yes, he'd stop by, he'd stop over about that time in the afternoon, usually after work between 4:00 and 6:00.'

And then the prosecutor wanted to know how long he was there on December 15th, so you told him, 'Fifteen, twenty minutes.' Does that bring it back to you?

A. Yes, but that wasn't every day. Used to be every day, but that wasn't every day.

Q. You do remember telling this jury that as of November he didn't come around any more?

A. No, I didn't say that. I said it thinned out.

Q. OK. He still came to the birthday party for Mark and he happened to be there on December 15th?

A. That's because there was a lot of people around.

Q. OK. Sir, this Decatur Avenue address, you admitted, I believe you admitted today, that you had been to that Decatur Avenue address before December 16, 1979. I mean, you did admit that in court today, didn't you?

A. Yes, I did.

Q. And you said that you'd been there with two people: Person number one, Salvatore 'Chuckie' Merlino, person number two, Vincent Falcone; is that right?

A. Yes, sir.

Q. Now, let's go back eight years, nine years, both when you talked to the police and when you testified under oath in court, you left out the fact that you had been there with Vincent Falcone, didn't you?

A. I don't remember. I don't recall.

Q. Sir, if I tell you that in your direct testimony you do not mention Vincent Falcone having been there with you at all and it was called to your attention in your cross-examination, will you accept my representation or do you want to see both sequences?

A. I'd like to see it, please.

Q. The first is at Page 122, for Counsel's reference, of the September 15 proceeding. The – well, actually, I guess to make it make sense, start at Page 121. Question: 'Have you been to that house?' Answer: 'Yes, I have.' Question: 'Approximately when, if you recall?' Answer: 'A month ago. From that time I guess maybe three months ago, three and a half months ago.' Question: 'Who were you with?' Answer: 'Chuck Merlino,' and we can go on and on, forward or backward, and we won't find any reference to Vince Falcone until you're cross-examined, which occurs at Page 155, I'm sorry, of the next session, September 16th.

> MR GORDON: Your Honor, in the interests of saving time I'll agree that it does not appear in the direct examination and the answer appears in the cross-examination.

BY MR JACOBS:

Q. Well, will you agree with him, will you take his word?

A. Yes. Yes, I do.

Q. OK. So you didn't mention to that jury that you had been at the murder scene with Vince Falcone until it was specifically brought up to your attention by me?

> MR GORDON: Objection, that question is misleading.
>
> MR JACOBS: How is that—
>
> MR GORDON: It wasn't a murder scene at the time he had been to it with Vince Falcone.
>
> MR. JACOBS: Judge, I'll accept that very technical amendment.

BY MR. JACOBS:

Q. You didn't tell that jury that you were testifying to under oath that you had been to the Decatur Avenue address with Vince Falcone until it was specifically brought up in front of the jury by me; is that right?

A. I've only been to the place two times in my life.

Q. Sir, did you withhold that from the jury until you were confronted with it?

A. No, I didn't withhold anything from the jury.

Q. OK. Did you say that the black Cadillac was on the scene at Decatur Avenue until 6 or 7 o'clock?

A. Yes.

Q. Did you say that? So therefore, it was there from around 2:30 p.m. to 6:30 – to 6:00 or 7:00 o'clock, maybe four, four and a half hours?

A. I'd say so.

Q. And you say there was one police officer right around?

A. One police officer what?

Q. Right in the area, right?

A. I said there was a police officer that parked on the lot.

Q. You have no idea how many police officers drove by?

A. No.

Q. And you also told us that there was other traffic there, there was the Lawrence Merlino car, there was the Vince Falcone car there in that same four and a half hour period, right?

A. Yes, sir.

Q. None of them photographed, none of them surveilled, nothing to confirm what you say but you?

MR GORDON: Objection.

THE WITNESS: Yes. Excuse me, sir—

MR GORDON: I'll withdraw it.

THE WITNESS: Can I finish the question now, please?

BY MR JACOBS:

Q. It's up to the Government, is that—

A. Can you ask me that question again, please?

Q. Do you remember it?

A. I'd like you to ask me the question again.

Q. The question is, sir, there were three cars there during that four and a half hour period, Mr Scarfo's you say, Mr Merlino's you say and Mr Falcone's you say, right?

A. Yes. Yes.

Q. Is there anything, any hard, concrete evidence to establish their presence, other than what you say, any surveillance photographs, for instance?

A. No, I don't think so.

Q. Talking about the Falcone car, where was that found parked with the body of Vince Falcone in it?

A. I don't know the exact name of the street.

Q. Well, do you know the name of the person who owned the house in front of which the car was parked?

A. No.

Q. Well, the name of the person is McCausland; does that ring a bell with you?

A. I can't recall right now.

Q. Well, let me help you some more. Mr McCausland was a man that you had just gone to see about putting a heater into his house.

A. Two, two heaters.

Q. Excuse me?

A. Two heaters.

Q. I'm sorry, two heaters. Now, Mr McCausland paid you $700 I believe, right?

A. That's correct.

Q. But you bought the heaters with this money but you never installed them; is that right?

A. I left the heaters on the premises.

Q. Well, sir, you previously testified you left the heaters at the home of Rick Casale?

A. That's right, because the people weren't there at the property and I left them across the street where Rick Casale lives so no-one would steal them.

Q. Well, here's the point, sir. The car, the Falcone car with the Falcone body in it was found right in front of the house you were familiar with and had just had some business dealings with, wasn't it?

A. Yes, it was.

Q. And that's just an enormous coincidence?

A. I don't know, sir; that's where the car was parked.

Q. Sir, you didn't put the car there, did you?

A. No, I did not.

Q. You knew the neighborhood though?

A. Not hardly. I said that I'm – I don't go down that neighborhood much.

Q. Well, that guy didn't have a heater if he was hiring you to put one in, did he?

A. Yes, so I went down to that neighborhood and I can't recall the name of the street because I never really did the job after, you know.

Q. Did the guy have a heater to start with or were you putting in a heater?

A. I don't think he had heat in the house.

Q. So if he didn't have heat in the house he wouldn't be living there in December, would he?

A. No, he was not there.

Q. And if he wouldn't be living there in December that would be a pretty neat place to leave a car with a body in it, wouldn't it?

A. I wouldn't know; I wouldn't know that question. I don't leave bodies around.

Q. I see. OK, sir, I think I heard you say that Phil Disney was not in that Decatur Avenue residence when you got there; you did say that, didn't you?

A. Yes, I did.

Q. Not there even for a second?

A. Not there for a second. That day he was not there for a second.

Q. So that day, the whole time you were there, Phil Disney was not there even for one second?

A. Yes, sir.

Q. Not even long enough to say hello or shake anybody's hand?

A. He was not there.

Q. OK. Now, sir, when you told another jury in 1980 what happened when you pulled up at the Decatur Avenue residence, all the prosecutor said to you was, quote, 127, the 15th, all the prosecutor said to you was quote, 'After you entered, I want you to convey to the jury what then happened and what transpired during the next couple of minutes,' open ended question. And your answer was, 'Well, everybody shook hands and Nick Scarfo says to Phil Disney, "We're going to be back in five minutes." He's the man that owns the house, he asked Vince to go make some drinks.' Did you say that?

A. Repeat that again.

Q. You don't need my preamble, I'll just read the question and answer.

A. Yeah, can you read a little slower for me, please?

Q. Yes. Question: 'After you entered, I want you to convey to the jury what then happened and what transpired during the next couple minutes.' Answer, by you: 'Well, everybody shook hands and Nick Scarfo says to Phil Disney, "We're going to be right back in five minutes." He's the man that owns the house. He asked Vince to go make some drinks.'

A. That's an incorrect statement.

Q. It's also quite different from what you told this jury, isn't it?

A. No, it's not.

Q. Weren't you testifying about a murder charge?

MR GORDON: Objection. Your Honor—

THE COURT: The objection is sustained.

MR GORDON: I would ask at this time in the interests of completeness that all that testimony about what happened in the house be read to this jury to see if at any other time Phil Disney is ever mentioned as being there.

MR SIMONE: I object to that.

MR JACOBS: Judge, that's a hundred pages. That's for the jury to remember.

THE COURT: Why don't you do that on your side of the case?

MR GORDON: Yes, sir.

BY MR JACOBS:

Q. . . . Sir, I want to ask you something. Tell me if I got this right or I got this wrong. Didn't you claim about two hours ago or three hours ago that Vince Falcone was killed because the motive that you told us about, because Vince Falcone told Chuck Merlino that Philip Leonetti was – I'm sorry, that Scarfo was crazy and Philip Leonetti shouldn't be in the concrete business and then Chuck tells that to Nick who says, 'Well, we'll kill him.' Isn't that basically what you said?

A. That's exactly what I said.

Q. And you claim that you heard this at the dinner table?

Q. Yes, sir.

Q. You've been a witness a lot of times, haven't you?

A. I wouldn't say a lot of times.

Q. Well, what's a lot to you?

MR GORDON: Objection.

BY MR JACOBS:

Q. How many times have you been a witness?

A. I don't know. I can't – I can't recall.

Q. You have no idea, it could have been 3,000, it could have been 2?

A. No, just a few times, I'd say; maybe five, six times.

Q. Five, six times you've been a witness. And each time you're a witness against the usual suspects, aren't you?

A. Yes, sir.

Q. OK. Now, for counsel's reference this is October 3, 1986, Federal Grand Jury Newark, testimony of Joe Salerno, Page 30. Do you remember this question, and you're being questioned by Jerome Bartoletto and Mr Gordon, who's seated here. Question: 'Now, Mr Salerno, approximately three months before the murder of Vincent Falcone did you meet with Vincent Falcone at a bar?' Answer by you: 'Yes.' Question: 'Did you have a conversation with him? Answer by you: 'Yes, I did.' Question: 'And did Vincent Falcone say to you in substance that Nicky Scarfo was crazy and that Philip Leonetti shouldn't act the way he acts, and did Vincent Falcone further say to you that they're not going to get away with this?' Answer: 'Yes, he did say that.' Do you remember saying that?

A. Yes, I do.

Q. So you told this group of 23 Federal Grand Jurors that this statement made by Falcone was made to you. You didn't tell them this statement was made to Salvatore Chuckie Merlino and then repeated to Nick Scarfo; different things, aren't they?

A. It was made to me and it probably was also made, probably was telling everybody about it, not only me.

Q. Was there a reason, sir, that you decided you would tell the Federal Grand Jury sitting in Newark that Falcone made the statement to you and you would tell this jury sitting in Philadelphia that Falcone made the statement to Salvatore Chuckie Merlino who repeated it to Nick Scarfo?

MR GORDON: Objection. That's assuming that it was only said the one time. Your Honor, if it was said to both people, then he hasn't decided what to tell either jury.

MR JACOBS: Well, Judge, isn't that something he can deal with on redirect? That's not an objection, that's—

THE COURT: You can ask him what the situation is. Are you going to be longer yet?

MR JACOBS: I do have a few more questions, Judge.

THE COURT: Well, if it's five minutes, we'll finish it

tonight. If it's going to be longer, we'll start tomorrow morning.

MR JACOBS: It's over five, Judge.

THE COURT: It's what?

MR JACOBS: It's over five.

THE COURT: Well, then in that case, let's adjourn until tomorrow morning at 9:30.

The jury is excused until tomorrow morning at 9:30.

(Jury out and court adjourn at 8:30 p.m.)

* * *

(Court convenes at 9:45 a.m., jury in the box.)
(Excerpt of testimony.)

JOSEPH SALERNO, JR, resumed.

CROSS-EXAMINATION (Continuing)

BY MR JACOBS:

Q. Good morning Mr Salerno.

A. Good morning.

Q. When we left off last night, I was in the midst of asking you about some of your testimony before the Federal Grand Jury convened in Newark, New Jersey on October 2, 1986, you remember, don't you? . . .

Q. When we left last night I had read to you an excerpt which says, in your own words, that you and Vincent Falcone had a chat three months before he was killed and during that chat he made complaints to you about Nick Scarfo and Philip Leonetti and said that Philip shouldn't be in the concrete business and Nick was crazy and stuff like that, you remember that, don't you?

A. Yes, I do.

Q. Now, sir, as I said last night here in court before this jury, you told us that you learned at the dinner table, at the Scarfo dinner table on December 16, 1979 that Vincent Falcone had said those things and then you involved my client, Salvatore 'Chuckie' Merlino, to him and it got back to Mr Scarfo and that is why he was killed, right?

A. That's correct.

Q. Do you concede that you said two different things to two different bodies, under oath, each time?

> MR GORDON: Objection, your Honor, they are not two different things.
> MR JACOBS: Judge, that's argumentative, isn't it?
> THE COURT: Why don't you—
> MR JACOBS: Isn't it really?
> THE COURT: It is somewhat—
> MR GORDON: It's a misleading question.
> THE COURT: —it is somewhat argumentative what you're saying. I'm going to permit it if you put it in the form of a question.

BY MR JACOBS:

Q. Sir, what you said to the Federal Grand Jury in Newark, in 1986—

A. Mm-hmm.

Q. —is not the same as what you said to this Grand Jury in 1988, now is it?

A. No, it's not the same.

Q. OK, and each time you took an oath and the oath—

A. Let me explain, sir? Can I explain, sir?

Q. Go ahead.

A. There were two different occasions.

Q. Does that mean you tell two different stories?

> MR GORDON: Objection.
> THE WITNESS: No, no, no.
> MR GORDON: Objection. Now, he's in the middle of an answer—

THE COURT: Sustained, sustained, you may continue to answer.

THE WITNESS: There was two different situations, Mr Jacobs. What I said to the jury yesterday, OK, was one occasion. What I had said to the Federal Grand Jury was another occasion, OK? Two different, separate situations.

BY MR JACOBS:

Q. Is that all of your explanation?

A. That's my explanation, yes.

Q. And you're telling us that what you told the Grand Jury in Newark in 1986 is the truth, right?

A. Yes.

Q. And you're telling us what you told this jury yesterday is the truth?

A. Yes, sir.

Q. Did you listen to the oath when it was administered here yesterday?

MR GORDON: Objection.

THE COURT: The objection is sustained.

MR JACOBS: Judge, whether he listened to and understood the oath is certainly germane, what could more go to the heart of credibility than whether he appreciates or understands or abides by an oath.

MR GORDON: I'll withdraw the objection, your Honor.

MR JACOBS: Thank you.

THE COURT: All right. You can ask him if he understood the oath. Whether or not – I'll let you go that far.

THE WITNESS: Of course, I understood the oath.

BY MR JACOBS:

Q. Doesn't the oath require you to tell not just the truth but the whole truth?

A. I did tell the whole truth.

Q. The whole truth?

A. Yes, sir.

Q. You told this jury – you told this jury both things. You told this jury that you learned at the dinner table that Vincent Falcone had complained to Chuckie Merlino and you also told this jury that you sat three months earlier with Vincent Falcone and he told you all these awful things?

A. That's true also.

> MR GORDON: Objection. Your Honor, I could not have asked this witness to repeat the conversation he had with Vincent Falcone. The Rules of Evidence forbid it.
>
> THE COURT: It's overruled.
>
> MR JACOBS: Thank you, Judge . . .

Q. Let's talk about the gun for a moment, the .32 gun, that's a gun that you had for some time, didn't you?

A. Yes, sir.

Q. And you fired it many times, didn't you?

A. Not many times.

Q. Well, how many is not many?

A. I don't know. I fired it a half a dozen times.

Q. A half a dozen times you took it out and you shot it, right?

A. Mm-hmm.

Q. And you previously estimated that you shot 30, 40, 50 shells out of that gun?

A. Correct.

Q. Some of them right in Brigantine, in your back yard?

A. That's correct.

Q. So, you knew how to handle and you knew how to use that gun?

A. I want to explain that my back yard was in Brigantine, OK?

> MR JACOBS: Well, Judge, is it really necesary that we know what his back yard is?
>
> MR GORDON: Objection.
>
> THE WITNESS: Can I do that?
>
> THE COURT: Well, let's find out.

BY MR JACOBS:

Q. All right. Tell us about your back yard?

A. My back yard had a beach and an ocean behind it.

Q. Is that all you want to tell us about your back yard?

A. There was no people around. The neighbors were all gone and we shot it New Year's Eve, OK, to make some noise, that's when I shot the gun, in my back yard.

Q. OK, that's one time. You used the gun about six times, didn't you?

A. Yeah, I used it a half a dozen times, yeah.

Q. Always on New Year's Eve in your back yard?

A. No, I would bring it to Philadelphia and shoot blanks out of it on New Year's Eve at my dad's house.

Q. So, it was a New Year's Eve gun?

A. Yeah, that's what I used it for, yeah.

Q. I see. All right, sir. Sir, you have told us that you moved out of your apartment on Georgia Avenue but you haven't made clear, at least to me, when that was, when was that?

A. I can't exactly recall it's been nine years ago. Do you want the date and the hour?

Q. Well, if you can fix a day in September that would be fine?

A. I can't do that.

Q. It certainly was in December, wasn't it?

A. Did you say September or December?'

Q. December?

A. Yes, it was in December.

Q. OK, but you can't tell us just when it was?

A. No.

Q. If I tell you that previosuly you have testified that it was December 22nd, 1979 would that refresh your recollection?

A. What I testified in 1979, OK, is not today. What I recollect and said to the jury yesterday is what I know now in 1988, OK.

Q. Are you telling us that your memory is getting better or worse?

A. I'm not saying either if my memory is getting better or worse.

Q. Sir, what—

A. I'm saying what I recollect today, OK, is not nine years ago, that testimony you're reading, OK, you guys did a good job on me. You switched the words around, you crossed me up—

322

Q. How did we switch the words around. Did we get to the court reporter or something?

A. You know how to switch – you're an attorney, sir, I'm a plumber.

Q. All right. Does any particular trade attorneys or plumbers or anybody else have a monopoly on the truth?

A. I'm saying the truth——

Q. Mr Salerno, you've drawn our attention to these transcripts of your sworn testimony back in 1980 and I want the jury to understand something. When you testified here, you testified about the Falcone murder and your direct testimony took about an hour and a half, didn't it?

A. I don't know how long it took. I did not time it, sir.

Q. OK, I saw you looking at your watch a few times and I was under the impression that you were aware of how long you were on the stand, but does it seem to you that you spent about an hour and a half?

A. Yes.

Q. Back in 1980 when you testified about the same Falcone murder case—

A. Mm-hmm.

Q. —did it also take you about an hour and a half to tell your story then?

A. I don't remember back then in 1979 how long it took.

Q. Sir, do you agree with me that you underwent five days of virtually full-time preparation in May and June of 1980? Five days of virtually full-time preparation for the testimony you gave in the Falcone murder case back then?

A. I don't recall that.

Q. If I tell you that you have admitted it under oath in these same transcripts, that you underwent five days of preparation, would you concede the fact—

A. If it's in the transcripts that's what happened, yes, sir.

> MR JACOBS: It's in the transcripts and if counsel wishes to check it's the testimony of the 16th, pages 99, 101 and 107.
>
> MR GORDON: Thank you.

MR JACOBS: You're welcome.

BY MR JACOBS:

Q. Yet you concede there are differences between what you said today and what you said in 1980?

A. Of course there is.

Q. OK, Mr Salerno, let's get back to when you moved out. In your testimony back in 1980, you remembered moving out on December 22, 1979. Now, did you do anything else that day?

A. I don't recollect. I don't remember what day it was, was it Thursday, Friday, I have no—

Q. Well, it was December 22nd. Let me help you. Did you also go hock your jewelry at a local jewelry store?

A. Yes, I did.

Q. So, on the same day you moved out of Mr Scarfo's apartment and you hocked your jewelry at a local store. Was that because you were going to blow town?

A. No, sir.

Q. You weren't going—

A. I had family there. My father-in-law was millionaire, OK. Blow town, and so were parents.

Q. Was your father-in-law Mr Hall?

A. Excuse me?

Q. Is your father-in-law Mr Hall?

A. Yes, he is.

Q. Now, you were at the time estranged, separated from his daughter, weren't you?

A. Yes, I was.

Q. Well, how was the millionaire father-in-law going to help you when you had left his daughter?

A. That's for me to know, sir.

Q. You won't tell us?

A. That's for me to know.

Q. I just have to accept that you didn't need any money?

A. Yes, you have to accept that, yes.

MR JACOBS: Judge, do I have—
THE WITNESS: I had three kids.

MR JACOBS: Judge, do I have to accept that or is the witness obliged to answer, how the father of the woman, he left, was going to help him.

MR GORDON: Objection, your Honor, that's completely irrelevant.

MR JACOBS: Well, he said it though, Judge.

THE COURT: If you really feel it has some relevance, of course, I'll order the witness to answer it. If you really feel it is relevant to this case, fine. I'll order him to answer it.

MR JACOBS: Judge, when you put it that way, I'll withdraw the question.

BY MR JACOBS:

Q. All right, sir, let's move past your father-in-law. The clothes and the bullets that you told us that were disposed of on December 16th, do you remember what you said about that?

A. Yes, sir.

Q. The way you described it, they were disposed of right near the offices of Scarf, Inc. isn't that right?

A. Yes.

Q. Within blocks?

A. Yes.

Q. OK, and was that your idea to dispose of these things within blocks of Scarf, Inc?

A. No, sir.

Q. That would be a convenient way to put some evidence in the proximity of Scarf, Inc.; wouldn't it?

MR GORDON: Objection.

THE COURT: I'll permit it.

BY MR JACOBS:

Q. Wouldn't it?

A. Ask the question again, sir?

Q. That would be a convenient way to put some evidence, place some evidence in the proximity of Scarf, Inc; wouldn't it?

A. I don't know if that would or not.

325

Q. Those clothes of yours were never found, were they?

A. No.

Q. And you know from your dealings with the Atlantic County prosecutor, that $20,000 was spent trying to locate the trash from this dumpster that you told that jury about and they never found the clothes?

A. I don't know anything about $20,000.

Q. You don't know about them digging up the whole dump and tracing the route to the garbage trucks and trying to find—

A. I know they dug up the whole the dump, sir.

Q. —what you told them was there?

A. I'm answering your question. I know they dug the dump up but I don't know what it cost them to do it.

Q. OK. So, you don't know how much it cost but you know that based on your—

A. They did.

Q. —story they dug up the whole dump trying to find—

A. Yes, they did.

Q. —the trash that you said was there, right?

A. Yes.

Q. OK. Now, sir, if I have it right both before and after the homicide of Vince Falcone, you said to your wife that Vince Falcone may be killed and Vince Falcone was killed, you said that to your wife, didn't you?

A. Yes, I did.

Q. OK. Did you do that because in your mind, in your mind, that might corroborate your later story that you only knew about it but you didn't have anything to do with the killing?

A. Sir, I didn't have anything to do with that killing and to corroborate my story, ask Mr Scarfo, Leonetti and Lawrence Merlino, they know what happened that day. They'll corroborate my story.

Q. Well, you say you know what happened that day, don't you?

A. I know what happened that day, too.

Q. But you, yourself can see that your story needs corroboration, can't you?

A. Yes, and they're the people that can do it for me.

Q. OK. Now, sir, one last thing. Didn't you realize in

December of 1979 when the Atlantic County Prosecutor's Office sat you down, didn't you realize that unless you could blame this murder on somebody else you, yourself, were going to be a prime suspect for killing Vince Falcone, didn't you realize that?

A. That's ridiculous, sir. Mr Jacobs, no way.

Q. Mr Jacobs, no way?

A. No.

Q. Mr Salerno, page 125, is the number 16th proceedings. The question to you, 'You know if you didn't say somebody else killed Mr Falcone that you would be prime suspect yourself in this case; isn't that a fact?' Mr Salerno, 'I would imagine so, yes.' Which one is true, Mr Salerno?

A. What I'm saying is what I said in 1979, OK, you guys got me up on a stand, you and Mr Simone, OK, and made a liar out of me in front of the jury.

Q. You admit you were a liar?

A. No, you made a liar out of me because—

Q. Well, it doesn't matter who made the liar, you admit you were lying?

> MR GORDON: Objection, the witness is trying to answer the question and Mr. Jacobs interrupts him.
> THE COURT: I'll permit him to answer.
> THE WITNESS: You and Mr Simone made a liar out of me in front of a jury, OK, and they got acquitted of a murder, for nine years they walked and I'm here today testifying and I told the jury yesterday what happened in my direct examination and I'm not lying today.

BY MR JACOBS:

Q. And you want this jury to believe, you're not lying today, right?

A. Yes, I think do they do believe it.

> MR JACOBS: No other questions.

★ ★ ★

(The following excerpted testimony occurred in open court:)

JOSEPH SALERNO, JR, Government Witness,
previously sworn.

REDIRECT EXAMINATION

BY MR GORDON:

Q. Mr Salerno, you were asked if you had seen any statements and you testified that I didn't give you any statements. But in fact I did let you look at testimony from the proceeding that Mr Simone just referred to, isn't that correct?

A. Yes, testimony, yes.

Q. OK. Now, you were asked how you knew that the bullets used to kill Vincent Falcone were not the bullets that you supplied. What conversation, if any, did you have with Phil Leonetti about the kinds of bullets used?

A. I asked him what kind of bullets he used, 'the long bullets?' He says, 'No.' He said, 'I used the short ones because the long ones would make too much of a mess in the house.'

Q. What did you understand him to mean by that?

A. Excuse me?

Q. What did you understand him to mean by that, what would have happened if they used the long bullets?

A. Too much blood all over the place.

Q. Now, you were asked if you had only been socially friendly with Nicodemo Scarfo for a short time in 1979 on cross-examination and you said yes, but how long by 1979 had you known and been friendly with Phil Leonetti?

A. I'd say seven to eight years . . .

Q. Now, did you also testify that Vincent Falcone told you something about Nicodemo Scarfo and Phil Leonetti?

A. Yes, he did.

Q. What did he tell you?

A. He told me that Philip shouldn't be in the concrete business and Nicky Scarfo's crazy.

328

Q. And is that similar to what Chuck Merlino had told Nicodemo Scarfo Vincent Falcone had told him?

A. It's the same thing exactly.

Q. But they were two separate conversations, is that correct?

A. That's correct.

Q. Once Vincent Falcone told it to you and once Vincent Falcone, according to them, told it to Chuck Merlino?

A. Yes, sir.

Q. Now, when you bid for different jobs when you were in business did you compete with Vincent Falcone for work?

A. Not at all.

Q. You were a plumber, is that correct?

A. Yes.

Q. Vincent Falcone did what kind of business?

A. Concrete.

Q. Now, you were asked about this testimony at the bottom of Page 27 on September 15, 1980, the other day on cross-examination where the transcript says, 'Well, everybody shook hands and Nick Scarfo says to Phil Disney, "We're going to be right back." ' Now that's in reference to you're inside the Decatur Avenue address and you say you never said that.

Now, was there any conversation at all about Phil Disney inside the Decatur address?

A. Yes.

Q. What was – first of all, who said or who mentioned Phil Disney's name?

A. Nick Scarfo.

Q. And what did Nick Scarfo say if anything about Phil Disney inside the address?

A. He said that Phil Dis – Phil Disney will be back in five or ten minutes.

Q. Now, after that answer do you recall this series of questions and answers. 'When you say Vince' – and this is from page 128 – 'When you say Vince you're referring to whom?' Answer: 'Vince Falcone. Then he went to the refrigerator first, got some ice out, then he went to the countertop, got some glasses and poured a couple drinks. Then he went back again, put some drinks on the table, went back again to the countertop.'

Question: 'All right, at that point I'm going to show you another photograph, that being a photograph that's now marked S-7 into evidence. I ask you if you can identify that particular photograph?'

Answer: 'Yes, that's the house where I was.'

Question: 'That's the kitchen area?'

Answer: 'Yes.'

Question: 'Now where is the refrigerator portrayed in that photograph?'

Answer: 'It's portrayed in the kitchen.'

Question: 'Where is the corner that you're indicating that Mr Falcone was standing at this time?'

Answer: 'Next to the range here.'

Question: 'Now I'm going to ask you'—

Answer: 'In the corner.'

Question: 'Come off the witness stand and take a look at this particular diagram. Is the refrigerator portrayed on that diagram?'

Answer: 'Yes, it is.'

Question: 'I want you to stand on the side so the jury can see it as well. Is the corner of the kitchen where Mr Falcone is, is that portrayed on the diagram?'

Answer: 'Yes, it is.'

Question: 'Where is that?'

Answer: 'It's here.'

Question: 'All right. Now, if Mr Falcone was in the corner of the kitchen area, where was everybody else positioned?'

Answer: 'There's a couch here.'

Question: 'All right, I'm going to give you a marking pen. I want you to draw on there where the couch was.'

Answer: 'Couch.'

Question: 'And who was sitting on the couch?'

Answer: 'Nick Scarfo.'

Question: 'I want you to put an X there and put NS. Where was everybody positioned?'

Answer: 'Vincent Falcone was positioned here.'

Question: 'Put VF. Where were you positioned?'

Answer: 'I was positioned right here.'

Question: 'JS.'

Answer: 'And Philip Leonetti was positioned right here.'

Question: 'And how about Mr Merlino?'

Answer: 'Lawrence Merlino was positioned here.'

Question: 'Was there a table in the kitchen?'

Answer: 'Yes.'

Question: 'Approximately where?'

Answer: 'Should I make it?'

Question: 'Yes.'

Answer. 'About here.'

Question: 'All right, I ask you to return back to the witness stand. At this point I want you to relate to the jury what happened, what you saw.'

Answer: 'OK, I had a drink up to my hand, in my hand to my mouth.'

MR GOODMAN: Your Honor, if it please the Court, I'm going to object. I don't know – this is not a question. This is a recitation of five pages of transcripts. That's not proper.

MR GORDON: After I finish reciting this, your Honor, I'm going to ask the witness where Phil Disney was at this time when he was receiving this—

MR SIMONE: Well, why don't you just ask him?

THE COURT: How much further do you have to go?

MR GORDON: I'm sorry, sir?

THE COURT: How much further do you have to go?

MR GORDON: Three lines.

THE COURT: All right, finish the lines and ask him.

BY MR GORDON:

Q. 'And Philip Leonetti pulled a gun out of his jacket and shot Mr Vincent Falcone, extended his arms and shot him in the back of the head.'

Now, at any point in that testimony did you mention Phil Disney being in the house?

A. No, sir.

Q. Was he in the house at any time that day?

A. Not at all.

> MR GORDON: Now, I would ask counsel at this time in the interests of saving time that there'd be a stipulation that there is never any direct testimony other than one spot about Phil Disney being in that house either on direct or cross-examination.

> MR SIMONE: If he says that there's no – if he says it, not if he says it, I'll accept that the testimony doesn't reflect Disney was in the house.

> MR GOODMAN: Well, it does in one spot, I won't accept that, your Honor.

> MR GORDON: I said but with one exception where we read on Page 127.

> MR SIMONE: Otherwise you've got to read the whole thing.

> THE COURT: All right, it's so agreed then? Is it? I don't know.

> MR SIMONE: Except for the one spot.

> THE COURT: Yes, except for the one spot. OK, thank you.

BY MR GRODON:

Q. Now, if you were going to pick three people to blame a murder on, you testified on cross-examination that these people, Scarfo, Leonetti, Lawrence Merlino, instead of being the first would be the last people you'd pick. Why is that?

A. I'd be scared to pin a murder on them. No way. They'd be the last people in the world I'd pin a murder on. They'd retaliate me – retaliate on me in a minute, that's why.

Q. In fact, was there any retaliation against you or your family?

> MR SIMONE: Objected to.

BY MR GORDON:

Q. Did anything happen to you or your family?

> MR SIMONE: Objected to. Mistrial.
> THE WITNESS: My father got shot.
> MR GORDON: Excuse me.

332

THE WITNESS: My father was shot, sir.

THE COURT: Just a minute.

MR SIMONE: Excuse me. I object and move for a mistrial. He's just testified as to motive, he's just – the question itself needs no explanation. I move for a mistrial.

THE COURT: The motion is denied. I will strike the testimony, however. You can ask what happened to—

MR SIMONE: I object to him asking what happened to anybody but him. What's that have to do with—

THE COURT: The objection is overruled.

MR SIMONE: It's the same thing, I move for a mistrial again.

THE COURT: The motion is denied again.

MR SIMONE: OK.

BY MR GORDON:

Q. Sometime after you testified did anything happen to your father?

MR SIMONE: Objected to.

THE WITNESS: Yes, he got shot.

MR SIMONE: Excuse me.

THE COURT: The objection is overruled.

BY MR GORDON.

Q. Now, at various times during cross-examination you were asked how many jobs did Phil Leonetti get you and you said two or three and then it was pointed out that you had testified earlier that it was five or six. You were asked on what day a particular thing occurred and you said you don't remember or what month something happened, you said you don't remember that. Is there any question about your memory today of the events inside of Phil McFillin or Phil Disney's house in Margate?

A. Not at all, sir, no.

Q. Is there any question in your mind, do you have any trouble at all remembering who it was that shot Vincent Falcone in the back of the head?

A. No, not at all.
Q. Who was that?
A. Philip Leonetti.
Q. Is there any question in your mind—

> MR SIMONE: Your Honor, objected to. Six times the same question, is there any question in your mind. I mean, why don't you just put a sign up. I object to it.
> THE COURT: Objection is overruled. Let's proceed.
> MR SIMONE: He can ask him six times the same question.

BY MR GORDON:

Q. Are you having any difficulty at all remembering who it was that talked about giving him another one?
A. Not at all.
Q. Who was that?
A. Mr Scarfo.
Q. Is there any difficulty remembering who it was that shot Vincent Falcone in the chest?
A. No, sir.
Q. Who was that?
A. Philip Leonetti.
Q. Do you have any difficulty remembering who it was that helped you carry Vincent Falcone's body down those steps?
A. No, sir.
Q. Who was that?
A. Lawrence Merlino.
Q. And why is it that your memory of those events is so good when you've forgotten some other facts?
A. That's just something that I'll never forget for the rest of my life.

> MR GORDON: No further questions.

★ ★ ★

WISEGUY
by Nicholas Pileggi

Now a major film *GOOD FELLAS*

'ONE OF THE FEW TRUE PICTURES OF THE CRIMINAL LIFE, A FASCINATING BOOK.'
Mario Puzo

WISEGUY is the life story of Henry Hill, a career criminal who literally grew up in the mob. For the first time, often in Hill's own words, the reader is swept into the day-to-day workings of a life of crime, from the truth about the Lufthansa heist (and the ten murders that followed) to the inside story of the Sindona case – which nearly caused the collapse of the Vatican bank – as well as countless other infamous crimes, all brought to life by a major player in the deadly high-stakes game some people call the Mafia.

WISEGUY is more extraordinary – and more compelling – than any novel. It is the firsthand account of a secret world, more brutal and far more fascinating than any of the novels that have glamorized it, and it is based on the searing testimony of a man who has run-and-done it all.

'The whole truth and nothing but the truth . . . WISE-GUY is a book of wisdom on the underworld – it penetrates the private space of crooked men'
Gay Talese

'Hurls you into a world you've never known, and before you finish reading this book, you feel you have been living in that world, so filled are his pages with vivid, authentic, fascinating detail'

0 552 13094 X

A SELECTION OF TRUE CRIME TITLES
AVAILABLE FROM CORGI BOOKS

☐	13639 5	**DEATH SHIFT**	*Peter Elkind*	£4.99
☐	13626 3	**A GATHERING OF SAINTS**	*Robert Lindsey*	£4.99
☐	13094 X	**WISEGUY**	*Nicholas Pileggi*	£3.99
☐	13304 3	**SMALL SACRIFICES**	*Ann Rule*	£4.99
☐	13058 3	**THE MARILYN CONSPIRACY**	*Milo Speriglio*	£3.99
☐	12858 9	**JACK THE RIPPER: SUMMING UP AND VERDICT**	*Colin Wilson & Robert Odell*	£4.99
☐	17204 2	**THE SICILIAN**	*Mario Puzo*	£4.99
☐	13451 1	**TO ENCOURAGE THE OTHERS**	*David Yallop*	£4.99
☐	13452 X	**THE DAY THE LAUGHTER STOPPED**	*David Yallop*	£5.99

All Corgi/Bantam Books are available at your bookshop or newsagent, or can be ordered from the following address:

Transworld Publishers Ltd, Cash Sales Department,
P.O. Box 11, Falmouth, Cornwall TR10 9EN

Please send a cheque or postal order (no currency) and allow £1.00 for postage and packing for one book, an additional 50p for a second book, and an additional 30p for each subsequent book ordered to a maximum charge of £3.00 if ordering seven or more books.

Overseas customers, including Eire, please allow £2.00 for postage and packing for the first book, £1.00 for the second book, and 30p for each subsequent title ordered.

NAME (Block Letters) ....

ADDRESS ....

....